Acing

Criminal Procedure

Third Edition

**A Checklist Approach to
Solving Procedural Problems**

Leslie W. Abramson
Frost Brown Todd Professor of Law
University of Louisville
School of Law

Series Editor
A. Benjamin Spencer

WEST.
A Thomson Reuters business

Mat #41308221

© West, a Thomson business, 2007
© 2010 Thomson Reuters
© 2013 Thomson Reuters
    610 Opperman Drive
    St. Paul, MN 55123
    1-800-313-9378

Printed in the United States of America

ISBN: 978-0-314-28273-6

For Lisa, Sam, Shel and Will

Table of Contents

Introduction

Most students spend a good deal of time developing an outline for each course—a lengthy (sometimes well over 100 pages) and exhaustive document that purports to compile the universe of information presented in a course into an organized, accessible format that would simplify studying and provide a useful source for information during the exam (provided the exam is open-book).

Unfortunately, personal outlines often do no more than provide anything more than a restatement of various principles of law or doctrine organized by topic. It remains for you to take those doctrines and apply them to the fact patterns presented on exams. That process of applying legal principles to facts is a large part of what exams and lawyering are all about; knowing the relevant law is only half (oftentimes less than half) of the battle. So why are you and your fellow students devoting all of this time and energy into developing these miniature volumes on the course material and not putting more energy into developing a tool that could help guide your legal analysis of problems presented on exams?

In addition to an outline, another document that some students occasionally develop as an examination aid: the checklist. There is not a single definition for a checklist or a consistent approach to drafting one. But a checklist is meant to present in a sparse and simplified way the basics about a topic that you want to be sure to remember to discuss or evaluate in the course of your examination answer. Some checklists are simply elements or rules under larger topical headings. Others are more involved in linking various concepts together in a logical pattern that facilitated the analysis of legal problems. Regardless of the format, most checklists do not make much of a contribution beyond being a condensed form of the lengthier outline prepared for the course.

Properly conceived and crafted, checklists can fulfill the role of providing a tool that truly aids you in your effort to analyze legal problems in your courses. There is a general structure to legal analysis that involves identifying the issue, articulating the applicable legal rules and principles, applying those principles to a given set of facts, and then arriving at and stating a conclusion. A checklist is the document that organizes a collection of rules, identifying all of the relevant questions and issues that you must consider in order to completely analyze a question.

The purpose of this book is to present you with a comprehensive set of checklists pertaining to each of the topics typically covered in a criminal procedure course. The checklists are meant to provide you with a tool that facilitates their analysis of procedural problems. Each chapter focuses on a different topic, first presenting a brief review of the subject followed by the checklist for the subject. After the checklist is presented, problems are analyzed to illustrate how the checklists can be used to resolve such problems. Each chapter concludes with a section entitled "Points to Remember" to recapitulate key points that you need to remember when answering exam questions. A concluding chapter provides some final thoughts on preparing for and taking exams generally. At the end of the book there is an Appendix that presents condensed "mini-checklists" for each topic. You may find these useful during the time crunch of an exam when you need quick access to the full range of major concepts that are pertinent to an issue.

You should use this book to assist yourself in developing your own analytical process for resolving the questions you will face on your examinations. The steps outlined in the checklists presented here can provide you with a map for how you should proceed when evaluating any given legal issue. Funneling your analysis through the checklist will also improve the chances that your answer will fully display a reasoned analysis while also arriving at a sound conclusion. But these checklists can only be used effectively if you have a thorough understanding of the substantive material.

This book does not attempt to explain constitutional criminal procedure doctrines in any great detail; rather, it merely seeks to organize doctrine into a dynamic tool that you can use to apply legal principles to fact patterns you will face on exams. You should use these checklists in conjunction with substantive course material to prepare for your exams. Use of these checklists should enhance your ability to write reasoned and sound responses to examination questions. Further, these checklists should be helpful in putting the course material in perspective and providing a clearer picture of how the concepts you are learning should be integrated into a legal analysis. Finally, you should make sure to modify these checklists according to the areas of emphasis and coverage of your professor.

CHAPTER 1

Incorporation & Retroactivity

A. INCORPORATION

The constitutional rights included in the first ten amendments to the United States Constitution—the "Bill of Rights"—do not apply to the States; they apply automatically only to the federal government. *Barron v. Baltimore*, 32 U.S. (7 Pet.) 243 (1833).

Prior to the adoption of the Fourteenth Amendment, the Bill of Rights was not applied to the States. Since then, the Court has been willing to apply the individual rights in the Bill of Rights to the States, using constitutional analysis and interpretation, discussed below.

1. Fundamental Rights Approach

For the first half of the 20th century, the Supreme Court decided the applicability to the States of the Bill of Rights on a right-by-right (not amendment-by-amendment) basis, using a standard of whether the asserted right violated in a particular case involved a "fundamental right." If the Court found that the right was fundamental, the right applied to the States through the authority of the Fourteenth Amendment Due Process Clause.

The test used by the Court to decide whether a right was fundamental was whether the right was "implicit in the concept of ordered liberty." *Palko v. Connecticut*, 302 U.S. 319 (1937). In *Rochin v. California*, 342 U.S. 165 (1952), the Court held that a person had a fundamental right not to have his stomach pumped forcibly, because such conduct "shocks the conscience." On the other hand, warrantless eavesdropping on bedroom conversations was permitted in *Irvine v. California*, 347 U.S. 128 (1954). The majority found that this police conduct was not as or more shocking than in *Rochin*, while the dissenters either disagreed or proposed that this whole fundamental rights approach be replaced. The dissenters' position ultimately prevailed.

2. Total Incorporation

Some Justices in the past have advocated a simple incorporation and application of *all* parts of the Bill of Rights to the States through the Fourteenth Amendment Due Process Clause. *See, e.g., Adamson v. California*, 332 U.S. 46, 71–72 (1947) (Black, J., dissenting). However, a majority of the Court rejected total incorporation for two reasons: it was an improper interpretation of the legislative history of the Fourteenth Amendment, and it failed to allow experimentation by the States about what and how liberties should be protected. *See, e.g., Adamson v. California*, 332 U.S. at 67 (Frankfurter, J., concurring).

A "total incorporation plus" approach also failed; it would incorporate not only all of the rights in the Bill of Rights, but also other rights deemed by the Court to be fundamental.

3. Selective Incorporation

Selective incorporation is a hybrid between earlier analytical methods. The Fourteenth Amendment Due Process Clause includes rights which are essential to "ordered liberty," and the protections in the Bill of Rights are the only fundamental protections. Advocates of selective incorporation believe that the fundamental rights approach is too subjective and unstructured.

Duncan v. Louisiana, 391 U.S. 145 (1968) is the leading selective incorporation decision, applying the Sixth Amendment right to a jury trial through the Fourteenth Amendment Due Process Clause to the States.

To determine whether a protection from the Bill of Rights applies to the States under the selective incorporation approach, a court looks at the entirety of the right (not just as it applies to a particular set of facts, as with the fundamental rights approach) and whether the provision is fundamental to Anglo–American jurisprudence.

Using the selective incorporation approach, the Supreme Court has applied almost every right in the Bill of Rights to the States through the Fourteenth Amendment. Although it may be regarded as fundamental, the Eighth Amendment prohibition on excessive bail does not apply to the States. As recently as the 1990s, the Court noted that the Fifth Amendment requirement for a grand jury indictment in felony cases is inapplicable to the States. *Albright v. Oliver*, 510 U.S. 266 (1994).

4. Scope of Selective Incorporation

When the Supreme Court selectively incorporates a right from the Bill of Rights to the States, a majority of the Court believes that the right as well as the case law relating to that right apply to the States as though the right is being applied in a trial in a federal court. *Duncan v. Louisiana*, 391 U.S. at 149.

Not every Justice has agreed with this principle. In *Duncan*, for example, Justice Harlan, in dissent, argued against the selective incorporation approach entirely, but he also argued that, even if a right were to be incorporated in this fashion, it should not be incorporated so as to include necessarily "the sometimes trivial accompanying *baggage* of judicial interpretation in federal contexts." In other words, some Justices argued that, even after a right was selectively incorporated, it could apply differently to the States than it does to the federal government.

Justice Harlan's view has from time to time influenced the Court's interpretation of the scope of some constitutional rights. For example, in *Apodaca v. Oregon*, 406 U.S. 404 (1972) and *Johnson v. Louisiana*, 406 U.S. 356 (1972), the Court examined whether States could constitutionally convict accused individuals with less-than-unanimous, criminal trial juries. The Court had to look at the

Sixth Amendment jury-trial right which had been selectively incorporated to the States in *Duncan*. Justice Powell concluded that the Sixth Amendment criminal jury trial right required verdict unanimity in the federal courts, but not in the State courts. Because Justice Powell's opinion also provided the fifth and the deciding vote, the Supreme Court judgment was that federal criminal juries must be unanimous, but that State criminal juries need not be.

B. RETROACTIVITY—THE SCOPE OF APPLICATION OF A CASE THAT GENERATES A NEW RULE OF LAW

1. Case-by-case Analysis

Traditionally, the prevailing litigant in a case establishing a new constitutional rule is entitled personally to the benefit of that new rule. Application of the decision to the prevailing litigant is justified as satisfying the case or controversy requirement as well as inducing challenges to improve the law.

The issue of retroactivity asks about the application of the new rule to others whose cases involve the same issue. What rule applies to them, the old or the new one? In *Linkletter v. Walker*, 381 U.S. 618 (1965), the Court held that "the Constitution neither prohibits nor requires retrospective effect." *Id.* at 629. Instead, it decided to "weigh the merits and demerits in each case by looking to the prior history of the rule in question, its purpose and effect, and whether retrospective operation will further or retard its operation." *Id.*

Applying a case-by-case, balancing approach, the *Linkletter* Court concluded that *Mapp v. Ohio*, 367 U.S. 643 (1961), the landmark decision overruling prior Supreme Court precedent and applying the exclusionary rule to the States, did not apply retroactively, i.e., it did not apply to any cases that had been finally decided prior to the date when *Mapp* was decided.

Subsequently, in *Stovall v. Denno*, 388 U.S. 293 (1967), the Court organized the retroactivity analysis: what mattered was "(a) the purpose to be served by the new standards, (b) the extent of the reliance by law enforcement authorities on the old standards, and (c) the effect on the administration of justice of a retroactive application of the new standards."

The Court did not even specify a bright-line rule for determining the operative date from which a new constitutional ruling applies when the Court rules that it applies prospectively only. It is up to the Court to decide whether a prospective decision applies from the date of the decision or from the date of the police conduct in question.

The Court's decisions over the next two decades lacked a unifying theme and produced inconsistent results, in turn making it difficult to predict how the Supreme Court would apply the *Linkletter* and *Stovall* tests to new constitutional rulings.

2. Cases Pending and Not Yet Final

There is clarity about whether a particular case was pending or "final" at the time that a new constitutional ruling was issued. A "final" decision is "a case in which a judgment of conviction has been rendered, the availability of appeal exhausted, and the time for a petition for certiorari elapsed or a petition for certiorari finally denied." *Griffith v. Kentucky*, 479 U.S. 314 (1987). And a case is deemed to be final, even though it is theoretically possible that a State court might, as a discretionary matter, decline to enforce a procedural bar to raising an issue and choose to apply a new rule of law. *Beard v. Banks*, 542 U.S. 406 (2004).

Rejection of the "Clear Break" Exception. The Court soon held that a new rule for the conduct of criminal prosecutions is to be applied retroactively to *all* cases, State or federal, pending on direct review or not yet final, with no exception for cases in which the new rule constitutes a "clear break" with the past. *Griffith v. Kentucky*, 479 U.S. 314 (1987). In *Griffith*, the Court concluded that its new constitutional ruling in *Batson v. Kentucky*, 476 U.S. 79 (1986) should be applied retroactively, even though it was a "clear break" with the Court's past precedent.

"New Rules." Retroactivity or prospectivity only becomes an issue when a court announces a *new* constitutional rule, as opposed to a ruling or clarification driven by precedent. *Schriro v. Summerlin*, 542 U.S. 348 (2004). It is not always easy, however, to figure out whether a new Supreme Court decision has stated a new constitutional rule or, instead, whether it is simply applying an existing rule to new and different circumstances. While conceding the difficulty in making the distinction, the Supreme Court has observed that "[i]n general, . . . a case announces a new rule when it breaks new ground or imposes a new obligation on the States or the Federal Government." *Teague v. Lane*, 489 U.S. 288 (1989).

3. Collateral Review

In contrast to the application of new rulings to cases still pending on direct appeal when a new constitutional ruling is handed down (i.e., not "final"), the Supreme Court concluded in 1989 that "[u]nless they fall within an exception to the general rule, new constitutional rules of criminal procedure will not be applicable to those cases which have become final before the new rules are announced." *Teague v. Lane*, 489 U.S. 288 (1989). However, *Danforth v. Minnesota*, 552 U.S. 264 (2008) held that state courts are free to give broader retroactive application than the *Teague* non-retroactivity standard which applies only in federal habeas corpus cases.

Two exceptions exist to this general rule: (1) "a new rule should be applied retroactively if it places 'certain kinds of primary, private individual conduct beyond the power of the criminal law-making authority to proscribe' "; and (2) "watershed rules of criminal procedure: . . . those new procedures without which the likelihood of an accurate conviction is seriously diminished." *Id.* at 311, 313.

Forbidden Punishment Exception. The first *Teague* exception "cover[s] not only rules forbidding criminal punishment of certain primary conduct but also rules prohibiting a certain category of punishment for a class of defendants because of their status or offense." *Penry v. Lynaugh*, 492 U.S. 302 (1989).

Watershed Rules of Criminal Procedure Exception. A watershed rule is sweeping and implicates the fundamental fairness and accuracy of a criminal proceeding. It changes the Supreme Court's understanding of the fundamental procedural elements essential to a proceeding's fairness. *Whorton v. Bockting*, 549 U.S. 406 (2007). The class of watershed rules is "extremely narrow." *Schriro v. Summerlin*, 542 U.S. 348 (2004). Since *Teague*, the Court has rejected every attempt to label a new holding as a watershed rule.

Retroactivity Inquiry Process. Federal district courts applying *Teague* in a retroactivity inquiry in habeas corpus proceedings should follow three steps. "First, the court must determine when the defendant's conviction became final. Second, it must ascertain . . . whether the rule is actually 'new.' Finally, if the rule is new, the court must consider whether it falls within either of the two exceptions to nonretroactivity." *Beard v. Banks*, 542 U.S. 406 (2004).

INCORPORATION AND RETROACTIVITY CHECKLIST

I. Incorporation

A. **Application of the Bill of Rights to the States** The rights included in the first ten amendments to the United States Constitution apply only to the federal government. ***Barron v. Baltimore***, 32 U.S. (7 Pet.) 243 (1833). Prior to the adoption of the Fourteenth Amendment, the Bill of Rights was not applied to the States.

B. **Fundamental Rights Approach**

   1. For the first half of the 20th century, the Supreme Court decided the applicability to the States of the Bill of Rights on a right-by-right basis.

   2. If the Court found that the right was fundamental, it held that the right applied to the States through the authority of the Fourteenth Amendment Due Process Clause.

   3. The test used to decide whether a right was fundamental was whether the right was "implicit in the concept of ordered liberty." ***Palko v. Connecticut***, 302 U.S. 319 (1937).

C. Total Incorporation and Total Incorporation Plus

1. The total incorporation theory for applying the Bill of Rights to the States involves an application of *all* parts of the Bill of Rights to the States through the Fourteenth Amendment Due Process Clause. *See, e.g.*, ***Adamson v. California***, 332 U.S. 46 (1947) (Black, J., dissenting).

2. A majority of the Court has rejected total incorporation, because it a) was an improper interpretation of the legislative history of the Fourteenth Amendment, and b) failed to allow experimentation by the States about what and how liberties should be protected. ***Id.*** at 67 (Frankfurter, J., concurring).

3. A "total incorporation plus" approach also failed; it would incorporate not only all of the rights in the Bill of Rights but also other rights deemed by the Court to be fundamental.

D. Selective Incorporation

1. Selective incorporation is a hybrid between the earlier analytical methods.

2. ***Duncan v. Louisiana***, 391 U.S. 145 (1968) is the leading selective incorporation decision, applying the Sixth Amendment right to a jury trial through the Fourteenth Amendment Due Process Clause to the States.

3. Under the selective incorporation approach, it is necessary to look at the entirety of the right (not just as it applies to a particular set of facts, as with the fundamental rights approach) and whether the provision is fundamental to Anglo–American jurisprudence.

4. When the Supreme Court selectively incorporates a right from the Bill of Rights to the States, a majority of Justices believes that the right as well as the case law relating to that right apply to the States as if the right is being applied in a trial in a federal court. ***Id.*** at 149.

5. The Supreme Court has applied almost every right in the Bill of Rights to the States through the Fourteenth

Amendment. The Eighth Amendment prohibition on excessive bail and the Fifth Amendment requirement for a grand jury indictment in felony cases are inapplicable to the States.

II. Retroactivity

A. A Case That Generates a New Rule of Law

1. The prevailing litigant in a case where the Supreme Court establishes a new constitutional rule is entitled personally to the benefit of that new rule.

2. The issue of retroactivity addresses the application of the new constitutional rule to others whose cases involve the same issue when the case announcing the new rule was decided.

   a. Retroactivity or prospectivity only becomes an issue when a court announces a new constitutional rule, as opposed to a ruling or clarification driven by precedent. ***Schriro v. Summerlin***, 542 U.S. 348 (2004).

   b. "In general, . . . a case announces a new rule when it breaks new ground or imposes a new obligation on the States or the Federal Government." ***Teague v. Lane***, 489 U.S. 288 (1989).

3. In ***Linkletter v. Walker***, 381 U.S. 618 (1965), the Court held that "the Constitution neither prohibits nor requires retrospective effect." Instead, the Court must "weigh the merits and demerits in each case by looking to the prior history of the rule in question, its purpose and effect, and whether retrospective operation will further or retard its operation."

4. In ***Stovall v. Denno***, 388 U.S. 293 (1967), the Court organized the retroactivity analysis. What mattered was

   a. the purpose to be served by the new standards,

   b. the extent of the reliance by law enforcement authorities on the old standards, and

  c. the effect on the administration of justice of a retroactive application of the new standards.

 5. There is no bright-line rule for determining the operative date from which a new constitutional ruling applies when the Court rules that it applies prospectively only. The Court decides whether a prospective decision applies from the date of the decision or from the date of the police conduct in question.

B. **Cases Pending and Not Yet Final**

 1. A bright-line rule does exist on the issue of whether a particular case was pending or "final" at the time that a new constitutional ruling was issued.

 2. A "final" decision is "a case in which a judgment of conviction has been rendered, the availability of appeal exhausted, and the time for a petition for certiorari elapsed or a petition for certiorari finally denied." *Griffith v. Kentucky*, 479 U.S. 314 (1987).

 3. A new rule is to be applied retroactively to all cases, State or federal, pending on direct review or not yet final, with no exception for cases in which the new rule constitutes a "clear break" with the past. *Id.*

C. **Collateral Review**

 1. "Unless they fall within an exception to the general rule, new constitutional rules of criminal procedure will not be applicable to those cases which have become final before the new rules are announced." *Teague v. Lane*, 489 U.S. 288 (1989). However, state courts are free to give broader retroactive application than the *Teague* nonretroactivity standard which applies only in federal habeas corpus cases. *Danforth v. Minnesota*, 552 U.S. 264 (2008).

 2. Federal district courts applying *Teague* in a retroactivity inquiry in habeas corpus proceedings, should "determine when the defendant's conviction became final, . . . ascertain . . . whether the rule is actually 'new,' [and], if the rule is new, . . . consider whether it falls within either of the two exceptions to nonretroactivity." *Beard v. Banks*, 542 U.S. 406 (2004).

3. Two exceptions to the general rule

    a. The first *Teague* exception "cover[s] not only rules forbidding criminal punishment of certain primary conduct but also rules prohibiting a certain category of punishment for a class of defendants because of their status or offense." ***Penry v. Lynaugh***, 492 U.S. 302 (1989).

    b. The second exception is "extremely narrow" and relates to "watershed rules of criminal procedure: . . . those new procedures without which the likelihood of an accurate conviction is seriously diminished." *Id.* at 311. Since *Teague*, the Court has rejected every attempt to label a new holding as a watershed rule.

POINTS TO REMEMBER

- The federal Bill of Rights does not apply automatically to the States.

- Most Bill of Rights protections have been "selectively incorporated" through the Fourteenth Amendment Due Process Clause to apply to the States.

- The Supreme Court is not required to apply a new constitutional ruling retroactively or prospectively, but looks at the merits and demerits in each case to determine retroactivity or from what point it will apply.

- A Supreme Court decision construing the Fourth or Fifth Amendment is to be applied retroactively to all convictions that were not yet final at the time the decision was rendered.

- Unless they fall within an exception to the general rule, new constitutional rules of criminal procedure will not be applicable to those cases which have become final before the new rules are announced.

CHAPTER 2

Right to Counsel

A. SCOPE OF THE CONSTITUTIONAL RIGHT

1. Appointed Counsel for Indigents

Source of the Constitutional Right. In 1938, the Supreme Court held that *federal* criminal defendants who could not afford an attorney had a Sixth Amendment right to have criminal defense counsel appointed for them. *Johnson v. Zerbst*, 304 U.S. 458 (1938). Twenty-five years later, the Court held in *Gideon v. Wainwright*, 372 U.S. 335 (1963) that this same Sixth Amendment right to appointed criminal defense counsel is "fundamental and necessary," and also applies to criminal defendants charged with a felony in State court criminal proceedings. Counsel is a necessity due to the State's belief that attorneys are essential to the public's prosecutorial interest. Defendants who can afford attorneys hire them. A fair and impartial system can be a reality only if indigents also face their accusers with the assistance of an attorney.

The Meaning and Consequences of "Indigency." Because the Supreme Court has never defined the meaning of "indigency" for the Sixth Amendment purposes, each jurisdiction defines this constitutional entitlement, usually by statute or court rule, in its own way. Courts consider such factors as defendant's income, property owned, outstanding obligations and the number and ages of her dependents. If the trial court finds that defendant is indigent, it must appoint counsel unless defendant waives counsel. The court may terminate the appointment upon proof that defendant is financially able to hire counsel.

Federal and State courts use different types of service-delivery systems to provide counsel for indigent defendants: public-defender programs; contract-attorney programs; or simply by means of an appropriate judge assigning the indigent's defense to a private attorney by order of appointment.

Choice of Appointed Counsel. Indigent defendants do not have the right to choose the defense attorney who will be appointed to represent them, *Wheat v. United States*, 486 U.S. 153 (1988), because a defendant has no right to a "meaningful attorney-client relationship" with appointed counsel. *Morris v. Slappy*, 461 U.S. 1 (1983). Nonetheless, a judge may use judicial discretion to appoint the particular attorney desired by an indigent defendant, if that attorney is available, if she is willing to accept the appointment, and if she is also agreeable to accepting the (typically low) compensation made available for provision of such appointed services. For example, when a defendant facing a death sentence requests that his appointed counsel be replaced, the correct standard is for the trial court to use its discretion and determine whether the "interests of justice" justify the request. *Martel v. Clair*, 132 S.Ct. 1276 (2012).

When the Right Attaches. Because the Sixth Amendment text applies to "all criminal prosecutions," not simply to "all criminal trials," the Supreme Court has held that the right to appointed counsel attaches prior to trial, at any "critical stage of the criminal prosecution" after the "initiation of adversary judicial criminal proceedings—whether by way of formal charge, preliminary hearing, indictment, information, or arraignment." *Kirby v. Illinois*, 406 U.S. 682 (1972).

A critical stage is when "potential substantial prejudice to the defendant's rights inheres in the particular confrontation, and the ability of counsel [to] help avoid that prejudice." *United States v. Wade*, 388 U.S. 218 (1967). In application to specific proceedings, the Court has found the right to counsel to apply, for example, when a criminal defendant appears at her preliminary hearing, at a guilty-plea hearing, and at a sentencing proceeding.

Rothgery v. Gillespie County, 554 U.S. 191 (2008) strongly suggested that where a first appearance involves no more than making an *ex parte* probable cause determination, giving notice of the charges, and setting bail, that first appearance does not constitute a "critical stage" requiring counsel. The right to counsel attached at the first appearance "to allow for adequate representation at any critical stage before trial, as well as the trial itself." *Id.* at 212.

"Day in Jail" Rule. In *Argersinger v. Hamlin*, 407 U.S. 25 (1972), the Supreme Court established that an indigent defendant changed with a misdemeanor cannot be imprisoned for *any* period of time unless she had the opportunity to have appointed counsel. *Argersinger* also requires appointment of counsel for defendants who receive suspended sentences (i.e., cases where imprisonment is imposed but may or may not actually occur), rather than actual, immediate incarceration, because such a sentence may ultimately result in incarceration. *Alabama v. Shelton*, 535 U.S. 654 (2002).

The so-called "day in jail" rule does not mean, however, that an indigent defendant has a right to counsel when she is charged with an offense conviction of which could result in potential imprisonment. *Scott v. Illinois*, 440 U.S. 367 (1979). A valid uncounseled misdemeanor conviction, because of no sentence of imprisonment, may be relied upon to enhance the sentence for a subsequent offense, even one that entails imprisonment. *Nichols v. United States*, 511 U.S. 738 (1994).

2. Retained Counsel

In contrast to indigent defendants, a criminal defendant who possesses sufficient financial resources to retain her own private criminal defense counsel has the right to be represented at trial by any criminal defense attorney she chooses to employ. *United States v. Gonzalez–Lopez*, 548 U.S. 140 (2006). Retained counsel must be admitted to practice law in the place where the criminal proceedings are to occur, unless the trial court exercises discretion to grant counsel special admission to the Bar of that jurisdiction for the limited purpose of representing defendant in that criminal proceeding ("*pro hac vice* admission"). The trial court's authority is discretionary, because "the Constitution does not require that because a lawyer has been admitted to the bar of one State, he or she must be allowed to practice in another." *Leis v. Flynt*, 439 U.S. 438 (1979).

B. WAIVER OF THE RIGHT TO COUNSEL

1. Knowing & Intelligent Waivers

A criminal defendant may waive her Sixth Amendment right to counsel, provided that such waiver is made knowingly and intelligently. A court must engage in careful precautions before approving a waiver of the right to counsel, i.e., the defendant has assured the court on the record that she fully understands the significance and consequences of such a waiver. *Johnson v. Zerbst*, 304 U.S. 458 (1938). A defendant must understand "the nature of the charges, the statutory offenses included within them, the range of allowable punishments thereunder, possible defenses to the charges and circumstances in mitigation thereof, and all other facts essential to a broad understanding of the whole matter." *Von Moltke v. Gillies*, 332 U.S. 708 (1948).

Since 1948, the Court has backed away from requiring the detail required by the *Von Moltke* plurality. To waive counsel in order to plead guilty, a defendant does *not* have to be advised "specifically: (1) [that] 'waiving the assistance of counsel in deciding whether to plead guilty [entails] the risk that a viable defense will be overlooked'; and (2) 'that by waiving his right to an attorney he will lose the opportunity to obtain an independent opinion on whether, under the facts and applicable law, it is wise to plead guilty.' " *Iowa v. Tovar*, 541 U.S. 77 (2004).

According to *Tovar*, a waiver of counsel is intelligent when the defendant "knows what he is doing and his choice is made with eyes open." But the Court has rejected any "formula or script to be read to a defendant who states that he elects to proceed without counsel. The information a defendant must possess in order to make an intelligent election [will] depend on a range of case-specific factors, including the defendant's education or sophistication, the complex or easily grasped nature of the charge, and the stage of the proceeding." *Id.* at 88.

2.   Representing   Oneself

Right to Represent Oneself and Proceed *Pro Se*. Despite the "strong presumption" against defendants' waivers of the Sixth Amendment right to counsel, and despite the Supreme Court's admonition that such waivers can only be accepted if made knowingly and intelligently, the Court has nonetheless permitted defendants to waive counsel and represent themselves in appropriate circumstances. In 1942, the Supreme Court ruled that "the Constitution does not force a lawyer upon a defendant. He may waive his Constitutional right to assistance of counsel if he knows what he is doing and his choice is made with eyes open." *Adams v. United States ex rel. McCann*, 317 U.S. 269 (1942).

The Supreme Court later extended the right to proceed *pro se* to criminal defendants being tried in State court criminal proceedings. *Faretta v. California*, 422 U.S. 806 (1975). Before invoking the right to self-representation, the defendant must make an unequivocal request which also must be timely. In response, the trial court holds a hearing to determine whether the defendant is competent to make the decision to completely or partially waive the right to counsel, and whether to appoint standby counsel. The standard for waiving the right to counsel is the same as the competency standard for standing trial. *Godinez v. Moran*, 509 U.S. 389 (1993).

Indiana v. Edwards, 554 U.S. 164 (2008), recognized a trial court's authority to deny *pro se* representation in cases where the defendant's mental illness interferes with self-representation, even when the defendant is mentally competent to stand trial and understands the disadvantages of self-representation described in *Faretta*. For the waiver to be intelligent and knowing, the defendant's "technical legal knowledge" is irrelevant.

Standby Counsel. In *Faretta*, the Supreme Court acknowledged that "a State may—even over objection by the accused—

appoint a 'standby counsel' to aid the accused if and when the accused requests help, and to be available to represent the accused in the event that termination of the defendant's self-representation is necessary." *Faretta*, 422 U.S. at 836. In *McKaskle v. Wiggins*, 465 U.S. 168 (1984), the Supreme Court offered guidance on the proper role of standby counsel. Against his periodic wishes, McKaskle's standby criminal defense attorneys made motions, questioned witnesses, and conducted colloquies with the judge. The Court recognized that "the *Faretta* right must impose some limits on the extent of standby counsel's unsolicited participation." *Id.* at 834 n. 46.

The *pro se* defendant is entitled to preserve actual control over the case he chooses to present to the jury. The *Faretta* right is eroded if standby counsel's participation over the defendant's objection effectively allows counsel to make or substantially interfere with any significant tactical decisions, or to control the questioning of witnesses, or to speak instead of the defendant on any matter of importance. In addition, the trial court cannot permit standby counsel's participation without the defendant's consent to destroy the jury's perception that the defendant is representing herself.

C.   INEFFECTIVE ASSISTANCE OF COUNSEL

In 1932, the Supreme Court concluded that a criminal defendant's Sixth Amendment right to counsel includes the right to the "effective" assistance of counsel. *Powell v. Alabama*, 287 U.S. 45 (1932). The right to effective assistance applies not only to trial, but also to guilty pleas, sentencing, and a first appeal of right. Whether a defendant has a right to effective assistance of counsel during state post conviction proceedings is still an open question after *Martinez v. Ryan*, 132 S.Ct. 1309 (2012).

Conversely, if there is no right to counsel, no right to effective assistance exists. A defendant whose counsel is unable to provide effective representation is in no better position than one who has no counsel at all. The standard of review applied to all types of ineffectiveness claims does not vary with the status of counsel as retained or court-appointed. *Cuyler v. Sullivan*, 446 U.S. 335 (1980). The remedy for ineffective assistance is automatic reversal of the conviction.

1. *Per Se* Ineffectiveness

The question that is raised when a criminal defendant claims that her defense counsel was guilty of "extrinsic ineffectiveness" is whether some factor or factors *extrinsic* to counsel's *actual* performance created a permissible inference of Sixth Amendment ineffectiveness. Such claims focus commonly, for example, on counsel's age, her inexperience overall or in criminal cases, disability, personal or emotional problems, alcoholism or substance abuse problems, problems with the law, insufficient preparation time, or disciplinary issues with the Bar.

In *United States v. Cronic*, 466 U.S. 648 (1984), the Supreme Court established criteria for evaluating when claims of extrinsic ineffectiveness establish ineffective assistance of counsel. The criteria make it almost impossible for a criminal defendant to make a successful claim. After appointment, Cronic's trial-inexperienced, young, real estate attorney had only twenty-five days to prepare a complicated case that the prosecution had investigated for four and one-half years and which involved thousands of documents and hundreds of checks.

The Court refused either to make an inference of ineffective assistance or to accept a hypothetical basis for finding ineffectiveness, concluding that ordinarily a defendant can "make out a claim of ineffective assistance only by pointing to specific errors made by trial counsel."

The *Cronic* Court recognized exceptions to the general rule that ineffectiveness cannot ordinarily be established extrinsically. Besides a complete denial of counsel at a critical stage of the trial, "if counsel entirely fails to subject the prosecution's case to a meaningful adversarial testing, then there has been a denial of Sixth Amendment rights that makes the adversary process itself presumptively unreliable." *Id.* at 659.

Despite the exceptions, rarely does an appellate court reverse a conviction due to extrinsic ineffectiveness. For example, extrinsic ineffectiveness did not exist when defense counsel conceded his client's guilt of the murder with which he was charged. A "concession of . . . guilt does not rank as a 'fail[ure] to function in any meaningful sense as the Government's adversary.' " *Florida v. Nixon*, 543 U.S. 175 (2004).

An "attorney's failure must be complete." *Bell v. Cone*, 535 U.S. 685 (2002). Accordingly, allegations of a defense counsel's failures at specific points (e.g., failure to introduce mitigating evidence, waiver of closing argument) may raise issues of *actual* ineffectiveness under *Strickland* (discussed in the next section), but not under *Cronic*. Similarly, a trial court's order denying a defendant the opportunity to consult with his attorney during a fifteen-minute recess taken while the defendant was continuing to testify was not extrinsic ineffective assistance because the order did not amount to "[a]ctual or constructive denial of the assistance of counsel altogether." *Perry v. Leeke*, 488 U.S. 272 (1989).

2.   Actual   Ineffectiveness

In a companion case to *Cronic*, *Strickland v. Washington*, 466 U.S. 668 (1984), the Supreme Court established the criteria for ineffective assistance of counsel when claims of *actual* episodes of ineffectiveness are alleged. Counsel's action or inaction as to a particular matter must be judged in the context of her total representation and the strength of the government's evidence.

In *Strickland*, defendant Washington ignored his counsel's advice, and pleaded guilty to all offenses for which he was indicted, including three counts of first-degree murder. During Washington's guilty-plea colloquy, in which he "accepted responsibility for the crimes," the trial judge told him that he respected people who admitted their criminal responsibility "but that he was making no statement at all about his likely sentencing decision." The trial judge sentenced Washington to death at his capital sentencing hearing.

Washington's counsel admitted to having done little preparation for the capital sentencing hearing: his client discussed his background, and he spoke by phone with Washington's wife and mother. He did not otherwise seek out character witnesses or request a psychiatric examination, since the conversations with his client gave no indication that Washington had psychological problems. The Supreme Court explained why counsel intentionally decided to do nothing more to prepare. "That decision reflected trial counsel's sense of hopelessness about overcoming the evidentiary effect of respondent's confessions to the gruesome crimes." *Id.* at 673. He also decided to rely on the plea colloquy for evidence about Washington's background and his claim of emotional stress, in order to prevent the prosecutor from cross-examining the defendant at a sentencing hearing. "Counsel also excluded from the sentencing hearing other evidence he thought was potentially damaging." *Id.* For example, he did not request preparation of a presentence report which would have included his client's criminal history.

On the basis of the record, the Supreme Court concluded that Washington had *not* proved ineffective assistance of counsel. The Court's standard involves a fact-sensitive analysis which measures the quality and impact of counsel's representation under the circumstances of the individual case. The federal constitutional standard for reviewing an allegation of ineffective assistance of counsel involves: (1) a finding of an error in counsel's performance, and (2) prejudice resulting from that error which had an adverse effect on the outcome, i.e., but for counsel's unprofessional errors, a reasonable probability exists that the result of the proceeding would have been different or that the defendant would have chosen a different course of action. *Strickland v. Washington*, 466 U.S. 668 (1984); *Hill v. Lockhart*, 474 U.S. 52 (1985).

The two parts of the test are independent of one another. A defendant must show *both* that her defense counsel performed deficiently *and* that the deficient performance actually prejudiced her defense. The Court pointed out that "there is no reason for a court deciding an ineffective assistance claim to approach the [two-pronged] inquiry in [a certain] order or even to address both components of the inquiry if the defendant makes an insufficient showing on one."

The Performance Prong. To apply the prejudice standard, a court must assess the strength or weakness of the prosecution's case and the importance of defense counsel's error, viewed at the time of counsel's conduct. For example, if the evidence against the defendant is overwhelming, a conviction will be affirmed no matter how fundamental is counsel's error. In making this determination, reviewing courts examine the totality of circumstances.

No one specific task by defense counsel qualifies counsel as effective. The Court rejected an approach using a "checklist for judicial evaluation of attorney performance." Instead, as the *Strickland* Court stressed, "the proper standard for attorney performance is that of reasonably effective assistance." "There are countless ways to provide effective assistance in any given case. Even the best criminal defense attorneys would not defend a particular client in the same way." *Id.* at 689.

The Court did define general duties that defense counsel *must* undertake on behalf of the client. "[C]ounsel owes the client a duty of loyalty, a duty to avoid conflicts of interest." Counsel has a duty to advocate the defendant's cause, to consult with the defendant on important decisions, to inform the defendant about important developments in the case, and to use her skills and knowledge in order to "render the trial a reliable adversarial testing process." *Id.*

In general, a defendant is likely to establish incompetency where counsel's alleged errors of omissions or commission are attributable to a lack of diligence. For example, in *Evitts v. Lucey*, 469 U.S. 387 (1985), counsel's failure to follow a simple court rule about filing a statement of appeal with an appellate brief constituted ineffective assistance of counsel rather than an exercise of judgment. By contrast, *Burger v. Kemp*, 483 U.S. 776 (1987) held that counsel's strategic decision not to mount an extensive investigation into the defendant's background in search of mitigating circumstances was supported by the attorney's reasonable professional judgment which is afforded a heavy measure of deference.

Courts find incompetency far more readily where there has been an abdication rather than an exercise of professional judgment. The crucial factor is how far a court is willing to go in assuming that counsel's actions are strategic, in accord with the general presumption of competence. For example, in *Wiggins v. Smith*, 539 U.S. 510 (2003), defense counsel in a capital case decided not to expand their penalty phase investigation beyond a presentence investigation report and a social services report. The Court held that this performance level was below professional standards prevailing in the State at the time of the trial.

In *Wiggins*, standard practice at the time included preparation of a social history report. Although funds existed to retain a forensic social worker, a report was not commissioned. Because counsel knew from the social services report about defendant's alcoholic mother and his problems in foster care, the decision to cease investigating was unreasonable. A reasonably competent attorney would have known that those leads would assist in making an informed choice among possible defenses. In addition, counsel discovered nothing to suggest that mitigation evidence would have been counterproductive or that further investigation would have been fruitless. This distinguished the case from precedents in which the Court had found limited investigations into mitigating evidence to be reasonable. The record showed that counsel's failure to investigate thoroughly resulted from inattention, not a strategic judgment.

Similarly, in *Rompilla v. Beard*, 545 U.S. 374 (2005), trial counsel failed to present mitigating evidence in the penalty phase about the defendant's childhood, mental capacity and health, and alcoholism. The Supreme Court held that "even when a capital defendant's family members and the defendant himself have suggested that no mitigating evidence is available, his lawyer is bound to make reasonable efforts to obtain and review material that counsel knows the prosecution will probably rely on as evidence of aggravation at the sentencing phase of trial." Although no one allegation of ineffectiveness may be sufficiently meritorious, a finding of ineffective assistance may be based upon the cumulative effect of the errors.

Strategic Decisions. A defendant is most likely to establish defective performance by proving a lack of diligence rather than an exercise of judgment such as deciding whether to investigate, whether to file a motion to dismiss the charge or to suppress evidence, or whether to raise substantive defenses. Some decisions belong to the defendant, e.g., decisions as to guilty plea, jury trial, appeal, and whether the defendant will testify. *Brookhart v. Janis*, 384 U.S. 1 (1966); *Jones v. Barnes*, 463 U.S. 745 (1983).

While strategic choices are not regarded as constituting deficient performance, defense counsel *is* subject to an ineffectiveness claim when such choices are made after less than complete investigation. *Rompilla v. Beard* suggested, however, that a reasonable lawyer is not required to look "for a needle in a haystack, when [she] truly has reason to doubt there is any needle there." When counsel informs the defendant of the strategy counsel believes to be in the defendant's best interest and the defendant is unresponsive, counsel's strategic choice is not impeded by any blanket rule demanding the defendant's explicit consent.

If counsel's strategy, given the evidence bearing on the defendant's guilt, satisfies the *Strickland* standard, that is the end of the matter; no tenable claim of ineffective assistance would remain. For example, in *Florida v. Nixon*, 543 U.S. 175 (2004), defense counsel was not presumptively ineffective by failing to obtain client's express approval of a strategy to concede guilt to a capital offense and focus on urging mercy during the penalty phase. In *Knowles v. Mirzayance*, 556 U.S. 111 (2009), the Court held that, after the guilt phase, defense counsel's recommendation that the client withdraw his insanity defense was not deficient performance; the recommendation instead was based on counsel's reasonable belief that the insanity defense was doomed because medical testimony had already been rejected and the defendant's parents were unavailable to testify.

Decisions on a substantially larger group of matters, such as objecting to evidence, *Wainwright v. Sykes*, 433 U.S. 72 (1977), or selecting witnesses are for counsel. Decisions within the client's control are simply described as involving "fundamental rights," while those within the lawyer's control are said to involve matters requiring the superior ability of trained counsel in assessing strategy.

In *Strickland*, applying the performance prong to the facts was not difficult, because the Court viewed counsel's decisions as strategic.

> Although counsel understandably felt hopeless about respondent's prospects, nothing in the record indicates that counsel's sense of hopelessness distorted his professional judgment. Counsel's strategy choice was well within the range of professionally reasonable judgments, and the decision not to seek more character or psychological evidence than was already in hand was likewise reasonable. 466 U.S. at 699.

The Prejudice Prong. *Strickland* ruled that a defendant must show both that her defense counsel performed deficiently *and* that the deficient performance actually prejudiced the defense. Prejudice may be presumed or proved by the defendant. *Strickland* stated that prejudice may be presumed in three circumstances. First, it may be presumed when there is an actual or constructive denial of counsel, such as where counsel is asleep for long periods of time during the proceeding, or where counsel is not a member of the bar. Second, when the state interferes with the lawyer's assistance, prejudice is presumed as where there is a late appointment of counsel or where the judge denies the defense counsel the right to cross-examine witnesses. Finally, prejudice is presumed where defense counsel is burdened by an actual conflict of interest.

If prejudice is not presumed, the defendant must show that trial errors prejudiced the defendant by depriving her of a fair trial whose result is reliable. Defendant must show a reasonable probability that, but for defense counsel's errors, the results of the case would have been different. "A reasonable probability is a probability sufficient to undermine confidence in the outcome."

As with the performance prong, *Strickland* established a presumption against a finding of prejudice. Applying the standard to the facts, the Court concluded that defendant Washington had not in fact been prejudiced by his counsel's conduct. The Court explained that "[g]iven the overwhelming aggravating factors, there is no reasonable probability that the omitted evidence would have changed the conclusion that the aggravating circumstances outweighed the mitigating circumstances and, hence, the sentence imposed."

"[T]he 'prejudice' component of the *Strickland* test focuses on the question whether counsel's deficient performance renders the result of the trial unreliable or the proceeding fundamentally unfair. Unreliability or unfairness does not result if the ineffectiveness of counsel does not deprive the defendant of any substantive or procedural right to which the law entitles him." *Lockhart v. Fretwell,* 506 U.S. 364 (1993). An argument that focuses "solely on mere outcome determination, without attention to whether the result of the proceeding was fundamentally unfair or unreliable, is defective."

In decisions after *Strickland*, the Court has found no prejudice where defense counsel threatened to withdraw if his client perjured himself at trial, *Nix v. Whiteside*, 475 U.S. 157 (1986), where defense counsel failed to make an objection in a capital sentencing hearing that would have (then) been supported by a decision that was subsequently overruled, *Lockhart v. Fretwell*, 506 U.S. 364 (1993), and where defense counsel had misinformed his client of his parole eligibility date in explaining to him the consequences of his contemplated guilty plea, *Hill v. Lockhart*, 474 U.S. 52 (1985).

On the other hand, the Court has also concluded that defense counsel's failure to object to a legal error that affected the calculation of a prison sentence, thereby resulting in additional incarceration, is clearly prejudicial to a defendant. "[A]ny amount of actual jail time has Sixth Amendment significance." *Glover v. United States*, 531 U.S. 198 (2001).

Ineffective Assistance in Plea Bargaining. Defense counsel may be ineffective if she fails to properly inform the defendant of a beneficial plea agreement offered by the prosecution, or if she incorrectly advises the defendant on the state of the law, leading the defendant to reject a beneficial plea agreement. *Missouri v. Frye*, 132 S.Ct. 1399 (2012); *Lafler v. Cooper*, 132 S.Ct. 1376 (2012).

The *Frye* Court held that defense counsel has a duty under the Sixth Amendment to communicate formal plea offers from the prosecution. Exceptions to that duty were not "explored" by the Court. In *Lafler*, the Court held that counsel's assistance is prejudicially ineffective where the defendant shows that 1) but for the ineffective advice of counsel there is a reasonable probability that the plea offer would have been accepted and brought before the court, 2) that the court would have accepted its terms, and 3) that the conviction or sentence would have been lesser than under those imposed after trial. The proper remedy is not specific performance of the original plea; on remand, the prosecution should re-offer the plea and, if the defendant accepts it, the trial court can decide how to amend the original sentence.

3. Ineffective Assistance Analysis in Federal Habeas Corpus Proceedings

In 1996, Congress enacted the Antiterrorism & Effective Death Penalty Act of 1996 ("AEDPA"), which provides in part that

> [a]n application for a writ of habeas corpus on behalf of a person in custody pursuant to the judgment of a State court shall not be granted with respect to any claim that was adjudicated on the merits in State court proceedings unless the adjudication of the claim * * * resulted in a decision that was contrary to, or involved an unreasonable application of, clearly established Federal law, as determined by the Supreme Court of the United States.

28 U.S.C. § 2254(d)(1).

For purposes of evaluating Sixth Amendment claims of defense counsel's ineffectiveness, the fact that a State court may have made an *incorrect* constitutional ruling on an ineffectiveness inquiry does not suffice under the AEDPA provision to entitle a defendant to habeas corpus relief. *Williams v. Taylor*, 529 U.S. 362 (2000). As *Williams* stated, "an *unreasonable* application of federal law is different from an *incorrect* application of federal law. . . . Congress specifically used the word 'unreasonable,' and not a term like 'erroneous' or 'incorrect.' " Thus, it is insufficient to conclude that counsel's decision was erroneous or incorrect; counsel's judgment must also have been unreasonable.

The Court has repeated its distinction between an unreasonable and an incorrect State court decision. In *Woodford v. Visciotti*, 537 U.S. 19 (2002), the Court concluded that, while the California Supreme Court may have *incorrectly* concluded that a capital defendant whose defense counsel failed to introduce available mitigating evidence was not prejudiced given the severity of the aggravating factors also in evidence, such a conclusion was not unreasonable. Again, in *Bell v. Cone*, 535 U.S. 685 (2002), the Court concluded that a Tennessee appellate court did not act unreasonably in concluding that defense counsel at a capital sentencing hearing was not ineffective (1) for failing to present sufficient mitigating evidence, and (2) by waiving final argument.

However, the Court has not always justified incorrect State court decisions relating to ineffective assistance of counsel as reasonable, for AEDPA purposes. For example, in *Rompilla v. Beard*, 545 U.S. 374 (2005), the Court found that the Pennsylvania Supreme Court had acted incorrectly and objectively unreasonably in concluding that defense counsel in a capital case were not ineffective when they failed to make reasonable efforts to obtain and review critical material relating to a prior conviction that counsel knew the prosecution would probably rely upon as evidence of aggravation at the sentencing phase of trial.

4. When Ineffective Assistance Claims Can Be Brought

In *Massaro v. United States*, 538 U.S. 500 (2003), the Supreme Court unanimously concluded that "an ineffective assistance of counsel claim may be brought in a collateral proceeding," whether or not the defendant could have raised the claim on direct appeal. In addition, a defendant may claim that state counsel in a collateral proceeding was ineffective in failing to raise his ineffective-assistance-at-trial claim; in a federal habeas proceeding, i.e., collateral proceeding counsel's ineffectiveness may excuse the procedural default. *Martinez v. Ryan*, 132 S.Ct. 1309 (2012).

D. CONFLICTS OF INTEREST

The constitutional right to effective assistance of counsel entitles the defendant to the "undivided loyalty" of counsel. The defendant loses the full benefit of the adversary process when counsel's decisions are influenced by obligations owed to other persons. The situation producing the most frequent conflict claims is the representation of more than one codefendant by the same attorney.

Although codefendants may start out with identical concerns, a divergence of interests may develop at almost every point in the progress of the litigation. One defendant may receive an attractive plea bargain, while the other may receive a less attractive offer or none at all. Codefendants may raise conflicting defenses, or have different levels of culpability, which may affect defense counsel's closing arguments or approach to sentencing. One defendant's decision to testify may highlight the lack of testimony from the other.

A lawyer may also be placed in a conflict situation when there is a professional relationship with both the defendant and a third party who has some interest in the case, or when someone with an interest in the case pays the legal fees of defense counsel. *Wood v. Georgia*, 450 U.S. 261 (1981).

A criminal defense attorney's conflict of interest by representing a defendant can amount to ineffective assistance of counsel. *Glasser v. United States*, 315 U.S. 60 (1942). When there are conflicting interests, "the evil . . . is in what the advocate finds himself compelled to *refrain* from doing, not only at trial but also as to possible pretrial plea negotiations and in the sentencing process." *Holloway v. Arkansas*, 435 U.S. 475 (1978) (emphasis in original).

The Court did not establish a *per se* rule against joint representation. However, the Court stated that, when trial counsel timely alerts the trial court to the risk of a conflict of interest, the trial judge must "either [appoint] separate counsel or [take] adequate steps to ascertain whether the risk was too remote to warrant separate counsel."

When faced with a possible conflict, a court can hold a remoteness-of-risk hearing to determine whether or not the risk of conflict is real. The hearing must include a thorough, meaningful inquiry into any and all potential for conflict. Given the nature of the hearing inquiry and of applicable ethical rules, trial courts can appoint separate counsel when current counsel raises the conflict of interest issue. Where counsel raises the potential conflict issue but the trial court fails to either grant the motion or hold a hearing, reversal of a defendant's conviction is "automatic," even without a showing of prejudice. *Mickens v. Taylor*, 535 U.S. 162 (2002).

Cuyler v. Sullivan, 446 U.S. 335 (1980) addressed the issue left open in *Holloway*: when does an alleged conflict of interest, not raised prior to or during trial, amount to ineffective assistance of counsel? The Court concluded that the timing of when the issue was raised required a different approach. "[A] defendant who raised no objection at trial must demonstrate that an actual conflict of interest adversely affected his lawyer's performance." In *Holloway*, the Court had concluded that a trial court's failure to adequately respond to defense counsel's motion for separate counsel automatically required a reversal of the defendant's conviction without showing, as *Cuyler* required, that "an actual conflict of interest" existed which "adversely affected [the defendant's] lawyer's performance."

A trial judge has the discretion to refuse waivers of conflicts of interest in both actual and potential conflict situations, without violating a defendant's Sixth Amendment right to her counsel of choice. In *Wheat v. United States*, 486 U.S. 153 (1988), the Court held that a defendant may waive a conflict of interest with regard to her attorney and a trial judge must recognize a presumption in favor of a defendant's counsel of choice, but that presumption may be overcome by a demonstration of either an actual conflict or a serious potential for conflict.

E. THE *GRIFFIN–DOUGLAS* DOCTRINE

The government has a constitutional obligation to redress the consequences of indigency in the criminal justice system. In *Griffin v. Illinois*, 351 U.S. 12 (1956), the Supreme Court concluded that an indigent prisoner appealing from his conviction in State court had a Fourteenth Amendment right (under both the Due Process and Equal Protection Clauses) to a free trial transcript where such transcripts were often a practical necessity for success on appeal.

In *Douglas v. California*, 372 U.S. 353 (1963), the Court held that indigent defendants convicted at trial have a Fourteenth Amendment right (again, under both the Due Process and Equal Protection Clauses) to the assistance of counsel on a first appeal where the State has granted them the right to appeal (as contrasted with situations where appeal is only discretionary).

However, in *Ross v. Moffitt*, 417 U.S. 600 (1974), the Court changed the focus of the standard. Instead of focusing on whether an indigent defendant could obtain the same sort of services that a non-indigent defendant could or would receive, the Court concluded that "[t]he duty of the State under our cases is not to duplicate the legal arsenal that may be privately retained by a criminal defendant in a continuing effort to reverse his conviction, but only to assure the indigent defendant an adequate opportunity to present his claims fairly. . . . "

Applying this less-demanding test, *Ross* ruled that indigents undertaking State discretionary appeals (as opposed to appeals as of right) and appeals to the United States Supreme Court (which are also discretionary) are not entitled to the appointment of counsel, even though a non-indigent would have the resources and, hence, could retain such appellate counsel. "Unfairness results only if indigents are singled out by the State and denied meaningful access to the appellate system because of their poverty."

Halbert v. Michigan, 545 U.S. 605 (2005) addressed whether there is a constitutional entitlement to appointed counsel on an appeal as of right when a convicted defendant has pleaded guilty or *nolo contendere*. The Court stated that

> Halbert's case is framed by two prior decisions of this Court concerning State-funded appellate counsel, *Douglas* and *Ross*. The question before us is essentially one of classification: With which of those decisions should the instant case be aligned? We hold that *Douglas* provides the controlling instruction."

"[I]ndigent defendants pursuing first-tier review in the Court of Appeals are generally ill equipped to represent themselves.

Other post-*Ross* Supreme Court decisions raising *Griffin–Douglas* doctrine issues have focused on what constitutes "meaningful access to justice." For example, in *Ake v. Oklahoma*, 470 U.S. 68 (1985), the Court held that a defendant was entitled to have access to a psychiatrist and a psychiatric examination when raising an insanity defense, because such services are a necessary, basic tool when the issue of sanity is raised at trial or sentencing. Thus, indigent defendants have the right to expert services under *Griffin–Douglas* in order to have "an adequate opportunity to present their claims fairly within the adversary system."

Indigent defendants also have constitutional rights relating to transcripts and filing fees: (1) a trial transcript for use in a collateral attack upon a conviction, *United States v. MacCollom*, 426 U.S. 317 (1976); (2) a transcript of a habeas corpus proceeding to be used on appeal from a denial of habeas relief, cf. *Eskridge v. Washington State Bd. of Prison Terms and Paroles*, 357 U.S. 214 (1958), or in filing a second habeas petition, *Gardner v. California*, 393 U.S. 367 (1969); and (3) a transcript of a preliminary hearing to be used in preparing for trial, *Roberts v. LaVallee*, 389 U.S. 40 (1967).

Transcripts for use on appeal have generally been required where they were the usual and preferable means of presenting a claim of the type asserted by the indigent defendant. Where the grounds of appeal make out a colorable need for a transcript, the burden is on the prosecution to establish the adequacy of a less costly alternative. *Mayer v. City of Chicago*, 404 U.S. 189 (1971). Courts will look more closely at alternatives, however, where a transcript is no longer available through no fault of the prosecution. *Norvell v. Illinois*, 373 U.S. 420 (1963).

Filing fees for appeals and post-conviction proceedings do not apply to indigent defendants. *Burns v. Ohio*, 360 U.S. 252 (1959); *Smith v. Bennett*, 365 U.S. 708 (1961).

RIGHT TO COUNSEL CHECKLIST

I. Scope of the Constitutional Right to Counsel

A. **Appointed Counsel for Indigents**

    1. **Source of the Constitutional Right**

        a. Federal criminal defendants who cannot afford an attorney have a constitutional right to have criminal defense counsel appointed for them under the Sixth Amendment. *Johnson v. Zerbst*, 304 U.S. 458 (1938).

        b. In *Gideon v. Wainwright*, 372 U.S. 335 (1963), the same Sixth Amendment right to appointed criminal defense counsel is "fundamental and necessary," and also applies to criminal defendants in State criminal proceedings.

        c. Counsel is a necessity, because States believe that attorneys are essential to the public's prosecutorial interest. Defendants who can afford attorneys hire them. A fair and impartial system can be a reality only if indigents face their accusers with the assistance of an attorney.

    2. **The Meaning & Consequences of "Indigency"**

        a. Each jurisdiction defines this constitutional entitlement, usually by statute or court rule.

        b. Federal and State courts use different types of service-delivery systems to provide counsel for indigent defendants: public-defender programs, contract-attorney programs, or simply by appointment.

    3. **Choice of Appointed Counsel**. An indigent defendant does not have the right to choose the defense attorney who will be appointed to represent her. *Wheat v. United States*, 486 U.S. 153, 159 (1988).

4. **When the Right Attaches**

    a. The right to appointed counsel attaches prior to trial or at any critical stage of the criminal prosecution.

    b. Case law has defined a critical stage as "at or after the initiation of adversary judicial criminal proceedings, whether by way of formal charge, preliminary hearing, indictment, information, or arraignment."

5. **"Day in Jail" Rule**

    a. An indigent defendant who has a right to cannot be imprisoned for *any* period of time unless she had the opportunity to have appointed counsel. ***Argersinger v. Hamlin***, 407 U.S. 25 (1972).

    b. Appointed counsel is also necessary for defendants who receive suspended sentences (i.e., cases where imprisonment is imposed but may or may not actually occur), rather than actual, immediate incarceration. ***Alabama v. Shelton***, 535 U.S. 654 (2002).

    c. However, an indigent defendant has no right to counsel when she is charged with an offense which could result in potential imprisonment. ***Scott v. Illinois***, 440 U.S. 367 (1979).

B. **Retained Counsel**

1. A criminal defendant with sufficient financial resources has the right to be represented at trial by any attorney she chooses to employ. ***United States v. Gonzalez–Lopez***, 548 U.S. 140 (2006).

2. A defendant does not have the right to retain any counsel. Even the right to retained counsel must yield to overriding governmental interests.

    a. Counsel with a conflict of interest may have to withdraw from representing the defendant. See Part IV of this Checklist.

b. Counsel must be admitted to practice in the
       court, permanently or (within the court's dis-
       cretion) temporarily. *Id.*

II. Waiver of the Right to Counsel

A. Knowing and Intelligent Waivers

   1. A criminal defendant may waive her Sixth Amendment
       right to counsel knowingly and intelligently. A court must
       engage in careful precautions on the record that the
       defendant fully understands the significance and conse-
       quences of such a waiver. *Johnson v. Zerbst*, 304 U.S. 458
       (1938).

   2. **Guilty Plea Waiver of Counsel**

       a. In a guilty plea situation, a judge must conduct
           a comprehensive dialogue with the defendant
           about all of the circumstances of the plea to
           assure that rights are waived knowingly and
           intelligently. *Von Moltke v. Gillies*, 332 U.S. 708
           (1948).

       b. To waive counsel in order to plead guilty, a
           defendant is not required to be advised "spe-
           cifically: (1) [that] 'waiving the assistance of
           counsel in deciding whether to plead guilty
           [entails] the risk that a viable defense will be
           overlooked'; and (2) 'that by waiving his right
           to an attorney he will lose the opportunity to
           obtain an independent opinion on whether,
           under the facts and applicable law, it is wise to
           plead guilty.' " *Iowa v. Tovar*, 541 U.S. 77
           (2004).

   3. A waiver of counsel is intelligently made even without a
       "formula or script." Relevant information is case-specific,
       "including the defendant's education or sophistication,
       the complex or easily grasped nature of the charge, and
       the stage of the proceeding."

B. **Representing Oneself**

    1. Despite the admonition that waivers can only be accepted if made knowingly and intelligently, the Court has none-theless permitted defendants to waive counsel and repre-sent themselves in appropriate circumstances.

        a. A defendant has the right to proceed *pro se*. ***Adams v. United States ex rel. McCann***, 317 U.S. 269 (1942).

        b. In ***Faretta v. California***, 422 U.S. 806 (1975), the Court reasoned that, despite the paternal-istic desire to assist defendants, assigned coun-sel cannot ordinarily be forced upon an accused.

        c. The defendant must be competent to waive counsel's assistance. See ***Godinez v. Moran***, 509 U.S. 389 (1993). A trial court has authority to deny *pro se* representation in cases where the defendant's mental illness interferes with self-representation, even when the defendant is mentally competent to stand trial and under-stands the disadvantages of self-representation. ***Indiana v. Edwards***, 554 U.S. 164 (2008).

        d. For the waiver to be intelligent and knowing, the defendant's "technical legal knowledge" is irrelevant. ***Faretta v. California***.

        e. A violation of *Faretta* cannot be harmless error, because the defendant is deprived of her choice of counsel.

    2. **Standby Counsel**. A court "may—even over objection by the accused—appoint a 'standby counsel' to aid the accused if and when the accused requests help, . . . [or if] termination of the defendant's self-representation is necessary."

        a. The *pro se* defendant is entitled to preserve actual control over the case. Standby counsel cannot substantially interfere with any significant tactical decisions by the defendant, or control the questioning of witnesses, or speak instead of the defendant on any matter of importance. ***McKaskle v. Wiggins***, 465 U.S. 168 (1984).

b. Ordinarily, the trial court cannot permit standby counsel's participation without the defendant's consent.

III. Ineffective Assistance of Counsel

A. A defendant's right to counsel includes the right to the "effective" assistance of counsel. ***Powell v. Alabama***, 287 U.S. 45 (1932). That right applies not only to trial, but also to guilty pleas, sentencing, and a first appeal of right. ***Evitts v. Lucey***, 469 U.S. 387 (1985). Conversely, if there is no right to counsel (e.g., ***Pennsylvania v. Finley***, 481 U.S. 551 (1987)), no right to effective assistance exists.

B. *Per Se* **Ineffectiveness**

1. A criminal defendant may claim *per se* or "extrinsic" ineffectiveness. The issue becomes whether some factor extrinsic to counsel's actual performance created a permissible inference of Sixth Amendment ineffectiveness.

   a. Claims focus commonly on counsel's age, inexperience, disability, personal or emotional problems, alcoholism or substance abuse problems, problems with the law, insufficient preparation time, or disciplinary issues with the Bar.

   b. ***United States v. Cronic***, 466 U.S. 648 (1984) established criteria for evaluating when claims of extrinsic ineffectiveness satisfy ineffective assistance of counsel criteria.

   c. After appointment, Cronic's trial-inexperienced, young, real estate attorney had only twenty-five days to prepare a complicated case that was more than four years old and involved thousands of documents.

        d.   The Court concluded that ordinarily a defendant can "make out a claim of ineffective assistance only by pointing to specific errors made by trial counsel."

    2. *Cronic* recognized exceptions to the general rule that ineffectiveness cannot ordinarily be established *per se.*

        a.   One example offered by the Court occurs "if counsel entirely fails to subject the prosecution's case to a meaningful adversarial testing. . . ."

        b.   Reversals are rare for *per se* ineffectiveness. For example, *per se* ineffectiveness did not exist because defense counsel conceded his client's guilt of the murder. ***Florida v. Nixon***, 543 U.S. 175 (2004).

        c.   An "attorney's failure must be complete" rather than at specific points during the trial. ***Bell v. Cone***, 535 U.S. 685 (2002). Defense counsel's failures at specific points (e.g., failure to introduce mitigating evidence, waiver of closing argument) raise issues of *actual* ineffectiveness rather than *per se* ineffectiveness.

C. Actual Ineffectiveness

    1. ***Strickland v. Washington***, 466 U.S. 668 (1984) established criteria for effective (or ineffective) assistance of counsel when claims of actual ineffectiveness are alleged. The Court described a two-pronged test for measuring the ineffective assistance of counsel.

        a.   Defendant must show that counsel's performance was deficient, and that the deficient performance prejudiced the defense.

        b.   The two prongs are independent of one another, i.e., a defendant must show *both* that her defense counsel performed deficiently *and* that the deficient performance actually prejudiced her defense.

2. **The Performance Prong**. No one specific task by defense counsel qualifies counsel as effective.

    a. The proper standard for attorney performance is that of reasonably effective assistance, with a strong presumption that counsel's conduct falls within the wide range of reasonable professional assistance.

    b. A defendant must overcome the presumption that, under the circumstances, the challenged action may be considered sound trial strategy.

    c. *Strickland* does not involve application of a set of mechanical rules. Defense counsel need wide discretion in making decisions about their client's case.

    d. For example, defense counsel's recommendation that the client withdraw his insanity defense after the guilt phase was not deficient performance, and instead was based on counsel's reasonable belief that the insanity defense was doomed because medical testimony had already been rejected and defendant's parents were unavailable to testify. ***Knowles v. Mirzayance***, 556 U.S. 111 (2009).

    e. Defense counsel's tasks on behalf of the client include: being loyal, avoiding conflicts of interest, advocating her case, consulting with her on important decisions, keeping her informed of important developments in the course of the prosecution, and using skills and knowledge so the trial will be a reliable adversarial testing process.

3. **Strategic Decision or Failure to Act?** Defense counsel may not (constitutionally) ignore investigation of her client's case.

    a. *Strickland*'s performance prong is not satisfied where defense counsel fails to do any pretrial discovery. ***Kimmelman v. Morrison***, 477 U.S. 365 (1986).

      b.   ***Rompilla v. Beard***, 545 U.S. 374 (2005) held that defense counsel was ineffective for failing to make reasonable efforts to obtain and review critical material about a prior conviction that counsel knew the prosecution would probably rely on at the sentencing phase of trial.

      c.   Counsel's decision not to conduct a thorough investigation may be regarded as a matter of strategy (***Burger v. Kemp***, 483 U.S. 776 (1987)) or deficient performance (***Wiggins v. Smith***, 539 U.S. 510 (2003)).

4. **The Prejudice Prong**

      a.   A court must assess the strength or weakness of the prosecution's case and the importance of defense counsel's error. For example, if the evidence against the defendant is overwhelming, a conviction generally will be affirmed no matter how fundamental is counsel's error.

      b.   Other than conflict of interest claims, actual ineffectiveness claims require that the defendant affirmatively prove prejudice, i.e., a reasonable probability that, but for defense counsel's errors, the results of the case would undermine confidence in the outcome. As with the performance prong, *Strickland* established a presumption against a finding of prejudice.

      c.   For example, there was no prejudice when defense counsel threatened to withdraw if his client perjured himself at trial. ***Nix v. Whiteside***, 475 U.S. 157 (1986). On the other hand, the Court has concluded that defense counsel's failure to object to a legal error, affecting the calculation of a prison sentence and resulting in additional incarceration, is clearly prejudicial to a defendant.

5. **Ineffective Assistance in Plea Bargaining**. Defense counsel may be ineffective if she either:

a. fails to properly inform the defendant of a beneficial plea agreement from the prosecution, or causes the defendant to reject a plea agreement because she incorrectly advises the defendant on the law. ***Missouri v. Frye***, 132 S.Ct. 1399 (2012); ***Lafler v. Cooper***, 132 S.Ct. 1376 (2012).

b. Prejudice is proved by the defendant when he shows that:

- but for the ineffective advice of counsel there is a reasonable probability that the plea offer would have been accepted and brought before the court;

- the court would have accepted the terms of the plea agreement; and

- the conviction or sentence would have been lesser than under those imposed after trial.

D. **Ineffective Assistance Analysis in Federal Habeas Corpus Proceedings**

1. In 1996, Congress enacted the Antiterrorism & Effective Death Penalty Act of 1996 ("AEDPA"), which provides in part that a writ of habeas corpus cannot be granted unless the claim involved an unreasonable application of clearly established Federal law.

2. The fact that a State court may have made an incorrect constitutional ruling on an ineffectiveness inquiry does not entitle a defendant to habeas corpus relief; counsel's judgment must also have been unreasonable.

E. An ineffective assistance of counsel may be brought in a collateral proceeding whether or not the petitioner could have raised the claim on direct appeal.

IV. Conflicts of Interest

A. Defense counsel's conflict of interest by representing a defendant can amount to ineffective assistance of counsel. ***Glasser v. United States***, 315 U.S. 60 (1942).

B. A lone attorney's representation of codefendants is not *per se* unconstitutional.

    1. When counsel timely alerts the trial court about the risk of a conflict of interest, the trial judge must "either [appoint] separate counsel or [take] adequate steps to ascertain whether the risk was too remote to warrant separate counsel." *Holloway v. Arkansas*, 435 U.S. 475 (1978).

    2. Where counsel raises the potential conflict issue but the trial court fails to either grant the motion or hold a hearing, reversal of a defendant's conviction is "automatic," even without a showing of prejudice. *Mickens v. Taylor*, 535 U.S. 162 (2002).

    3. In *Cuyler v. Sullivan*, 446 U.S. 335 (1980), the Court concluded that a defendant who raised no objection at trial "must demonstrate that an actual conflict of interest adversely affected his lawyer's performance."

C. **Waiver**

    1. All lawyers' professional responsibility rules permit clients to waive conflicts of interest in most situations, if clients are fully informed of the consequences of such a waiver.

    2. Trial courts have broad discretion to decide whether to permit criminal defendants to accept such a waiver under the Sixth Amendment.

V. The *Griffin–Douglas* Doctrine

A. An indigent prisoner appealing from his conviction in State court has a Fourteenth Amendment right to a free trial transcript, where such transcripts are often a practical necessity for success on appeal. *Griffin v. Illinois*, 351 U.S. 12 (1956).

B. An indigent defendant has a Fourteenth Amendment right to counsel on a first appeal, where the State has granted the right to appeal (contrasted with situations where appeal is only discretionary). *Douglas v. California*, 372 U.S. 353 (1963).

C. In *Ross v. Moffitt*, 417 U.S. 600 (1974), the Court changed the focus of the "*Griffin–Douglas*" doctrine.

1. The Court concluded that "[t]he duty of the State under our cases is . . . only to assure the indigent defendant an adequate opportunity to present his claims fairly."

2. Indigents undertaking discretionary appeals (as opposed to appeals as of right) are not entitled to the appointment of counsel, even though a non-indigent would have the resources and could retain appellate counsel.

3. Post–*Ross* decisions have focused on what constitutes "meaningful access to justice." For example, an accused is entitled to have access to a psychiatrist and a psychiatric examination that are necessary as basic tools to raise an insanity defense. *Ake v. Oklahoma*, 470 U.S. 68 (1985).

ILLUSTRATIVE PROBLEMS

■ PROBLEM 2.1 CHOICE OF COUNSEL ■

On May 8, the defendant was indicted and arraigned in State court on four counts of rape and one count of kidnaping. Defendant's retained counsel requested that the judge reschedule the trial from May 18 to sometime in early June. She stated that other obligations prevented her from adequately preparing for trial on the 18th. When the judge refused to reschedule the trial, counsel withdrew from the case. The judge then instructed the defendant to hire another attorney for trial on May 18. When the defendant stated that he could not hire another lawyer, the judge appointed one for him.

Appointed counsel immediately moved for a continuance, which the judge denied. On the 18th, counsel again moved for a continuance so that defendant's original retained counsel could resume her representation of the defendant. While the judge denied the motion, he did move the trial to May 22 because of his own scheduling problems. On May 22, with appointed counsel representing the defendant, trial commenced. On May 24, the jury returned a verdict of guilty on four of the five counts, and the judge ultimately sentenced the defendant to seven to twenty-five years imprisonment. Was the defendant denied his counsel of choice?

Analysis

Yes. The Sixth Amendment guarantees a defendant the right to have counsel of his own choosing. The right, however, is not absolute, because it cannot be used to unreasonably delay a trial. A trial court must take into account both the accused's interest in counsel of his choice and the public interest in the efficient administration of justice. In the problem, there is no evidence that counsel was trying to manipulate the system or take advantage of the prosecution. This request appears to have been the first request for a continuance, and the period of delay was relatively short. The defendant was charged with five serious felonies. Finally, the judge moved the trial four days because of his own scheduling problems. No prejudice has to be shown to get appellate relief. A requirement that prejudice be shown would defeat the right.

■ PROBLEM 2.2 APPOINTED COUNSEL ■

Richard Peters was arrested six months ago on several misdemeanors, including illegally entering the United States, and transporting illegal aliens in violation of federal law. The authorized penalty for both charges includes jail time and/or monetary fines. Appearing *pro se*, Peters entered a plea of guilty. You are the law clerk for the trial judge in *United States v. Peters*. The judge inadvertently forgot to appoint counsel for Peters. What are her options for sentencing Peters on the misdemeanor charges? Sentence him to serve time in jail? Fine him for the violations? Sentence him, suspend the sentence and place him on probation? Place him on probation without suspending the sentence?

Analysis

The right to counsel applies to all misdemeanor defendants who receive an actual jail sentence. The right to counsel is unavailable to defendants who could be, but are not, sentenced to a jail term. Peters cannot be given jail time for the misdemeanors, because he did not have counsel at the time he entered his guilty plea. However, he could be fined for the misdemeanors.

The Sixth Amendment does not allow later activation of a suspended sentence that was imposed along with probation in a proceeding when defendant had no counsel. The suspended sentence is regarded as an incarceration "actually imposed." The incarceration that would result after a probation revocation hearing would be the result of the underlying offense, rather than for the later probation violation. Thus, without counsel, Peters could not be given a suspended sentence involving incarceration, even if the sentence is immediately suspended and he is placed on probation.

Courts, though, probably can create probation-only sentences for defendants like Peters that shift incarceration decisions and the accompanying right to counsel to later probation revocation hearings. Why? Because probation-only sentences probably do not give rise to concerns about the focus of the right to counsel cases: when jail time that is actually imposed or authorized.

■ PROBLEM 2.3 *PRO SE* COUNSEL ■

Charged with first-degree murder, defendant moved to dismiss his appointed lawyer and to represent himself. After noting that defendant's speech impediment might cause him considerable difficulty, but after also concluding that defendant's waiver of counsel was knowing and intelligent, the judge reluctantly granted the motion. For the next two months, defendant attended hearings and filed and argued motions.

Thereafter, following a hearing in which the judge concluded that defendant's speech impediment was so severe that it would effectively preclude him from articulating his defense to the jury, the trial judge appointed attorney Kehoe to act as co-counsel. The judge ruled that defendant would not be permitted to question

jurors or witnesses, make objections, or argue to the jury. On the
other hand, defendant would retain privileges in jail, including
access to the law library and private meetings with the court-
appointed investigator. Defendant also retained the right to file
motions.

Defendant subsequently objected to Kehoe's appointment:

I—it is my understanding that I have a constitutional right
to—that I have a right to waive counsel and to—to proceed
with—with—without the assistance—without the assistance of
counsel, which I would—which I would—which I would—
which I would request at—at—which I would request at this
time here. I would like to call to the court's a—to the court's
a—attention that I have also filed similar motions—similar
motions on—on July 29 and on September—on September—
excuse me—Sep—Sep—September 26.

After conviction, what are the arguments that defendant's conviction be reversed, given Kehoe's assumption of the role envisioned
by the court?

Analysis

The judge appointed a lawyer to act as co-counsel because of
concern that defendant's speech impediment would preclude him
from articulating his defense to the jury. Is the speech impediment
a valid basis for denying the defendant the right to proceed *pro se*?
On the other hand, is the court justified in denying the right to
proceed *pro se* to a defendant who is unable or unwilling to abide by
the rules of procedure and courtroom protocol?

If the defendant, even with the speech impediment, had the
right to represent himself, the appellate court must decide whether
the appointment of Kehoe as co-counsel violated that right. Here,
the defendant was not permitted to participate in voir dire, to
question witnesses, to make objections, or to argue to the jury. The
opposing argument would be that the defendant's speech impediment made him unable to follow the rules of procedure and
protocol and therefore the right to proceed *pro se* could be denied.

■ PROBLEM 2.4 *PER SE* INEFFECTIVENESS ■

On September 23, Assistant Public Defender Shelton attended a lineup for defendant Williams, who had been arrested for raping a thirteen-year-old girl. Between then and the preliminary hearing on November 11, at which Shelton represented Williams, Shelton spoke to Williams several times. Williams gave Shelton the names of several witnesses, some of whom Shelton or his investigator interviewed. Shelton also examined the prosecutor's file, interviewed the arresting officers, and examined statements that Williams had given the police.

After the preliminary hearing, Williams indicated to Shelton his desire to retain counsel, and Shelton confirmed this in a letter to Williams. Shelton presented a formal motion to withdraw on December 1, the day Williams was indicted, but because Williams had not succeeded in retaining counsel, the court denied the motion. Trial was scheduled for December 4. On December 3, Shelton asked for a continuance, stating that he was unprepared because he had been in court on other cases every day since December 1. The court denied the motion, but told Shelton that another Assistant Public Defender, Samuels, who had no familiarity with Williams's case, should help him prepare any legal issues.

On December 3, Shelton was in court on another matter until 11:00 p.m. Thereafter, Shelton and Samuels worked on Williams's case until 2:00 a.m. When trial began on the 4th, Shelton and Samuels unsuccessfully moved for a continuance. After a one-day trial at which no defense witnesses testified, the jury found Williams guilty of rape. Was counsel ineffective?

Analysis

Defendant has not pointed to any acts or omissions of counsel that constitute ineffective assistance. Rather, he is alleging that the circumstances surrounding the representation supports an inference of ineffectiveness—the failure to grant a continuance and the limited time to prepare. The Court rejected such a claim in *United States v. Cronic*, 466 U.S. 648 (1984). The Court said that the right of effective assistance is recognized because of the effect it has on the accused's ability to get a fair trial. The defendant has to challenge some conduct that affected the outcome of the trial.

There are some circumstances so likely to prejudice the accused that the cost of litigating their effect in a particular case is unjustified, i.e., ineffective assistance is presumed without inquiry into counsel's performance at trial. The attorney had almost two months to prepare before the preliminary hearing, after which the defendant attempted to discharge him, and the lawyer used that time productively.

The one thing the defendant can cite in terms of counsel's actual performance is the failure to call any defense witnesses.

■ PROBLEM 2.5 ACTUAL INEFFECTIVENESS ■

An experienced lawyer who had represented scores of defendants was appointed to represent defendant Stearman in a murder trial. When Stearman said that he had been out of State with his family, his counsel responded that a "family alibi" often results in conviction. When the prosecutor offered life imprisonment if Stearman pleaded guilty, counsel recommended taking the plea. Insisting on his innocence, Stearman said he would plead not guilty. Counsel spoke to family members who credibly corroborated Stearman's story. She did not make any other efforts to speak with Stearman's codefendant or the eyewitnesses before trial.

At trial, despite vigorous cross-examination, the eyewitnesses remained certain in their identification of Stearman. After the witnesses testified, the prosecution called a fingerprint expert, who testified Stearman's prints were found at the murder scene. Counsel objected because she did not know about this witness. At this point, Stearman whispered to counsel that he had not told her the truth. Although counsel had said in her opening statement that Stearman and his family would testify that they were out of State, counsel decided not to call any witnesses for the defense. Instead, in closing argument, counsel stressed the codefendant's motivation to lie. Was counsel ineffective?

Analysis

No. The right to counsel is the right to the effective assistance of counsel. To prevail on a claim of ineffective assistance of counsel, defendant must show 1) that counsel's performance fell below the level of competence expected of lawyers in criminal cases, and 2) that counsel's deficient performance prejudiced the defense, i.e., that there is a reasonable probability that but for counsel's poor performance, the result of the proceeding would have been different.

Defense counsel talked to defendant and his family about the defendant's alibi. It would have been better if counsel also talked to the eyewitnesses and codefendant, but the issues are 1) whether these omissions amounted to counsel functioning below the range of competence expected of lawyers in criminal cases, and 2) whether the failure to talk with the witnesses prejudiced the defendant.

The lawyer's failure to learn of the fingerprint expert is more troubling. However, given the positive eyewitness identifications, learning about the expert before trial would not have had a reasonable probability of changing the outcome. The attorney also cannot be faulted for his actions concerning the defendant's alibi. He first tried to talk the defendant out of the "family" alibi. When the defendant persisted, he interviewed family members and came to believe them, only to be told by the defendant midway through the trial that the defendant had lied. At this point, counsel had to abandon the alibi defense.

■ PROBLEM 2.6 CONFLICT OF INTEREST ■

Charged with robbery and murder, Homer Ford and his brother, Thomas, jointly retained one lawyer to represent both of them.

Homer wanted to go to trial, but Thomas wanted to plead guilty and request mercy from the court. The prosecutor said that she would agree not to seek the death penalty, but only if both brothers pleaded guilty. Under pressure from his mother, Homer changed his mind and pleaded guilty. He received two consecutive life sentences. Should the convictions be reversed because of the conflict of interest?

Analysis

Absent special circumstances, the trial has no duty to inquire *sua sponte* into a possible conflict when a lawyer represents multiple clients. The judge may presume either that multiple representation entails no conflict or that the defendants knowingly assume the risk. The reviewing court should grant relief only if the defendant can demonstrate that an actual conflict of interest adversely affected counsel's performance.

An actual conflict existed here. The same lawyer represented two defendants, one of whom wanted to go to trial while the other wanted to plead guilty. Because the prosecutor would reject the death penalty only if both brothers agreed to plead, counsel was put in the position of divided loyalties. The conflict adversely affected counsel's performance. Counsel could not rigorously pursue Homer's right to contest his guilt while accommodating Thomas's interest in pleading guilty and avoiding the death penalty.

■ PROBLEM 2.7 *GRIFFIN–DOUGLAS* EQUALITY PRINCIPLE ■

Defendant was charged with murder. The victim died eight months after being shot. According to the coroner, the victim died from a pulmonary embolism that resulted from a thrombosis in her leg, which in turn resulted from immobilization caused by paralysis from the shooting. Prior to trial, appointed counsel requested that the court provide $600 for an independent forensic pathologist to evaluate the medical evidence. Counsel argued that she could not personally evaluate the accuracy of the medical examiner's conclusions, that blood clots have many causes, and that the question of causation was pivotal in the case. Stating that she had no authority to provide such funds, the judge denied the motion.

At trial, the coroner conceded that it is unusual for a pulmonary embolism to occur as long as eight months after a trauma. The coroner also indicated that the victim had cirrhosis of the liver, an ailment that may cause an embolism. Questioned about his certainty concerning the causal connection between the shooting and the embolism, the coroner responded that he could not be 100% sure about anything in medicine but that he had the highest degree of medical certainty. Should the conviction be reversed on appeal because the trial court refused to provide the funds for an expert?

Analysis

An indigent must be given a meaningful opportunity to present his claims fairly. This is not to say that the defendant has a right to an expert of his own choosing or a right to funds to hire his own expert. He just must have access to a competent expert. The State must furnish indigents the basic tools of an adequate defense.

Is an independent forensic pathologist a "basic tool" of the defense? The State's medical examiner admitted that it was unusual for a pulmonary embolism to occur eight months after a trauma, but he insisted with the "highest degree of medical certainty" that the shooting in this case was causally related to the embolism. The question of causation was pivotal in this case. The defendant would appear to have a strong argument. On the other hand, because the defendant had access to the medical examiner's report and an opportunity fully to question him at trial, was there really a need for a second expert?

POINTS TO REMEMBER

- Indigent defendants in federal and State cases have a right under the Sixth Amendment to appointed defense counsel at critical stages of the prosecution.

- Indigent defendants cannot receive even a "day in jail," whether or not their sentence is suspended, if they did not receive or waive their right to counsel.

- Waivers of the right to counsel must be "knowing and intelligent" but need not follow a formula or script in order to be effective.

- Competent defendants may waive their right to counsel and proceed *pro se*.

- Defendants have a right to the effective assistance of counsel.

- To establish ineffective assistance of counsel, a defendant must establish ordinarily that counsel committed actual, specific errors.

- Ineffective assistance of counsel is established by using a two-part test that assesses the reasonableness of counsel's performance and whether or not defendant was prejudiced by that performance.

- For a federal habeas corpus petitioner to establish ineffective assistance of counsel arising out of a State conviction after 1996, the State courts must not only have applied the Sixth Amendment incorrectly or erroneously, but "unreasonably" as well.

- Where counsel's alleged ineffectiveness is based on a conflict of interest, prejudice does not have to be demonstrated unless the conflict was not raised at trial.

- Indigent defendants must receive at government expense the basic tools necessary to assure that they have meaningful access to justice at trial and on appeal.

CHAPTER 3

Search and Seizure: Search and Arrest Warrants

1. The Significance of Using a Search Warrant

The Warrant Clause of the Fourth Amendment requires that "no Warrants shall issue, but upon probable cause, supported by Oath or affirmation, and particularly describing the place to be searched, and the persons or things to be seized."

The "Warrant Preference" There is a strong preference for search warrants. In cases where it is a close question whether probable cause exists, courts lean toward upholding searches based upon warrants and lean against warrantless searches.

The "Warrant Requirement" Searches conducted without prior approval by a judge are *per se* unreasonable under the Fourth Amendment, subject to a few well-delineated exceptions. *Thompson v. Louisiana*, 469 U.S. 17 (1984). "A warrant assures the citizen that the intrusion is authorized by law, and that it is narrowly limited in its objectives and scope. . . . A warrant also provides the detached and neutral scrutiny of a neutral magistrate, and thus ensures an objective determination whether an intrusion is justified in any given case." *Skinner v. Railway Labor Executives' Ass'n*, 489 U.S. 602 (1989).

Reasons for Using an Arrest Warrant. Absent exigent circumstances, an arrest warrant is required to arrest a person in her own home. *Payton v. New York*, 445 U.S. 573 (1980). Entry into the defendant's home without a lawful arrest warrant under such circumstances makes any seized evidence inadmissible.

2. Probable Cause

Probable Cause Test. Probable cause requires a showing of "a fair probability" on each of the points that the prosecution must establish in order for a warrant to issue. For an arrest warrant, the government must prove a fair probability that a crime has been committed and that the person to be arrested committed the crime. To demonstrate probable cause sufficient to obtain a search warrant, the government must establish a fair probability that the specified items sought are evidence of criminal activity and that those items are presently located at the specified place described in the search warrant application.

For probable cause, the issuing judge makes a "commonsense decision" whether under the circumstances articulated in the affidavit there is a fair probability that evidence of a crime will be found in a particular place. *Illinois v. Gates*, 462 U.S. 213 (1983). Using a "commonsense" test, the Supreme Court has concluded that probable cause existed to arrest a driver and both of his two passengers in a car where baggies of cocaine and cash had been discovered: "We think it an entirely reasonable inference from these facts that any or all three of the occupants had knowledge of, and exercised dominion and control over, the cocaine." *Maryland v. Pringle*, 540 U.S. 366 (2003).

Informant Information and Probable Cause. Prior to 1983, the Supreme Court used the so-called *Aguilar–Spinelli* test to evaluate the existence of probable cause based upon information obtained from an informant. Under *Aguilar–Spinelli*, the government needed to provide the judge with information that sufficiently explained: (1) how the informant obtained her information (the "underlying circumstances" prong), *and* (2) why the informant is reliable (the "credibility" prong). *Aguilar v. Texas*, 378 U.S. 108 (1964); *Spinelli v. United States*, 393 U.S. 410 (1969).

In 1983, in *Illinois v. Gates*, 462 U.S. 213 (1983), while finding the *Aguilar–Spinelli* test "highly relevant" to the probable cause determination, the Court rejected the rigid categories of proof as necessary to show probable cause. In its place, the Court adopted a "totality-of-the-circumstances" test to evaluate probable cause based upon informant information. As the *Gates* Court pointed out, "a deficiency in one category", e.g., basis of knowledge, may be offset by a strong showing as to the other category, e.g., why the informant is reliable, or by some other indicia of reliability. Other "indicia of reliability" may include corroboration by police of some of the informant's factual details (even if the specific corroborated facts show only otherwise innocent activity, e.g., the wearing of clothing of a particular color or style, the same color or style as a criminal suspect) and the informant's status as a "citizen" (as opposed to an informant with a criminal past).

Informer's Privilege. The government may try to keep informants' identities confidential out of fear for their safety and/or a desire for their continued effectiveness as informants. As a result, the Court recognizes an "informer's privilege" when defense counsel seeks an informant's actual identity. Judges have discretion to order disclosure of an informant's identity when there is some reason to believe that her information is not believable (or that the informant does not even exist). Disclosure of an informant's identity may occur out of the presence of the defendant and defense counsel.

Staleness. Probable cause information may be stale depending on the relationship between the length of time between discovery of the information and the time that a search warrant is sought. Some evidence may: 1) disappear quickly (a marijuana cigarette), or 2) persist for a long time (e.g., a corpse buried in a basement). Additional factors relevant to the staleness inquiry are: the nature of the criminal evidence sought (e.g., large or small, moveable or fixed), the location of the evidence (e.g., in plain view or buried), the condition in which the evidence was observed (e.g., solid or liquid, easily disposable or permanent), and the nature of the place to be searched (e.g., readily moveable vehicle or a residential home).

Anticipatory Warrants. In *United States v. Grubbs*, 547 U.S. 90 (2006), the Supreme Court upheld the constitutionality of an "anticipatory warrant," which is a search warrant issued based only upon a showing of prospective probable cause. In other words, there is a showing that evidence of crime will be or is likely to be present on the premises sought to be searched at some specified time in the future subsequent to the occurrence of some specified triggering condition.

Two prerequisites of probability must be satisfied: 1) if the triggering condition occurs, a fair probability exists "that contraband or evidence of a crime will be found in a particular place," and 2) "probable cause exists to believe the triggering condition will occur. The supporting affidavit must provide sufficient information to evaluate both aspects of the probable cause determination." The triggering condition does not have to be set forth in the warrant itself.

Many anticipatory warrants involve information that narcotics will be delivered to a certain place at a certain time in the future (the "triggering condition"). Often, law enforcement agents know for a virtual certainty that such a delivery will be made (and when it will be made), because their own agents are making or monitoring the delivery. Such anticipatory warrants become invalid and cannot be executed when and if the contingent event (e.g., the delivery of narcotics) that established prospective probable cause does not in fact occur (e.g., no delivery appears to have been made).

3. Obtaining Warrants

Affidavits. Information supporting the issuance of a search warrant or arrest warrant must be disclosed to the issuing judge at the time she is considering the application for a warrant. Ordinarily, the information is presented in the form of written affidavits, sworn to by the affiant under oath. Most jurisdictions go beyond this constitutional requirement, and further require that the issuing judge may consider only the information that is contained within "the four corners" of the affidavits in evaluating whether probable cause exists. In some jurisdictions, however, the issuing judge may also consider sworn oral statements made by affiants or other witnesses as supplements to information contained in the affidavits themselves.

Challenging Affidavits. Affidavits offered as support for probable cause may be challenged by defense counsel in two different ways: 1) "on their face," i.e., counsel argues that the facts in the affidavit are insufficient to establish probable cause; or 2) "going behind" an affidavit by showing that some or all of the statements in the affidavit were false. The mere falsity of affidavit information is not enough to make the warrant defective and unconstitutional, because search warrant affidavits are presumptively valid. *Franks v. Delaware*, 438 U.S. 154 (1978).

A *Franks* hearing is a pretrial hearing at which defense counsel attempts to show that the affiant deliberately lied or made a statement in reckless disregard for the truth. If the judge rules that particular statements in an affidavit were intentionally or recklessly made (and not merely false or simply negligently made) *or* that the affiant intentionally or recklessly omitted material information from the affidavit to the same effect, the offending statements are redacted from the affidavit (or the material omissions are included). The judge then re-evaluates the redacted (or amended) affidavit to determine whether it still supports a finding of probable cause. Therefore, even if an affiant intentionally lied in a search warrant affidavit, that affidavit may still establish probable cause on the basis of the remaining statements.

Review of Probable Cause Determinations. Probable cause determinations where a search warrant has been issued are reviewed for whether the issuing judge had a substantial basis for concluding that a search would uncover evidence of wrongdoing. *Illinois v. Gates*, 462 U.S. 213 (1983). *Gates* noted that a reviewing court must pay "great deference" to the trial judge's conclusion that probable cause existed.

Issuing Judges. A judge authorized by a jurisdiction to issue a warrant is generically referred to as an "issuing judge." She ordinarily may issue search warrants only for the search of places located within the issuing court's jurisdiction. Likewise, she may issue arrest warrants only for the arrest of persons in the issuing court's jurisdiction.

An issuing judge must be neutral, detached, and capable of determining whether probable cause exists for a requested arrest or search warrant. *Shadwick v. City of Tampa*, 407 U.S. 345 (1972). A State Attorney General, for example, is not sufficiently neutral and detached to be empowered to issue warrants. *Coolidge v. New Hampshire*, 403 U.S. 443 (1971).

A defendant may also attack the validity of a warrant by pointing to specific examples of partiality to show that the issuing judge was not acting in a neutral and detached manner in the particular case. For example, Georgia judges who received $5.00 each time they issued a search warrant (and received nothing each time that they declined to issue a warrant) had a pecuniary interest in the issuance of the warrants. *Connally v. Georgia*, 429 U.S. 245 (1977).

4.   The   Particularity   Requirement

Constitutional Requirement. The Fourth Amendment prescribes that "no Warrants shall issue, but upon probable cause, supported by Oath or affirmation, and particularly describing the place to be searched, and the persons or things to be seized." The requirement ensures that the search will not become an exploratory, wide-ranging rummaging. *Maryland v. Garrison*, 480 U.S. 79 (1987).

"The requirement that warrants shall particularly describe the things to be seized makes general searches under them impossible and prevents the seizure of one thing under a warrant describing another. As to what is to be taken, nothing is left to the discretion of the officer executing the warrant." *Marron v. United States*, 275 U.S. 192 (1927). The Supreme Court recently noted that the "Fourth Amendment . . . does not set forth some general 'particularity requirement.' It specifies only two matters that must be 'particularly describ[ed]' in the warrant: 'the place to be searched' and 'the persons or things to be seized.' " *United States v. Grubbs*, 547 U.S. 90 (2006).

Particularity of Person to be Seized. An arrest warrant must specify the name of the defendant or otherwise describe the defendant with information by which she may be identified with reasonable certainty.

Particularity of the Search Premises. When describing search premises, the important question is whether the description is so specific that it identifies only the premises intended to be searched, and no other place. If the description fails this test, the warrant is constitutionally deficient. Typical forms of descriptive information of the search premises are: street numbers; geographic indicators; apartment numbers; city, county, and State locations; legal property descriptions; plat map references; directions on a map (sometimes attached); descriptions of the house or building color, style, composition, or size; description of the neighborhood character (e.g., urban, suburban, rural); and the name of the owner and/or residents.

When the warrant authorizes a search of only part of a building, e.g., a single apartment in a multi-unit, residential building, that limitation must be expressed in the search warrant description to meet the constitutional test. Most courts are willing to evaluate the particularity of a warrant description (the place to be searched or things to be seized) on the basis of the description contained in the search warrant itself and in any physically attached affidavits or lists, assuming that appropriate words of reference to those documents are included in the warrant itself.

Particularity of Things to Be Seized. The description in the warrant must be only as particular as the circumstances require, e.g., a description of contraband like "narcotics" or "drugs" is sufficiently specific, but a reference to "stolen property" is too general and unconstitutionally deficient. A reference to stolen "jewelry," on the other hand, described by detailed reference to characteristics as to nature, appearance, dimensions and initialing is constitutional. A less-detailed description may be constitutional when that is the most that can be said under the circumstances, e.g., a "brown puppy."

Minor or Partial Errors Irrelevant. A minor error in the search warrant regarding the place to be searched does not automatically render the warrant constitutionally defective, e.g., "2620 McCoy Way" instead of "2620A McCoy Way." As long as the place where the search is to take place is clear to the executing officers, e.g., from an otherwise accurate description aside from the error in the address number, the warrant is constitutional despite the descriptive error. The same is true of minor errors in the description of the things to be seized contained in a search warrant, e.g., a serial number on an appliance when only one appliance of the type described is on the premises. Even if some items seized must be suppressed for violating the particularity requirement, any remaining items seized pursuant to the warrant and described particularly are admissible.

"All Persons" Warrants. Some search warrants list as search targets "all persons on the premises." Normally, if a person is a target of a search warrant, she must be described particularly (although not necessarily by name), just as with any non-human search target like a residence, business, or vehicle. The rationale justifying "all persons" warrants is that they are proper when the search premises are being used for such clearly criminal purposes, e.g., a "crack house," that all persons present are necessarily involved with criminal activity. The Supreme Court has expressly reserved judgment on the constitutionality of such "all persons on the premises" warrants, *Ybarra v. Illinois*, 444 U.S. 85 (1979), and the lower courts are split on the question.

5. Execution of Search or Arrest Warrants

Who May Execute? A search or arrest warrant may be executed by the specific law enforcement officers directed in the warrant itself or by any other law enforcement officers authorized by applicable statutes in that jurisdiction. The executing officers must be acting within their own jurisdiction but they may use the services of officers from other law enforcement agencies or, where necessary, private citizens.

Time Limits. Search warrants must be executed both within the jurisdiction's maximum time limit for execution (usually established by court rule or by statute) and prior to the time the probable cause information supporting the warrant becomes stale. Prescribed maximum time limits vary widely, from two to sixty days. After the time limit passes, unless it is renewed with a fresh showing of probable cause prior to its execution, evidence seized will be suppressed. A delay in the execution of an arrest warrant does not render the warrant invalid.

Nighttime Searches. Most jurisdictions (including the federal courts) require—by statute or court rule—a special showing if a search warrant is to be executed at night. Searches at night are more intrusive of individuals' privacy and raise a greater risk of a violent response from the occupants who may not realize who is forcing their way on the premises. Officers seeking a nighttime warrant must specify why they need to search at night, e.g., evidence of easily destructible or mobile evidence on the search premises.

Knock-and-Announce Doctrine. The common-law "knock-and-announce" doctrine for warrants is part of the Fourth Amendment and applicable to all federal and State executing officers. *Wilson v. Arkansas*, 514 U.S. 927 (1995). The doctrine requires executing officers to do four things: (1) audibly "knock" or otherwise make their presence known at the outer door, thereby giving notice to the occupants about the law enforcement presence; (2) "announce" the identity of the executing officers (e.g., "It's the Police!"); (3) "announce" the purpose of the executing officers (e.g., "We have a warrant!"); and (4) "delay" for a period of time sufficient to permit the occupants to reach and to open the door.

After a sufficient delay and no one has answered the door, . . . officers may then enter the premises forcibly, including breaking down doors and engaging in the destruction of other property, if it is necessary and reasonable to enter. *United States v. Ramirez*, 523 U.S. 65 (1998). There is no need to wait for someone to be at the premises before police may make a forcible entry. Nor do executing officers need to look for or obtain the cooperation of search premises' occupants before beginning their search of the premises named in the warrant or for the person designated in the arrest warrant.

In general, a delay of thirty seconds is sufficient in most jurisdictions to meet the Fourth Amendment delay requirement. The Supreme Court has upheld a delay of only 15 to 20 seconds, however, where the premises occupant was suspected of selling cocaine, which can be quickly destroyed. *United States v. Banks*, 540 U.S. 31 (2003). By contrast, "[p]olice seeking a stolen piano [i.e., evidence that cannot be quickly destroyed] may be able to spend more time to make sure they really need the battering ram."

Violation of the knock-and-announce doctrine by executing officers renders the search warrant defective as a constitutional matter, but the federal exclusionary rule does not apply to law enforcement officers' knock-and-announce violations. *Hudson v. Michigan*, 547 U.S. 586 (2006). "[T]he social costs of applying the exclusionary rule to knock-and-announce violations are considerable; the incentive to such violations is minimal to begin with, and the extant deterrences against them are substantial. . . . "

There are a number of permissible exceptions to the knock-and-announce doctrine: 1) nonviolent "entry by trick," e.g., law enforcement officer pretending to be a hotel desk clerk; 2) the exigency exception, which must be specific to the particular circumstances, see *Richards v. Wisconsin*, 520 U.S. 385 (1997); and 3) when adherence to the knock-and-announce doctrine would be futile. For the last two exceptions, police must have a reasonable suspicion that knocking and announcing their presence would be dangerous or futile, or that it would inhibit the effective investigation by, for example, allowing the destruction of evidence. Requiring executing officers who have already been spotted by search premises' occupants to follow all of the requirements of the knock-and-announce doctrine may be a futile gesture and not required.

When individuals obtaining a search warrant can show in advance that the conditions that would excuse compliance with the knock-and-announce doctrine at the scene will be present at the search premises (e.g., danger to the officers or the destructibility of evidence), the Court has stated in dicta that executing officers may obtain a no-knock warrant.

Post–Execution Requirements. By rule or statute, most jurisdictions require executing officers to leave a copy of the search warrant and a receipt for items seized at the search premises. They also must promptly file a "return" with the court, noting when the warrant was executed and specifying precisely what was seized. Most jurisdictions do not treat these requirements as requiring application of the exclusionary rule. Governments are not constitutionally required to give detailed instructions to individuals seeking to obtain their lawfully-seized property after the property is no longer needed for investigative or prosecutorial purposes. *City of West Covina v. Perkins*, 525 U.S. 234 (1999).

6. Seizures Pursuant to Search Warrant

What Can Be Seized? Items specified and particularly described in a search warrant as evidence of crime may be seized under the authority of the warrant. In addition, executing officers may seize non-described items that they see in "plain view" while they are lawfully present at a place to execute a search warrant, provided that the items are "incriminating on their face," i.e., connected with some criminal activity. *Horton v. California*, 496 U.S. 128 (1990).

Where Can Seizures Be Made? Executing officers may search anywhere on the search premises that the items particularly described in the search warrant may be hidden. As long as the officers are searching in such a place, they may lawfully seize items particularly described in the warrant and/or plain view items. Where probable cause exists to search a particular room or location in a residence but the warrant does not expressly limit the search to that room or location, the entire residence may be searched.

A search warrant description for a particular home, building or place usually includes permission to search the land immediately surrounding and associated with the search target, any and all buildings located thereon (e.g., a garage), and any vehicles found there. However, a search pursuant to a search warrant cannot extend to neighboring areas outside of or beyond the search premises.

The exception to this rule is where a neighboring area reasonably appears to the executing officers to be part of the search premises covered by a warrant. For example, the Supreme Court upheld a search of a third-floor apartment in a building where the executing officers reasonably did not realize that the third floor was divided into two separate apartments, and that they were searching the wrong one. *Maryland v. Garrison*, 480 U.S. 79 (1987). However, the Court warned that "the officers . . . were required to discontinue the search of [the wrong] apartment as soon as they discovered that there were two separate units on the third floor and therefore were put on notice of the risk that they might be in a unit erroneously included within the terms of the warrant."

Intensity of Search. The permissible intensity of a search is dictated and limited by the nature of the items being sought under the warrant.

> [A] warrant that authorizes an officer to search a home for illegal weapons also provides authority to open closets, chests, drawers, and containers in which the weapon might be found. A warrant to open a footlocker to search for marijuana would also authorize the opening of packages found inside. A warrant to search a vehicle would support a search of every part of the vehicle that might contain the object of the search.

United States v. Ross, 456 U.S. 798 (1982).

Property Damage or Destruction. Executing officers may damage or destroy property in conducting a search where such damage is reasonably necessary to effect the search. *Dalia v. United States*, 441 U.S. 238 (1979). Nonetheless, there are limits to the permissible extent of property destruction in the execution of a warrant. "Excessive or unnecessary destruction of property in the course of a search may violate the Fourth Amendment, even though the entry itself is lawful and the fruits of the search not subject to suppression." *United States v. Ramirez*, 523 U.S. 65 (1998). An excessive search also may lead to a civil action for damages.

Duration of Search. Searches are limited in duration by a similar rule of reasonable necessity. Searches of a home that last for several hours are not uncommon, but once all of the objects particularly described and sought under a warrant have been found, no further searches are permissible under the authority of that warrant.

Persons and Their Property On or Near Search Premises. Search premises' occupants can be detained (but not searched) under the authority of a search warrant for criminal evidence on the premises occupied, in order to minimize violence and the potential destruction of evidence. *Michigan v. Summers*, 452 U.S. 692 (1981). If there is reasonable suspicion that any person is armed, police may frisk the outer clothing of that person for weapons.

When executing officers either know or reasonably should know that property found on search premises belongs to a non-suspect third-party, e.g. a purse belonging to a social guest, that property cannot be searched pursuant to the search warrant. This rule is inapplicable to the search of property belonging to a non-suspect, third-party vehicle passenger subject to a lawful search of the car for contraband. "[P]olice officers with probable cause to search a car may inspect passengers' belongings found in the car that are capable of concealing the object of the search." *Wyoming v. Houghton*, 526 U.S. 295 (1999).

SEARCH AND ARREST WARRANT CHECKLIST

A. **The Warrant Clause**. The Fourth Amendment requires expressly that "no Warrants shall issue, but upon probable cause, supported by Oath or affirmation, and particularly describing the place to be searched, and the persons or things to be seized."

    1. Courts prefer searches conducted pursuant to a warrant. *Illinois v. Gates*, 462 U.S. 213 (1983).

    2. Searches without warrants are *per se* unreasonable under the Fourth Amendment, subject only to a few specifically established and well delineated exceptions.

      a. Warrants protect privacy interests against random or arbitrary acts of government agents.

      b. Warrants are narrowly limited in their objectives and scope.

      c. Warrants provide the detached and neutral scrutiny of a neutral judge.

3. Absent an emergency, an arrest warrant is required to arrest a person in her own home. *Payton v. New York*, 445 U.S. 573 (1980). Without such a warrant, any seized evidence is inadmissible.

B. **Probable Cause**. Probable cause requires a showing by the government of "a fair probability."

1. **Arrest Warrant**. The government must establish a fair probability that a crime has been committed *and* that the person to be arrested committed the crime.

2. **Search Warrant**. The government must establish a fair probability that the specified items sought are evidence of criminal activity *and* that those items are presently located at the specified place described in the search warrant application.

3. **Informant Information**. In *Illinois v. Gates*, the Supreme Court adopted a "totality-of-the-circumstances" test for deciding probable cause, considering factors like the basis for the information, why the informant is credible, and corroboration of some of the informant's factual details.

4. **Informer's Privilege**. The prosecution may wish to keep confidential the identities of informants who have provided information about criminal conduct, subject to disclosure when there is some reason to believe that her information is not believable or that the informant does not exist.

5. **Staleness.** Probable cause information that is stale cannot support the issuance of a search warrant. Staleness may be determined by the length of time between discovery of the probable cause information and the time that a

warrant is sought, the nature of the criminal evidence sought, the location of the evidence, the condition in which the evidence was observed, and the nature of the place to be searched.

6. **Anticipatory Warrants**. An anticipatory warrant is a search warrant issued based only upon a showing of prospective probable cause, i.e., a showing that evidence of crime is likely to be present on the premises sought to be searched at some specified time in the future subsequent to the occurrence of some specified triggering condition. *United States v. Grubbs*, 547 U.S. 90 (2006).

C. Obtaining Warrants

1. **Affidavits**. Ordinarily, the information presented to request a search warrant is in the form of written affidavits, sworn to by the affiant under oath. Information supporting issuance of a search warrant must be disclosed to the issuing judge at the time of the application for a search warrant.

2. **Challenging Affidavits**. Defense counsel can challenge affidavits in two ways:

   a. "On their face," i.e., the facts in the affidavit are insufficient to establish probable cause; or

   b. "Go behind" an affidavit at a suppression hearing by establishing that some or all of the statements in that affidavit were false.

   c. The offending statements are redacted from the affidavit, which is then re-evaluated to determine whether it still supports a finding of probable cause. *Franks v. Delaware*, 438 U.S. 154 (1978).

3. **Review of Probable Cause Determinations**. Probable cause determinations where a search warrant has been issued are reviewed by a deferential standard.

4. **Issuing Judges**. A judge who issues warrants must be neutral, detached, and capable of determining whether

probable cause exists for a requested arrest or search warrant. *Shadwick v. City of Tampa*, 407 U.S. 345 (1972).

D. **The Particularity Requirement**. The Fourth Amendment prescribes that "no Warrants shall issue, but upon probable cause, . . . and particularly describing the place to be searched, and the persons or things to be seized."

   1. **Particularity of Person to be Seized**. An arrest warrant must specify the name of the defendant or otherwise describe the defendant with information by which she may be identified with reasonable certainty.

   2. **Particularity of the Search Premises**. The description must be so specific that it identifies only the premises intended to be searched, and no other place, using, e.g., street numbers, geographic indicators, apartment numbers, city, county, and State locations, and legal property descriptions.

   3. **Particularity of Things to be Seized**. A description of seizable things must be particular as the circumstances require, e.g., a description of contraband like "narcotics" or "drugs" is sufficiently specific, but a reference to "stolen property" is too general and unconstitutionally deficient.

   4. **Minor or Partial Errors Irrelevant**. Minor errors in the search warrant description of the place to be searched do not render the warrant constitutionally defective, e.g., "2620 McCoy Way" instead of "2620A McCoy Way," as long as the place where the search is to take place is clear to the executing officers.

   5. **"All Persons" Warrants**. Usually, if a person is a search target of a search warrant, she must be described particularly (although not necessarily by name), just as with any non-human search target like a residence, business, or vehicle.

E. **Execution of Search Warrants**

   1. **Who May Execute a Warrant?** Warrants may lawfully be executed either by the specific law enforcement officers

directed in the warrant itself or by any other law enforcement officers authorized by applicable statutes in that jurisdiction.

2. **Time Limits**

   a. Search warrants must be executed both within the jurisdiction's maximum time limit for execution (usually established by court rule or by statute) and prior to the time the probable cause information supporting the warrant grows stale.

   b. A delay in the execution of an arrest warrant does not render the warrant invalid.

3. **Nighttime Searches**. Most jurisdictions (including the federal courts) require—by statute or court rule—that a special showing be made if a search warrant is to be executed at night.

4. **Knock-and-Announce Doctrine**. The common-law "knock-and-announce" doctrine for warrants requires executing officers to do several things *before* entering forcibly.

   a. Audibly "knock" or otherwise make their presence known at the outer door, thereby giving notice to the occupants inside of the law enforcement presence;

   b. "Announce" the identity of the executing officers (e.g., "It's the Police!");

   c. "Announce" the purpose of the executing officers (e.g., "We have a warrant!"); and

   d. "Delay" for a period of time sufficient to permit the occupants to reach and to open the door.

   e. A delay of only 15 to 20 seconds has been upheld where the premises occupant was suspected of selling cocaine, which can be quickly destroyed. ***United States v. Banks***, 540 U.S. 31 (2003).

f. The federal exclusionary rule does not apply to law enforcement officers' knock-and-announce violations. *Hudson v. Michigan*, 547 U.S. 586 (2006).

g. Permissible exceptions to the knock-and-announce doctrine include reasonable suspicion that knocking and announcing police presence, under the particular circumstances, would be dangerous or allow an opportunity for the destruction of evidence.

h. An officer seeking a warrant may present to the issuing judge specific information justifying an unannounced entry, but the type of suspected crime alone does not justify judicial permission for a no-knock entry.

F. **Seizures Pursuant to Warrant**

1. **What Can Be Seized?** Items specified and particularly described in a search warrant as evidence of crime may be seized, as well as non-described items that executing officers see in "plain view."

2. **Where Can Seizures Be Made?** Executing officers may search anywhere on the search premises that the items particularly described in the search warrant may be hidden. A warrant authorizing a search of a particular place usually permits a search of the area immediately surrounding and associated with the search target, and any and all buildings and vehicles located there.

3. **Intensity of Search**. The scope of the search is dictated and limited by the nature of the items being sought under the warrant, e.g., a warrant that authorizes a search for illegal weapons provides authority to open closets, chests, drawers, and containers in which the weapon might be found.

4. **Property Damage or Destruction**. Executing officers may damage or destroy property in conducting a search, if damage is reasonably necessary to effect the search.

However, excessive or unnecessary destruction may lead to a civil action for damages.

5. **Duration of Search**. Searches are limited in duration by a similar rule of reasonable necessity. Once all of the objects particularly described and sought under a warrant have been found, no further searches are permissible under that warrant.

6. **Persons and Their Property on or near Search Premises**. Anyone on the search premises may be detained (but not searched) under the authority of a search warrant, to minimize violence and the potential destruction of evidence. *Michigan v. Summers*, 452 U.S. 692 (1981).

G. The prosecution has the burden of proving the warrant's validity, and the defendant then has the burden of rebutting that showing. A reviewing court uses a "clear error" standard of review for warrant cases. *Ornelas v. United States*, 517 U.S. 690 (1996).

ILLUSTRATIVE PROBLEMS

■ PROBLEM 3.1 OBTAINING A SEARCH WARRANT: INFORMANT'S INFORMATION   ■

United States Drug Enforcement Administration [DEA] agents have applied for a search warrant for the home of Clarence Romero, who is suspected of being a major seller of heroin. A DEA agent received a tip from an anonymous informant that Romero had flown that morning from Albuquerque to Tucson to purchase a half-kilo of heroin and that he would probably ask a second person to return the heroin to Albuquerque on Omega Airlines flight #239 at 2:50 p.m. the same day. A DEA agent went to the Tucson International Airport, where she learned that "C. Romero" had a reservation on the described flight. The agent then observed defendant, whom he knew to be Romero's associate, board the plane. The DEA agent in Albuquerque applied for a warrant to search Romero's home there. Should the United States Judge issue a search warrant for Romero's Albuquerque home?

Analysis

This problem requires analysis of *Illinois v. Gates,* which allowed an informant's information to be used to prove probable cause through the totality of circumstances. It helps to analyze the problem under the old two-pronged test, basis of knowledge and credibility. The tip tells us nothing about the informant's honesty or how the informant got his information. In terms of the basis of knowledge prong, however, the tip is full of detail. It describes the precise flight Romero would be returning the drugs on, and it says Romero would ask another person to return the drugs. If the informant is telling the truth, then he probably got his information in a reliable way.

It is useful to show the Judge that the informant is truthful, and that he has not made the whole thing up. Detail cannot help with credibility, but corroboration can. An officer corroborated that Romero had purchased a ticket for the flight in question and that he had given his ticket to an associate. Under *Gates* there should be no doubt about probable cause. A deficiency in one prong can be made up by strength in the other. Here, like *Gates*, there is sufficient detail and corroboration.

■ PROBLEM 3.2 EXECUTION OF SEARCH WARRANT: KNOCK–AND–ANNOUNCE ■

Jon has moved to suppress the fruits of a no-knock search warrant on the basis that no circumstances existed to justify a no-knock search. He was staying at the home of his friend Jill in rural Frazier County. The home had been searched successfully for weapons and drugs under a warrant six weeks prior to the current search. A reliable informant bought drugs from Jill at her home two days before the search. The next day, based upon the information from the informant, a sheriff's deputy applied for a search warrant for Jill's property, vehicle and Jill herself. A judge signed the warrant and it was executed two days later. Prior to executing the warrant, officers parked about a quarter of a mile from Jill's house. Before entering, they observed Jill and Jon sitting at a table playing what appeared to be a word game. When one officer tried the front door and found it unlocked, the officers, in camouflage, helmets and masks, entered with their guns drawn, shouting, "Police." Jill did not move other than to raise her arms above her head. Jon, stunned by the entry, tossed the dictionary he was holding into the air and attempted to run from the room. He held his fist closed and then appeared to shove its contents down the front of his pants. Officers subdued him, finding a knife in his belt and drugs and an inhaler in his pants.

Analysis

In *Richards v. Wisconsin*, 520 U.S. 385 (1997), the Court held that a common law no-knock entry for warrants requires a reasonable suspicion that knocking and announcing under the particular circumstances would either be "dangerous or futile," or allow "the destruction of evidence." The reasonable suspicion standard strikes a balance between legitimate concerns in executing search warrants and individual privacy interests. It also differs in amount from the proof for probable cause necessary for issuance of a warrant.

Richards requires more than assumptions that the type of crime automatically permits a no-knock entry. The "particular circumstances" matter instead. Merely because people engaging in such offenses "normally" possess firearms, making them "dangerous," does not dispense with a proof requirement by the police officer or prosecutor seeking the warrant. The prosecution would be helped if there was a threat of violence, a history of violence, or a reliable indication that guns were in Jill's home.

The officer seeking the warrant may present to the judge specific information justifying an unannounced entry. An officer may be able to point to a particular fact about a particular place (weapons were found weeks prior to the warrant's execution) that, when coupled with the criminal activity, suggests an unannounced entry. Even if an unannounced entry is initially denied or not addressed during the warrant request, *Richards* still permits the executing officer to reappraise the situation and decide that such an entry is justified by unforeseen (i.e., different from those presented to the judge earlier) circumstances occurring during the warrant's execution.

POINTS TO REMEMBER

- The police are required to use a warrant to search unless an exception applies (which is frequent).

- To search, police officers must establish probable cause, i.e., a fair probability that evidence of a crime is or will be at the place to be searched.

- Whether probable cause exists is assessed by considering the "totality of the circumstances."

- Probable cause to support a search can be challenged in a *Franks* hearing by showing that erroneous information was included in a supporting affidavit intentionally or recklessly and that the information was necessary to a finding of probable cause.

- Search warrants must particularly describe the place to be searched and the evidence to be seized.

- Arrest warrants must particularly describe the person to be arrested.

- In executing a warrant, the executing officers must knock, announce their purpose and their identity, and delay a sufficient period of time to give the occupants a chance to answer the door. They may make a "no-knock" entry when they possess a reasonable suspicion that evidence is being destroyed or that they or others are in danger, but the federal exclusionary rule does not apply to violations of these rules.

- Evidence not described in a warrant may nonetheless be seized by executing officers if the officers are lawfully in the place from which they see this evidence in "plain view" and it is immediately apparent to them that the evidence has a connection with any criminal activity.

CHAPTER 4

Search and Seizure: Fourth Amendment Activity

The Fourth Amendment applies only to conduct that can be classified as a search or seizure, and seeks to protect conduct which an individual legitimately has the right to preserve as private. A court determines the reasonableness of a search by evaluating the degree of intrusion on a person's privacy and the extent to which the search is necessary to promote legitimate governmental interests. *Wyoming v. Houghton*, 526 U.S. 295 (1999).

Defining a Search and a Seizure. A search involves a visual observation or physical intrusion which infringes upon a person's reasonable expectation of privacy. *Kyllo v. United States*, 533 U.S. 27 (2001). For example, although passengers on a commercial bus expect fellow passengers to handle or move carry-on baggage, a police officer's "probing tactile examination" of soft-sided luggage constitutes a search. *Bond v. United States*, 529 U.S. 334 (2000).

A seizure in the Fourth Amendment context requires some meaningful interference with an individual's liberty (an arrest) or possessory interests (a seizure). *Michigan v. Chesternut*, 486 U.S. 567 (1988). A seizure such as an arrest is subject to Fourth Amendment scrutiny even though no Fourth Amendment search has occurred. See *Florida v. Bostick*, 501 U.S. 429 (1991).

Seizure of an individual connotes taking a person physically or constructively into custody and detaining that person, thus causing a deprivation of the person's freedom of movement in a significant way. A law enforcement officer's use of physical force is a seizure regardless of whether the suspect submits to detention. *California v. Hodari D.*, 499 U.S. 621 (1991). However, if an officer engages in a nonphysical show of authority, a seizure occurs only if a reasonable person would not feel free to leave and actually submits to authority. *Florida v. Bostick*, 501 U.S. 429 (1991).

***Katz* and the Reasonable Expectation of Privacy**. The modern Fourth Amendment privacy definition was articulated in *Katz v. United States*, 389 U.S. 347 (1967) (Harlan, J., concurring): "[T]here is a twofold requirement, first that a person have exhibited an actual (subjective) expectation of privacy and, second, that the expectation be one that society is prepared to recognize as 'reasonable.'" When the Court determines that a defendant's expectation of privacy is unreasonable, the police do not have to comply with the Fourth Amendment. When the Court rules that the expectation of privacy is reasonable, police conduct must satisfy the Fourth Amendment's requirements.

Katz held that a person inside a public phone booth had a reasonable expectation of privacy in his conversations. Therefore, agents' use of an electronic listening and recording device attached to the outside of the booth required compliance with the Fourth Amendment. *Katz* declared that "the Fourth Amendment protects people, not places." "What a person knowingly exposes to the public, even in his own home or office, is not a subject of Fourth Amendment protection. But what he seeks to preserve as private, even in an area accessible to the public, may be constitutionally protected."

The rationales for the *Katz* holding focus on the context of Katz's reliance on his expectation of privacy from police surveillance. "One who occupies [a public phone booth], shuts the door behind him, and pays the toll that permits him to place a call is surely entitled to assume that the words he utters into the mouthpiece will not be broadcast to the world." The Court's focus on the defendant's privacy expectation also reflected concern about the government's power to gain access to the contents of that communication anywhere, anytime.

Thus, the privacy interest is a constitutional right that depends in part on the person's behavior (e.g., talking loudly in a public place) and in part on the social context (e.g., using a telephone booth to conduct a phone conversation). Talking loudly in a booth may make the person's expectation unreasonable. If the expectation is unreasonable, an officer eavesdropping on the conversation from outside the booth does not have to satisfy the Fourth Amendment in order to listen and testify later about the what she heard.

Katz does not apply when government agents have access to a conversation through a participant in the conversation. *United States v. White*, 401 U.S. 745 (1971). Defendants cannot reasonably expect that the person to whom they are talking is not a government agent recording the conversation or is not reporting the conversation to the police. The Court has reached similar conclusions when defendants convey other information to third parties, who then provide that information to the authorities. See e.g., *United States v. Miller*, 425 U.S. 435 (1976) (bank); *Smith v. Maryland*, 442 U.S. 735 (1979) (phone company).

The Court's privacy doctrine also applies to the "curtilage" (the land "immediately surrounding and associated with the home"), which generally is a protected area. The difficulty relates to defining its boundaries. The status of a potential "curtilage" area is evaluated with reference to four factors: its proximity to the home, whether it is enclosed, the nature of its uses, and the steps taken to protect it from observation. See *United States v. Dunn*, 480 U.S. 294 (1987) (defining scope of curtilage). Police can observe activity on the curtilage from a public street, but police presence on the curtilage itself is Fourth Amendment activity.

On the other hand, "open fields," the area beyond the curtilage, are exempt from Fourth Amendment requirements and can be entered and searched without a warrant. The "open fields" exception is consistent with the *Katz* privacy analysis. *Oliver v. United States*, 466 U.S. 170 (1984). Thus, police presence on a person's property that is an open field (i.e., beyond the curtilage) does not require compliance with the Fourth Amendment (even though it constitutes a trespass). The police can stand in an open field and observe what is occurring on the curtilage.

However, the Court in *United States v. Jones*, 132 S.Ct. 945 (2012) held that police installation of a GPS tracking device on a vehicle and warrantless use of the device to monitor the vehicle's movements constitute a "search" and violate a defendant's Fourth Amendment rights. The Court disagreed about why this was a Fourth Amendment violation. Writing for the majority, Justice Scalia found that the *Katz* reasonable expectation of privacy standard had not changed the historical principle that the Government cannot engage in a physical intrusion of a constitutionally protected area in order to obtain information. In other words, the reasonable expectation of privacy standard was *an addition, not a substitute for*, the common-law trespass test.

Five other members of the Court concluded that Justice Scalia's trespass theory does *not* form a sufficiently comprehensive analysis of the Fourth Amendment implications of GPS monitoring. They instead argued that GPS monitoring should be analyzed to determine whether it has invaded a reasonable expectation of privacy. Even Justice Scalia noted that cases "involving merely the transmission of electronic signals without trespass would *remain* subject to *Katz* analysis." Because the collection of cell site location data does not involve a physical trespass to property, a trial court should continue to analyze Fourth Amendment implications under *Katz*.

An essential component of the Fourth Amendment claim thus requires that 1) one's own personal "effects" have been trespassed (e.g., Scalia's majority view that emphasized the trespassory nature of the secret installation of a GPS device on one's automobile), or 2) one's own expectation of privacy was impinged (e.g., the focus of the *Jones*'s concurrences and dissent upon the continuous monitoring and tracking of one's movements for a material period of time).

Human Surveillance and Enhanced Surveillance. The Court's cases also address issues of "human" surveillance and issues of "enhanced" surveillance, using technologies that are as varied as canine sniffs, tracking beepers, helicopter "fly overs," aerial mapping cameras, and thermal-imaging devices. In a controversial decision emphasizing public access, the Court held that a defendant had no reasonable expectation of privacy in garbage that was placed in opaque trash bags, left on the curb, and searched by police who procured the bags from the garbage collector. *California v. Greenwood*, 486 U.S. 35 (1988). The *Greenwood* defendants were in the unprotected *Katz* category of those who knowingly expose information about private items to the public, e.g., garbage collectors, scavengers.

Greenwood's logic did not prevail for carry-on luggage placed in an overhead bin by a bus passenger and squeezed by a police officer in *Bond v. United States*, 529 U.S. 334 (2000). While "public access" and "conveyance to a third party" were present in *Bond*, given that other passengers and bus employees could handle or touch the luggage, the Court recognized that public customs do not extend beyond mere "handling" to encompass the "exploratory" feeling of a bag. The Court also emphasized that "tactile" observation is "more intrusive than purely visual inspection."

Bond did not hold that luggage in a public area is protected *per se* from all intrusions. In a pre-*Bond* decision, the Court approved canine sniffs by narcotics detection dogs of the exterior of luggage in a public place; such an intrusion does not violate a reasonable expectation of privacy. *United States v. Place*, 462 U.S. 696 (1983). The Court relied on the sniff as: 1) minimally intrusive (contrasted with opening the luggage), and 2) disclosing "only the presence or absence of narcotics," thereby protecting innocent citizens from general police "rummaging" in their possessions. The Court later recognized in *City of Indianapolis v. Edmond*, 531 U.S. 32 (2000), that a canine sniff of the exterior of a car at a roadblock is not a "search" or a "seizure" under *Place*. However, the Court has not held that a canine sniff can never violate a reasonable expectation of privacy, e.g., a sniff of a person.

Other forms of "enhanced" surveillance have addressed whether to set limits for police use of technology. The Court approved of beepers as a substitute for visual surveillance in *United States v. Knotts*, 460 U.S. 276 (1983), when the police attached a tracking beeper inside a container, and then followed the defendant's car in which the container was located. After the police lost visual surveillance of the car, the beeper allowed them to track the car to the area of the defendant's cabin. *Knotts* limited its approval of "tracking beepers" to a situation where "there is no indication that the beeper was used in any way to reveal information as to the movement of the . . . container within the [defendant's premises]."

By contrast, *United States v. Karo*, 468 U.S. 705 (1984) held that police cannot use "tracking beepers" to obtain information that could not have been obtained through visual surveillance. *Karo* found that a violation of a reasonable expectation of privacy occurred when police used a beeper in a container to discover "a critical fact about the interior of the premises," i.e., the container was moved inside the home.

The Court's aerial surveillance cases indicate that there is no reasonable expectation of privacy from some police "fly overs" of property, aerial surveillance of a home's curtilage from a helicopter flying as low as 400 feet, and the use of an aerial mapping camera during "fly overs" of commercial property. *Florida v. Riley*, 488 U.S. 445 (1989); *Dow Chemical v. United States*, 476 U.S. 227 (1986). These cases rely on the "public access" rationale of *Greenwood*, because members of the "flying public" could make "naked eye" observations of the curtilage like the police in *Riley*, and could use a "conventional" mapping camera like the one in *Dow Chemical*. *Riley* noted, though, that the police observed marijuana growing in a greenhouse, but not "intimate details connected with the use of the home or the curtilage."

In *Kyllo v. United States*, 533 U.S. 27 (2001), a "thermal imaging device" was aimed at a private home from across the street, and the heat scan showed that the garage was hotter than the rest of the house and "substantially warmer than neighboring homes." That evidence established the probable cause required for the issuance of a warrant to search the home for an "indoor growing operation" using halide lights to grow marijuana. The *Kyllo* majority determined that the homeowner had a reasonable expectation of privacy from the use of the thermal imaging device: obtaining information about the interior of home by sense-enhancing technology by physical "intrusion into a constitutionally protected area" constitutes a search (requiring a finding of probable cause *prior* to using the imager), at least where the technology used is not available to the general public.

Kyllo's rationales relied on *Katz*, *Karo*, and *Dow Chemical*. The Court rejected the argument that the device detected heat only from the external surface of the home, reasoning that such a "mechanical interpretation" of privacy was rejected in *Katz*. *Karo* implies that a homeowner should not without probable cause be subject to police use of technology that may discern human activity inside the home. The majority also rejected the government's alternate argument that the heat device did not "detect private activities occurring in private areas," reasoning that "[i]n the home, all details are intimate details, because the entire area is held safe from prying government eyes."

FOURTH AMENDMENT ACTIVITY CHECKLIST

A. The Fourth Amendment privacy definition was articulated in **Katz v. United States**, 389 U.S. 347 (1967): a subjective expectation of privacy that society is prepared to recognize as objectively reasonable.

　　1. When a defendant's expectation of privacy is unreasonable, the police do not have to comply with the Fourth Amendment.

　　2. When a defendant's expectation of privacy is reasonable, police conduct must satisfy the Fourth Amendment's requirements.

　　3. The privacy interest is a constitutional right which depends in part on the person's behavior (e.g., talking loudly in a public place) and in part on the social context (e.g., using a telephone booth to conduct a phone conversation).

B. There is not a reasonable expectation of privacy when a person conveys information to third parties, who then provide that information to the authorities.

C. The area surrounding a person's home protected by a reasonable expectation of privacy is known as the "curtilage," i.e., the land "immediately surrounding and associated with the home," and is generally is a protected area. Whether land is characterized as the "curtilage" area depends upon four factors. See *United States v. Dunn*, 480 U.S. 294 (1987).

   1. Its proximity to the home,

   2. Whether it is enclosed,

   3. The nature of its uses, and

   4. The steps taken to protect it from observation.

D. There is no reasonable expectation of privacy in "open fields," i.e., the area beyond the curtilage. Open fields are exempt from Fourth Amendment requirements and can be entered and searched without a warrant or probable cause. *Oliver v. United States*, 466 U.S. 170 (1984).

E. After *United States v. Jones*, 132 S.Ct. 945 (2012) reintroduced the property element of trespass into the Fourth Amendment activity discussion, it would appear that an essential component of the Fourth Amendment claim requires that state actors 1) trespassed on the personal "effects" of another, or 2) impinged on one's own expectation of privacy.

F. **Human Surveillance and Enhanced Surveillance**, in relation to police compliance with Fourth Amendment requirements, have been explained by the Supreme Court in the following cases.

   1. *California v. Greenwood*, 486 U.S. 35 (1988). A defendant has no reasonable expectation of privacy in garbage placed in opaque trash bags on the curb and searched by police. The *Greenwood* defendants were in the unprotected *Katz* category of those who knowingly expose a private item to the public, e.g., garbage collectors, scavengers.

2. ***Bond v. United States***, 529 U.S. 334 (2000). A person has a reasonable expectation of privacy in carry-on luggage placed in an overhead bin by a bus passenger and squeezed by a police officer.

3. ***United States v. Place***, 462 U.S. 696 (1983). Canine sniffs by narcotics detection dogs of luggage in a public place do not violate a reasonable expectation of privacy.

4. ***United States v. Knotts***, 460 U.S. 276 (1983). Tracking beepers are acceptable as a substitute for visual surveillance when the beeper was not used to reveal information about what was going on inside the defendant's home.

5. ***Florida v. Riley***, 488 U.S. 445 (1989); ***Dow Chemical v. United States***, 476 U.S. 227 (1986). Aerial surveillance cases indicate no reasonable expectation of privacy from some police "fly overs" of property; aerial surveillance of home curtilage from a helicopter flying as low as 400 feet has been approved, and the use of an aerial mapping camera is acceptable during "fly overs" of commercial property.

6. ***Kyllo v. United States***, 533 U.S. 27 (2001). A homeowner has a reasonable expectation of privacy from the use of a thermal imaging device. In "the home, all details are intimate details, because the entire area is held safe from prying government eyes."

ILLUSTRATIVE PROBLEMS

■ PROBLEM 4.1 FOURTH AMENDMENT ACTIVITY: OPEN FIELDS AND CURTILAGE ■

Donald's home is in the middle of his 155 acre farm, about a half mile from a dirt road. Because of dense trees, the home and farm buildings are not visible from the road. The farm is surrounded by a low fence with an access gate. Several "No Trespassing" signs are posted, including one adjacent to the access gate. Police officers with a tip that did not establish probable cause went to Donald's farm looking for money from a robbery. Acting upon the tip, they used a shovel to probe the ground next to a chicken coop adjacent to the home. The officers discovered the money after displacing a few inches of soil. How will a court decide Donald's motion to suppress?

Analysis

The entry onto the farm is covered by the open fields doctrine. Fences and no trespassing signs are not effective in keeping the public from open fields. Fourth Amendment requirements do not apply.

The officers did not enter only upon the open fields. They removed a few inches of soil next to a chicken coop adjacent to the home, which may be within the curtilage. Curtilage questions are to be resolved by the proximity of the area to the home, whether the area is included within an enclosure surrounding the home, the nature of the uses to which the area is put, and the steps the person took to prevent observation. The first and fourth factors may cut in favor of finding this area to be within curtilage. If the coop was not within the curtilage and the police entered it, the issue is analogous to digging for money. The issue then becomes whether all unsecured premises in the open fields (i.e., not within the curtilage) are fair game for law enforcement.

■ PROBLEM 4.2 FOURTH AMENDMENT ACTIVITY: ENHANCED SURVEILLANCE ■

Officer Mattingly applied for and received a search warrant from a judge, to search the defendant's apartment for marijuana and other contraband. In support of the warrant request, Mattingly submitted an affidavit in which he referred to an anonymous tip that defendant lived in a particular apartment and that he may be growing marijuana there. The informant told Mattingly that he had seen defendant and another man carry a carbon dioxide tank and other equipment into defendant's apartment. He also told Mattingly that from the hallway of the apartment building he could smell the odor of marijuana plants emitting from the defendant's apartment. Through defendant's open windows, the informant also had observed a very bright white light, which he described as "growing lights," as well as the tops of the marijuana plants.

In the affidavit, Mattingly asserted that he checked the utility records for the defendant's apartment and two neighboring apartments in defendant's building that were the same size. The records showed the defendant's average kilowatt usage was more than three times that of either of the other two apartments for the preceding year. He also returned to defendant's apartment and aimed a thermal imager at the bedroom area of defendant's apartment. He did not physically cross any fence lines or enter any curtilage area while using the thermal imager. Based upon his prior training and experience with the imager, he concluded that the surface temperature of defendant's structure was significantly higher than that of similar adjacent structures. The search pursuant to the warrant yielded marijuana plants and seedlings, sprouts, seeds, bagged vegetable matter, and some drug paraphernalia. Defendant filed a motion to suppress the evidence, arguing that the police use of the thermal imager allowed them to gather information regarding the interior of the defendant's apartment which they otherwise could not have gathered without a search warrant. How should the motion be decided?

Analysis

In using the thermal imager, Mattingly was seeking to measure the amount of heat in defendant's apartment to acquire information about the interior of defendant's apartment. Any information about the interior of a person's home that cannot otherwise be obtained without a physical intrusion into a constitutionally protected area like the home constitutes a search. Thus, warrantless use of the thermal imager to measure heat flowing from the interior of the defendant's apartment violated the Fourth

Amendment. And the information gained from the imager's use cannot be considered in establishing probable cause.

POINTS TO REMEMBER

- It is a violation of a person's reasonable expectation of privacy for the police to intrude without complying with Fourth Amendment requirements:

  — Squeeze luggage to determine its contents when the luggage has been placed in the overhead rack of a bus by a passenger;

  — Use a thermal imaging device to determine the amount of heat emanating from the exterior walls of a home;

  — Conduct an electronic intrusion that captures the substance of phone conversations, as by using a device affixed to the outside of a public phone booth to record the conversations of the person within the booth;

  — Place a tracking beeper in an object and use it to obtain information about the location of that object when the location is inside a person's premises;

  — Enter on to property and perform visual surveillance there when the property constitutes the "curtilage" around a home.

- It is *not* a violation of a person's reasonable expectation of privacy for the police to perform any of these intrusions without complying with Fourth Amendment requirements:

  — Use a dog trained to detect contraband to perform a canine sniff of luggage in a public place or of the exterior of an automobile;

  — Enter on to property and perform visual surveillance there when the property constitutes the "open fields";

  — Obtain the substance of phone conversations from an undercover agent who records those conversations as a trusted participant;

— Obtain trash bags from a garbage collector, which bags were placed on the curb outside a house by the homeowner, and then search the garbage inside them;

— Conduct aerial surveillance of the "curtilage" surrounding a home at the height of 400 feet, or use an aerial mapping camera to take photographs of the areas surrounding commercial buildings;

— Place a tracking beeper in an object and use it to obtain information about the location of that object when the location is in the "open fields."

CHAPTER 5

Search and Seizure: Warrantless Searches and Seizures

Although the Fourth Amendment prohibits "unreasonable" searches and seizures, it does not require that all searches or seizures be conducted pursuant to a warrant. The Court has articulated a "preference" for warrants, but it has frequently found that warrantless searches are "reasonable." Even though warrantless arrests are generally permissible, warrantless searches are disfavored and are "*per se* unreasonable . . . subject only to a few specifically established and well-delineated exceptions." *Katz v. United States*, 389 U.S. 347 (1967). This chapter discusses those exceptions.

A. PLAIN VIEW EXCEPTION

"Plain view" is a frequently used exception to the warrant requirement. When the police are in a place where they have the right to be (as when they are conducting a lawful search), either pursuant to a warrant or pursuant to an exception to the warrant requirement, the exception allows them to seize items that they find in "plain view." While a seizure of property is an invasion of the owner's possessory interest, the search is justified by the fact that the officer found it in "plain view."

For the plain view exception to apply, the contraband's incriminating character must be "immediately apparent." If the police see the defendant carrying what looks like a cigarette, it must be "immediately apparent" that the cigarette contains marijuana rather than ordinary tobacco, i.e., the police must be able to ascertain the cigarette's incriminating character based on their training and experience.

Several cases illustrate the "immediately apparent" requirement. In *Coolidge v. New Hampshire*, 403 U.S. 443 (1971), the police seized the defendant's car from his driveway because they thought that it might contain microscopic fibers that would implicate him in a crime. The Court held that the seizure of the car was invalid, because the incriminating character of the car (containing the fibers) was not immediately apparent.

Similarly, in *Arizona v. Hicks*, 480 U.S. 321 (1987), although the police validly entered an apartment to search for evidence relating to a shooting, they observed expensive stereo components which they moved to observe the serial numbers. The Court invalidated the search, holding that the serial numbers were not "immediately apparent" before the police moved (i.e., seized) the components to observe the numbers.

In *Minnesota v. Dickerson*, 508 U.S. 366 (1993), a police officer stopped Dickerson and forced him to submit to a frisk for weapons. The frisk revealed no weapons, but the officer felt a small "lump" in his nylon jacket. The officer examined the lump by sliding it back and forth until he was able to determine that it was crack cocaine. The officer then seized the cocaine. The Court held that the contraband was not in plain view and that the seizure therefore was invalid, because the officer was unaware that the "lump" was contraband until he manipulated it.

The plain view exception also requires that the police have a right to be where they are when they make their observation. For example, suppose that a police officer walking down a city street looks through a window and sees marijuana on a table inside a house. If the officer does not possess a warrant to enter the house, and cannot enter under one of the recognized exceptions to the warrant requirement, the officer cannot justify entry under the plain view exception. However, the officer's observation of the marijuana in plain view may give her probable cause to obtain a warrant to search the house for the marijuana.

The plain view exception applies even if the discovery of contraband was not accidental or "inadvertent." *Horton v. California,* 496 U.S. 128 (1990). "The fact that an officer is interested in an item of evidence and fully expects to find it in the course of a search should not invalidate its seizure if the search is confined in area and duration by the terms of a warrant or a valid exception to the warrant requirement."

POINTS TO REMEMBER

- The "plain view" exception justifies the seizure of evidence that the police find in plain view, provided that the police are in a place where they have the right to be.

- Before contraband can be regarded as being in "plain view," its status as contraband must be immediately apparent.

- By itself, the plain view exception will not justify a warrantless entry into a residence even though the officer, standing in a public place, can see contraband lying in plain view.

- Under the plain view exception, the discovery of evidence need not be inadvertent.

B. SEARCH INCIDENT TO LEGAL ARREST

The search incident to legal arrest exception is a well-established exception to the warrant requirement. When the police make a legal arrest, they have the right to make a search incident to that arrest.

What constitutes a "legal" arrest? A custodial arrest occurs when the police take a suspect into custody in order to bring charges. *United States v. Watson,* 423 U.S. 411 (1976) held that the police may arrest a person in a public place without a warrant, provided that they have probable cause to believe that the arrestee committed a felony. Essentially, the Court reaffirmed the common law rule which allowed peace officers to arrest without a warrant "for a misdemeanor or felony committed in his presence as well as for a felony not committed in his presence if there [are] reasonable ground[s] for making the arrest."

The Court qualified *Watson* for an arrest at a person's home in *Payton v. New York*, 445 U.S. 573 (1980). The Court held that, absent exigent circumstances, police cannot arrest a person at his home without an arrest warrant. In *Steagald v. United States*, 451 U.S. 204 (1981), the Court extended *Payton* by holding that a law enforcement officer may not search for a person who is the subject of an arrest warrant in the home of a third party without first obtaining a *search* warrant.

Even if the arrest is a "sham" or "pretext" to allow the police to search, the police may arrest the suspect. In *Arkansas v. Sullivan*, 532 U.S. 769 (2001), the Court noted that individual officers' "[s]ubjective intentions play no role in ordinary, probable cause Fourth Amendment analysis."

The Scope of a Search Incident to Arrest. Once a legal arrest occurs, the police are allowed to make a search incident to arrest. A search incident to legal arrest is "reasonable" because the arrestee might have: 1) a weapon that she can use to endanger the police or to effect an escape, and 2) evidence in her possession that she might try to destroy.

In *Chimel v. California*, 395 U.S. 752 (1969), Chimel was legally arrested at his home for burglary, and the police searched the entire house and seized various stolen coins and other objects. Although the Court held that the police may conduct searches incident to arrest, it held that the police had exceeded the permissible scope of the search incident to the arrest. The scope of a search incident to arrest is limited to the arrestee's person and the areas within her immediate control. By searching all of Chimel's house, the police went beyond the area of her "immediate control."

Except in rare circumstances, the arrest must precede the search in order to fit within this exception. However, in *Rawlings v.*

Kentucky, 448 U.S. 98 (1980), after petitioner admitted ownership of a sizeable quantity of drugs, the police searched his person (the search revealed money and a knife) and placed him under arrest. The Court viewed the search of Rawlings' person as "incident to arrest" even though it preceded the arrest. After Rawlings admitted ownership of the drugs found in Cox's purse, the police clearly already had probable cause to arrest him. "Where the formal arrest followed quickly on the heels of the challenged search of petitioner's person, we do not believe it particularly important that the search preceded the arrest rather than vice versa."

The search incident to legal arrest exception applies, regardless of the type of crime for which the arrest is made and regardless of whether the police can prove that the arrestee is carrying a weapon or contraband. *United States v. Robinson*, 414 U.S. 218 (1973).

For purposes of safety or evidentiary concerns, "[p]olice may search a [passenger compartment of a] vehicle incident to a recent occupant's arrest only if the arrestee is within reaching distance of the passenger compartment at the time of the search *or* it is reasonable to believe the vehicle contains evidence of the offense of arrest." *Arizona v. Gant*, 556 U.S. 332 (2009). An automatic search incident to an arrest of the passenger compartment after the defendant is arrested, handcuffed and secured in a patrol car is unreasonable. A reasonable search may extend to items found in containers within the passenger compartment, e.g., the glove compartment.

Chimel and *Gant* are subject to temporal and spatial limitations. The police can search only the area within the arrestee's "immediate control." In *Coolidge v. New Hampshire*, 403 U.S. 443 (1971), the defendant was arrested inside his home and the police searched his car which was sitting outside on the driveway. The Court held that the car search did not fit within the scope of a permissible search incident to arrest.

The "temporal limitation" requires that the search incident to legal arrest be conducted relatively contemporaneously with the arrest. In *Preston v. United States*, 376 U.S. 364 (1964), Preston and his companions were arrested while riding in an automobile and taken to the police station for booking. A police officer towed their car to a garage. After the men were booked, police officers searched the passenger compartment of the car and found two loaded revolvers. The Court invalidated the search as "too remote in time or place to have been made as incidental to the arrest."

POINTS TO REMEMBER

- When the police make a lawful arrest, they are entitled to make a search incident to arrest.

- The search incident to legal arrest is justified by the need to remove weapons that the arrestee might use to effect an escape and the need to remove evidence that the arrestee might destroy.

- In general, warrantless arrests are permissible provided that the officer has probable cause to believe that the suspect committed a crime.

- Absent consent or some other exception, a suspect may not be arrested in his own home without an arrest warrant or in a third party's home without a search warrant.

- The search incident exception extends to those areas within the arrestee's "immediate control."

- The search must be relatively contemporaneous with the arrest.

- When the arrestee is traveling in an automobile, the search incident exception extends to the entire passenger compartment if the arrestee is within reaching distance of the passenger compartment at the time of the search or it is reasonable to believe the vehicle contains evidence of the offense of arrest.

C. BOOKING SEARCHES

Closely related to the search incident to legal arrest exception is the so-called "booking" exception. After the police arrest and "book" a suspect, and before they place the suspect in jail, the police usually conduct a "booking" search. In *Illinois v. Lafayette*, 462 U.S. 640 (1983), the Court upheld this type of search, noting that it "is reasonable for police to search the personal effects of a person under lawful arrest as part of the routine administrative procedure at a police stationhouse incident to booking and jailing the suspect." Under the booking exception, jail officials can remove both contraband and valuables. For example, in the case of a person with a backpack, the officials have the right not only to take the backpack but to search its interior as well.

A number of governmental interests justify booking searches. Jail officials: 1) prevent personal items from being stolen while the arrestee is in the jail population, 2) help protect themselves against false claims of theft, 3) prevent the arrestee from introducing contraband, weapons, etc. into the jail, and 4) are better able to ascertain a suspect's identity.

Courts loosely apply temporal limitations in this context. For example, in *United States v. Edwards*, 415 U.S. 800 (1974), the Court upheld a booking search which took place nearly ten hours after a defendant's arrest: "searches and seizures that could be made on the spot at the time of arrest may legally be conducted later when the accused arrives at the place of detention."

Striking "a reasonable balance between inmate privacy and the security needs of the institutions," the Court has upheld routine, suspicionless strip searches of all arrestees who end up in the general jail population, regardless of the seriousness of the crimes charged. *Florence v. Board of Chosen Freeholders of the County of Burlington*, 132 S.Ct. 1510 (2012).

POINTS TO REMEMBER

- Jail officials have the right to conduct "booking" searches before they put individuals in jail.

- Booking searches protect the detainee's valuables, protect the jail against false claims, prevent the introduction of dangerous items and contraband into the jail, and help jail officials ascertain and verify a detainee's identity.

- Corrections officials can strip search each person who enters the general jail population.

D. AUTOMOBILE EXCEPTION

When the police have probable cause to believe that an automobile contains the fruits, instrumentalities or evidence of crime, the automobile exception provides that they may search the vehicle without a warrant. In *Carroll v. United States*, 267 U.S. 132 (1925), the Court noted that, although owners or drivers have constitutionally protected privacy interests in their cars, they are given less protection than when they are at home because of the "ready mobility" of automobiles. This mobility creates exigent circumstances to justify a warrantless search.

In recent cases, the Court also has recognized that an automobile is subject to less rigorous warrant requirements "because the expectation of privacy with respect to one's automobile is significantly less than that relating to one's home or office" due to the "pervasive regulation" of vehicles on the highway. *California v. Carney*, 471 U.S. 386 (1985). "Pervasive regulation" includes the possibility of periodic inspections as well as licensing requirements.

In light of the mobility and diminished expectation of privacy, the existence of probable cause justifies an immediate warrantless search of an automobile "before the vehicle and its occupants become unavailable." It does not matter whether the car is being driven at the time of the stop and the subsequent search so long as it is capable of moving and therefore has "ready mobility."

In *California v. Carney*, the Court treated a mobile home like an automobile, concluding that its mobility is similar to an automobile and therefore is subject to the diminished expectation of privacy associated with automobiles. The Court emphasized that this particular mobile home was "readily mobile." In addition, it was subject to the pervasive regulation associated with vehicles, and the vehicle was so situated that an objective observer would conclude that it was being used not as a residence, but as a vehicle.

Most decisions have loosely applied the contemporaneous requirement to the automobile exception. For example, in *Chambers v. Maroney*, 399 U.S. 42 (1970), although petitioner was riding in an automobile at the time of his arrest, the vehicle was searched at the police station rather than at the scene. The court upheld the search even though the car had been immobilized and it would have been relatively easy to obtain a warrant. Given the existence of probable cause to search, the police may choose to search later at the police station or elsewhere.

For many years, the courts struggled with the question of the scope of a search conducted under the automobile exception. In *United States v. Ross*, 456 U.S. 798 (1982), the police armed with probable cause had the authority to search the entire car for contraband and to search any container where the contraband could be. By contrast, in *California v. Acevedo*, 500 U.S. 565 (1991), police had probable cause to seize and search only a paper bag which happened to be in a vehicle. If the police have probable cause to search for that bag, once they find the particular container they can open it. But that is the end of the search unless the container's contents suggest probable cause for a broader search. If the police come across criminal evidence in plain view on the way to finding the specific paper bag for which there is probable cause, they can seize that evidence as well. They also may open larger containers in which the paper bag for which probable cause exists could be located. The *Acevedo* Court refused to recognize a distinction "between a container for which the police are specifically searching and a container which they come across in a car." Therefore, as long as the police have probable cause to search the automobile, they can search anywhere in the automobile, including a search of containers found within the automobile.

POINTS TO REMEMBER

- The automobile exception allows the police to make a warrantless search of a vehicle provided that they have probable cause to believe that the automobile contains the fruits, instrumentalities or evidence of crime.

- The automobile exception is justified by the "diminished expectation of privacy" associated with automobiles, as well as by the fact that cars are readily mobile.

- The courts have loosely applied the contemporaneous requirement to automobile searches.

- The police can search parts of the car for which they have probable cause to believe that the fruits, instrumentalities or evidence of crime can be found.

- The automobile exception includes the search of closed containers in the vehicle.

E.   INVENTORY EXCEPTION

When the police impound vehicles, they routinely inventory the contents. Inventory searches may be conducted without probable cause or a warrant. Before an inventory search, the vehicle must have been legally impounded according to local standards. Once a vehicle is lawfully impounded, the scope of an inventory search is broad: police may search the passenger compartment, the trunk, and any closed containers.

The leading decision is *Colorado v. Bertine*, 479 U.S. 367 (1987), a case that involved an inventory search of a vehicle following its operator's arrest for drunk driving. Upholding the search, the Court emphasized that the inventory exception is justified by the need "to protect an owner's property while it is in the custody of the police, to insure against claims of lost, stolen, or vandalized property, and to guard the police from danger."

An inventory search cannot be conducted solely for criminal investigative motives. Indeed, before conducting an inventory search, the police are not required to show that the particular vehicle contains dangerous items. *Colorado v. Bertine*, 479 U.S. 367 (1987).

Courts sometimes require that inventory searches be conducted pursuant to departmental regulation so that the discretion of individual police officers is minimized. For example, in *Florida v. Wells*, 495 U.S. 1 (1990), Wells was arrested and his car was impounded. An inventory search at the impoundment facility revealed two marijuana cigarettes, and a locked suitcase that was found to contain a considerable quantity of marijuana. Because the Florida Highway Patrol "had no policy whatever with respect to the opening of closed containers encountered during an inventory search," the Court held that the search was "not sufficiently regulated to satisfy the Fourth Amendment." The Court does not preclude individual police officers from exercising all discretion, provided that "discretion is exercised according to standard criteria and on the basis of something other than suspicion or evidence of criminal activity."

POINTS TO REMEMBER

- The police may conduct routine inventory searches of lawfully impounded vehicles.

- The purpose of an inventory search is to protect valuables, protect the police against false claims, and remove items that may present a danger to the public.

- The scope of an inventory search is broad, extending to the passenger compartment, the trunk and closed containers.

- Inventory searches will sometimes be invalidated when department regulations fail to sufficiently limit the discretion of individual police officers (i.e., regarding the search of closed containers).

F. CONSENT

Voluntary Consent. The consent exception is not really an "exception" to the warrant requirement. Any constitutional right can be waived, including the Fourth Amendment right to be free from unreasonable searches and seizures.

Schneckloth v. Bustamonte, 412 U.S. 218 (1973), provides insight into the meaning of the term "consent." That case involved six men who were traveling in an automobile. When the vehicle was stopped (because one headlight and a license plate light were burned out), and the driver could not produce a driver's license, the officer asked the driver and passengers to step out of the vehicle. The officer then asked Alcala, a passenger who claimed that his brother owned the car, if he could search the vehicle. Alcala replied, "Sure, go ahead." The officer testified that it "was all very congenial at this time." The driver testified that Alcala actually helped in the search of the car by opening the trunk and glove compartment. In the car, the officer found three stolen checks which were introduced at Bustamonte's subsequent trial.

The Court held that consent searches are permissible, but that the State bears the burden of showing "that the consent was, in fact, freely and voluntarily given." Consent does not exist when the suspect was "coerced." In determining whether consent was voluntary or coerced, a "totality of the circumstances" test is applied, using a variety of factors peculiar to the suspect (e.g., if the suspect is particularly vulnerable because of lack of schooling) and factors that suggest coercion (e.g., police guns were drawn, police demanded the right to search).

One potential factor in the "totality of circumstances" analysis is whether the suspect knows that she has the right to refuse consent. However, the Court refused to require the police to inform a suspect of her right to refuse. Fourth Amendment rights are different because they were designed to protect the "security of one's privacy against arbitrary intrusion by the [police]," rather than to guarantee a fair trial. In addition, the community has an interest in encouraging consent, because "the resulting search may yield necessary evidence for the solution and prosecution of crime, evidence that may insure that a wholly innocent person is not wrongly charged with a criminal offense."

Schneckloth was followed and expanded in *Ohio v. Robinette*, 519 U.S. 33 (1996), where the defendant was lawfully stopped for speeding and given a verbal warning. The officer asked whether Robinette was carrying contraband. When Robinette answered in the negative, the officer asked for and obtained permission to search Robinette's car. The search revealed a small amount of marijuana. The Court held that the officer was not required to tell Robinette that he was "free to go" before asking for consent to search the vehicle. "The Fourth Amendment test for a valid consent to search is that the consent be voluntary, and '[v]oluntariness is a question of fact to be determined from all the circumstances.' "

The scope of consent can extend to closed containers. In *Florida v. Jimeno*, 500 U.S. 248 (1991), believing that respondent was carrying narcotics, a police officer asked for permission to search his car. Respondent consented, stating that he had nothing to hide. When the search revealed cocaine in a paper bag on the floorboard, the Court held that the consent extended to the paper bag because Jimeno "did not place any explicit limitation on the scope of the search. [I]t was objectively reasonable for the police to conclude that the general consent to search respondent's car included consent to search containers within that car which might bear drugs."

Even when consent is apparently given, it may be vitiated by police assertions of authority and right. In *Bumper v. State of North Carolina*, 391 U.S. 543 (1968), the police went to an elderly widow and asked for permission to search her house (the police believed that her grandson had committed a crime). One officer lied and stated, "I have a search warrant to search your house." The grandmother responded, "Go ahead," and opened the door. The Court held that the consent was invalid, noting that the State bears the burden of showing that the consent was "freely and voluntarily given" and that consent did not exist simply because the woman acquiesced to a "claim of lawful authority."

Third Party Consent. When a third party consents to a search of property, a court must decide not only whether the consent was voluntarily given, but also whether the third party could consent to the search. In *United States v. Matlock*, 415 U.S. 164 (1974), a woman consented to the search of a house that she shared with Matlock, including their bedroom, where police found evidence that they used against Matlock. The Court held that the woman could consent to a search of the room because she had "common authority" over the area. "Common authority" rests on

> mutual use of the property by persons generally having joint access or control for most purposes, so that it is reasonable to recognize that any of the co-inhabitants has the right to permit the inspection in his own right and that the others have assumed the risk that one of their number might permit the common area to be searched.

In *Illinois v. Rodriguez*, 497 U.S. 177 (1990), police made a warrantless entry into Rodriguez's apartment with the consent of his girlfriend who had lived there for several months and who possessed a key. She referred to the apartment as "our apartment" and she claimed to have clothing and furniture there. In fact, although she had lived in the apartment with Rodriguez, she had moved out more than a month before, her name was not on the lease, she did not pay rent, and she had taken the key without Rodriguez's knowledge or consent (although she had not yet moved all of her furniture out). Inside the apartment, the police found cocaine and seized the drugs and related paraphernalia.

Upholding the search, the Court stated that the girlfriend did not possess "common authority" over the apartment because she did not have "joint access or control for most purposes." Nevertheless, the Court upheld the search, focusing on the reasonableness of the police in believing that the consenting party had "apparent authority" to consent. The Court required only that the officers make a "reasonable" judgment regarding the facts before them. The Court noted that this approach would sanction a "reasonable mistake."

In the Court's view, the police act "reasonably" when they enter a dwelling based on a reasonable but erroneous belief "that the person who has consented to their entry is a resident of the premises." An objective standard applies: "would the facts available to the officer at the [moment] 'warrant a man of reasonable caution in the belief' that the consenting party had authority over the premises?" In *Rodriguez*, the Court concluded that the officers reasonably believed that the girlfriend had authority over the apartment to provide valid consent to search.

Georgia v. Randolph, 547 U.S. 103 (2006), held that a wife's consent to search did not validate the search in the face of the husband's objections. The Court distinguished *Matlock* because that case involved consent by a co-tenant against an "absent, nonconsenting person with whom that authority is shared."

The Court concluded that, unless there is some "recognized hierarchy" within a household (e.g., parent and child or barracks housing military personnel of different grades), "there is no societal understanding of superior and inferior" and "a physically present inhabitant's express refusal of consent to a police search is dispositive as to him, regardless of the consent of a fellow occupant."

As for children, *Randolph* suggested that the authority to consent depends on the circumstances.

> [A] child of eight might well be considered to have the power to consent to the police crossing the threshold into that part of the house where any caller, such as a pollster or salesman, might well be admitted . . . but no one would reasonably expect such a child to be in a position to authorize anyone to rummage through his parents' bedroom.

POINTS TO REMEMBER

- Consent searches are permissible because Fourth Amendment rights, like other rights, can be waived.

- In determining whether consent is valid, courts focus on whether the consent was voluntarily given or instead was coerced.

- Courts apply a "totality of the circumstances" test in determining the question of voluntariness.

- Under the "totality of circumstances" test, courts consider various factors, including factors particular to the suspect (e.g., lack of schooling).

- While lack of knowledge of the right to refuse consent is a factor to be considered, the police do not have a duty to warn a person that she has the right to refuse.

- Other relevant factors include the attitude and actions of the police (i.e., did they have guns drawn, did they request or demand permission to search).

- Third parties can consent to a search when they have common authority over the place or things to be searched.

- If the police reasonably (though incorrectly) believe that a person who gives them consent has the right to consent, the court might uphold the search even though the person who gave the consent lacked common authority over the place or things to be searched.

G. ADMINISTRATIVE INSPECTIONS

Administrative agencies regularly conduct various types of inspections, e.g., health inspectors enter restaurants to determine whether food preparation and service areas are clean. Government inspectors examine industrial sites for safe and healthy conditions. Sometimes, officials enter private homes or yards looking for abused or neglected children.

The Fourth Amendment applies to administrative inspections. *Camara v. Municipal Court*, 387 U.S. 523 (1967). A San Francisco city ordinance authorized city inspectors to enter buildings "to perform any duty imposed upon them by the Municipal Code." When Camara refused to allow inspectors to enter his apartment without a warrant, he was ultimately convicted of refusing to permit a lawful inspection. Overturning the conviction, the Court emphasized that the Fourth Amendment was designed to prevent "arbitrary invasions by governmental officials," and reiterated its long-standing preference for warrants.

Camara also noted that the Fourth Amendment warrant requirement could effectively function in the administrative context, because it both notifies the homeowner about the purpose of the inspection and about the limits of the inspector's power. It also checks administrative discretion by requiring a neutral judge to determine whether the inspection is justified.

An important aspect of *Camara* was the balancing of competing interests. In determining whether the search was "reasonable," the Court balanced the governmental interest against the private interest. The governmental interest in administrative inspections ensures "city-wide compliance with minimum physical standards for private property" and prevents "the unintentional development of conditions which are hazardous to public health and safety." The Court also recognized that administrative searches involve "significant intrusions" on individual privacy, and noted that warrants help protect individual security.

After balancing these interests, the Court held that the Fourth Amendment imposed a warrant requirement on administrative inspections based on "administrative" probable cause. Historically, the probable cause requirement applied in a defendant-specific/place-specific way, but in *Camara*, the Court did not require building-specific probable cause for building inspections. Instead, the Court held that the decision to inspect all buildings in a particular area could be based on an assessment of "conditions in the area as a whole, not on its knowledge of conditions in each particular building."

Camara held that "area inspections" required reasonable legislative or administrative standards that could focus on general criteria such as "the passage of time, the nature of the building (e.g., a multifamily apartment house), or the condition of the entire area." Many conditions (e.g., faulty wiring) "are not observable from outside the building and indeed may not be apparent to the inexpert occupant himself," and administrative inspections "involve a relatively limited invasion of the urban citizen's privacy."

The Court also recognized that there are situations when warrantless inspections are constitutionally permissible. For example, a warrant is not required in "emergency situations" involving the seizure of unwholesome food, smallpox vaccinations, health quarantines, or the inspection of a fire scene.

The Court has established an exception to the warrant requirement for certain "closely regulated" businesses that have "such a history of government oversight that no reasonable expectation of privacy could exist for a proprietor over the stock of such an enterprise." *Marshall v. Barlow's, Inc.*, 436 U.S. 307 (1978). In *Donovan v. Dewey*, 452 U.S. 594 (1981), the Court held that underground and surface mines qualified as closely regulated businesses, and in *United States v. Biswell*, 406 U.S. 311 (1972), the Court held that a businessperson who engages in a pervasively regulated business under a license knows that her business records, firearms, and ammunition are subject to effective inspection.

Not all businesses can be regarded as "closely regulated." Warrantless searches are upheld if: 1) there is a "substantial government interest that informs the regulatory scheme pursuant to which the inspection is made", and 2) the warrantless inspections are "necessary to further [the] regulatory scheme." *Barlow's*. The regulatory statute must perform the two basic functions of a warrant: 1) advising the owner of the commercial premises that the search is being made with a properly defined scope, and 2) limiting the discretion of the inspecting officers. Inspectors' discretion is limited by time, place, and scope.

The outer limits of the "closely regulated" exception were established in *New York v. Burger*, 482 U.S. 691 (1987), in which a junkyard was in the business of dismantling cars and selling car parts. Police officers sought to inspect under a New York law authorizing warrantless inspections of junkyards. During the inspection, officers recorded vehicle identification numbers on several vehicles that were later determined to be stolen. Burger was charged with possession of stolen property and operation of a junkyard in non-compliance with State law.

Upholding the search, the Court held that junkyards qualified as "closely regulated" businesses. Junkyards must maintain a book showing the acquisition and disposition of motor vehicles and vehicle parts, and these records must be available for inspection by governmental agents. Although junkyards and vehicle dismantlers had not existed very long and thus did not have a long history of regulation, the Court analogized the industry to secondhand shops and general junkyards which "long have been subject to regulation." As a result, the junkyard owners engaged in vehicle dismantling had a reduced expectation of privacy.

The New York statute met the criteria for warrantless inspections of closely regulated businesses. First, the interest in regulating the industry was substantial, "because motor vehicle theft has increased in the State and because the problem of theft is associated with this industry." Second, the statute provided a "constitutionally adequate substitute for a warrant," because it informed the operator of a vehicle dismantling business about regular inspections and the scope of the inspections. Finally, the administrative scheme is an adequate substitute for a warrant by limiting the discretion of inspectors regarding the "time, place, and scope" of the inspection.

The *Burger* search did not involve ordinary administrative inspections by administrative officials, but instead involved police searches for evidence of criminal activity. Still, the Court upheld the police search as an administrative inspection: "a State can address a major social problem both by way of an administrative scheme and through penal sanctions."

POINTS TO REMEMBER

- Administrative inspections are subject to the Fourth Amendment's prohibition against unreasonable searches and seizures.

- Before the government can compel a person or business to submit to an administrative inspection, the government must obtain a warrant based on probable cause.

- However, the definition of probable cause has been redefined in this area of the law to include "reasonable legislative or administrative standards" for periodic inspections.

- As in other areas of the law, warrants might not be required when an emergency situation is involved.

- Warrants are also not required for inspection of "closely regulated" businesses.

H. STOP AND FRISK

The "stop and frisk" exception has reshaped Fourth Amendment law in important respects. In *Terry v. Ohio*, 392 U.S. 1 (1968), a police officer observed suspicious behavior (three men walked back and forth in front of a business) and became concerned that a robbery was about to take place. Because robbers carry guns, the officer believed that the men were armed. He approached them and asked for their names. When they "mumbled" a response, he grabbed Terry, spun him around, and patted down the outside of his clothing, revealing a revolver. The officer then "patted down" the other two men and found a second weapon. The officer arrested the men and charged them with carrying concealed weapons.

Upholding the officer's actions, the Court provided detailed guidance for police-citizen street encounters. Because Terry was protected by the Fourth Amendment on public streets, the "stop" involved a "seizure" and the "frisk" involved a "search." A seizure occurs when the police "accost an individual and restrain his freedom to walk away," and a search occurs even when the police simply explore a person's outer clothing in an effort to discover weapons.

The Court concluded that a stop and frisk constituted a "serious intrusion . . . upon the sanctity of the person, which may inflict great indignity and arouse strong resentment." In reaching its conclusion, the Court applied the "need" versus "intrusion" balancing test which it had announced a year earlier in *Camara*.

The Court found a governmental interest in "effective crime prevention and detection." Because the officer believed that a "stick-up" might be in progress and that the suspects might be armed and dangerous, he was justified in believing that immediate action was needed. Because he did not have "probable cause" to arrest the suspects, he began with a limited intrusion as he approached the men and asked them to identify themselves. When he received an unsatisfactory response, he seized Terry to pat him down, which was justified by the circumstances.

Because the stop and frisk exception was designed to allow the police to protect themselves and others from a suspect who might be armed and dangerous, the search must be designed to discover hidden weapons. The frisk of Terry was permissible because the officer patted down only the outer clothing until he found a weapon, therefore confining "his search strictly to what was minimally necessary to learn whether the men were armed and to disarm them once he discovered the weapons." Police must be able to point to "specific and articulable facts which, taken together with rational inferences from those facts, reasonably warrant that intrusion." Courts apply an objective standard: "would the facts available to the officer at the moment of the seizure or the search warrant a man of reasonable caution in the belief that the action taken was appropriate?"

To summarize: a stop is a temporary seizure of a person short of an arrest; its purpose is to clarify ambiguous situations that a police officer observes. *Terry* establishes that a stop is proper when an officer reasonably concludes in light of his experience and observation that criminal activity may be afoot *and* that the person is armed and presently dangerous. Since *Terry*, the case law has de-emphasized the armed and dangerous requirement for a stop. The test for a stop has both objective and subjective aspects: the test is objective because it focuses on whether the officer reached a reasonable conclusion, but the test is also subjective because the officer is relying on his experiences and observations. A mere hunch that someone is involved in illegal activity is not enough to justify a stop. *Sibron v. New York*, 392 U.S. 40 (1968).

In measuring whether a stop has occurred, so that the requisite proof can be assessed, the Court has posed the issue as whether a reasonable person would have felt free to leave the scene. If the answer is yes, the situation constitutes an encounter and not even a stop.

The "free to leave" concept does not apply if the citizen's choice to stay is extraneous to the police presence, such as being on a common carrier. For example, in *Florida v. Bostick*, 501 U.S. 429 (1991), during a stopover in Ft. Lauderdale, armed police officers boarded a bus bound from Miami to Atlanta. Without any articulable suspicion, they asked Bostick for his bus ticket and identification, and returned them to him; then they asked if they could search his luggage. The Court concluded that he had not been "stopped" under the Fourth Amendment. Instead of applying the "free to leave" standard, the Court stated that the applicable question was whether a reasonable person would feel free to decline the officer's request or otherwise terminate the situation.

The Reasonable Suspicion Standard. The reasonable suspicion standard requires less proof than either probable cause or even a preponderance of evidence. *United States v. Sokolow*, 490 U.S. 1. The legal standard to stop expresses a concern for danger that flows from the nature of the crime for which reasonable suspicion exists. Measuring reasonable suspicion is based on an assessment of the totality of the circumstances for suspecting the person of criminal activity.

For example, in *Sokolow*, the Court found a "reasonable suspicion of criminal activity" when a suspect 1) paid $2,100 for two airplane tickets from a roll of $20 bills, 2) traveled under a name that did not match the name under which his telephone number was listed, 3) went to Miami as his original destination, a source city for illicit drugs, 4) stayed in Miami for only 48 hours, even though a round-trip flight from Honolulu to Miami takes 20 hours, 5) appeared nervous during his trip, and 6) checked none of his luggage.

As with probable cause, reasonable suspicion is based on an individualized assessment of the circumstances. Drug courier profiles have been used at least since the 1970s to support stopping persons based upon certain characteristics and behavioral traits. However, case law has held that reliance on such profiles does not necessarily amount to reasonable suspicion to justify a stop. *United States v. Cortez*, 449 U.S. 411 (1981) notes that reasonable suspicion is based upon the totality of circumstances, which involves the cumulative effect of facts rather than the presence of a fact that happens to match a profile.

Efforts to avoid police or avoid being seen may contribute to the reasonable suspicion necessary for a valid stop. In *Illinois v. Wardlow*, 528 U.S. 119 (2000), the suspect ran from police in a heavy drug trafficking area as soon as he saw them. After catching the suspect, police subjected him to a patdown search for weapons, during which they squeezed a bag he was carrying and felt a heavy, hard object with a shape similar to a gun. The officer opened the bag and found a handgun with ammunition. The Court upheld the stop and frisk. "Headlong flight . . . is the consummate act of evasion: it is not necessarily indicative of wrongdoing, but it is certainly suggestive of such."

Other facts that may support reasonable suspicion are the nature of the suspected crime, what conduct caused the suspicion, whether the area is a high crime area or a luxury home area, whether the suspect is engaged in conduct for which he already has a criminal record, the suspect's age, race, dress, demeanor, and the police officer's experience.

Reasonable suspicion may be based on a tip from an informant, even an anonymous tipster, to develop reasonable suspicion. "If a tip has a relatively low degree of reliability, more information will be required to establish the requisite quantum of suspicion than would be required if the tip was more reliable." *Alabama v. White*, 496 U.S. 325 (1990).

However, in *Florida v. J.L.*, 529 U.S. 266 (2000), an anonymous tipster called the Miami police to say that a young black male was wearing a plaid shirt while carrying a concealed weapon and standing with others at a bus stop. Apart from the tip, the officers had no reason to believe that any of the persons was engaged in illegal conduct. Nevertheless, the officers immediately frisked the defendant and found a gun in his pocket. The Court reversed the conviction because of the nature of the information in the tip, observing: "[R]easonable suspicion . . . requires that a tip be reliable in its assertion of illegality, not just in its tendency to identify a determinate person." In other words, police action must be based on objective criteria rather than simply a "hunch."

The police are not restricted to stopping people for crimes that have not yet been committed. They also may stop a suspect who is found near the scene of a recent or completed crime. *United States v. Hensley*, 469 U.S. 221 (1985). In these situations, reasonable suspicion may be based upon the specificity of the description of a person or vehicle, the elapsed time since the crime, the number of persons in the area, the known or probable direction of the offender's flight, and other suspicion that the person or vehicle stopped has been involved in other criminality of the type under investigation.

Stopping and Frisking People. A stop must be temporary and last no longer than is necessary to effectuate the stop's purpose. *Florida v. Royer*, 460 U.S. 491 (1983). In *Royer*, the officer's decision to remove the suspect from the initial location of the stop to the detective office rendered the seizure unreasonable. However, a stop does not become unreasonable simply because the police could have used a less intrusive means of investigation. "Such a rule would unduly hamper the police's ability to make swift, on-the-spot decisions." *United States v. Sokolow*, 490 U.S. 1 (1989). Police may justify a longer time period for a stop as long as they are diligently pursuing their investigation during the detention.

Although the Court has not fixed any outer time limit for the duration of a stop, the police must pursue a means of investigation that is likely to confirm or dispel their suspicion quickly. In each case, courts must consider the length and intrusiveness of the stop and "the enforcement purposes to be served by the stop as well as the time reasonably needed to effectuate those purposes." *United States v. Sharpe*, 470 U.S. 675 (1985). When the actions by the police exceed what is permitted for a stop, the seizure becomes an arrest, which must be supported by probable cause.

After a stop, if police still suspect that the person seized is about to or has committed a crime, *Terry* permits them to frisk him if they also have reasonable grounds to believe that the person is armed and dangerous. Even if the officer is not certain, a protective search is permitted if "a reasonably prudent man in the circumstances would be warranted in the belief that his safety or that of others was in danger," given "the specific reasonable inferences which he is entitled to draw from the facts in light of his experience." That standard of proof may be satisfied by the nature of the investigation, a bulge in the suspect's clothing, a sudden movement by the suspect toward a pocket or other place where a weapon may be hidden, and police awareness that the suspect was armed on a prior occasion.

A frisk typically must begin with a patdown. (An exception occurred in *Adams v. Williams*, 407 U.S. 143 (1972) when the officer was allowed to bypass the patdown and immediately reach beneath the suspect's clothing because an informant told him the exact location of a weapon and the suspect failed to exit the vehicle when requested.)

In a patdown, the officer is seeking a weapon which the suspect could reach to harm the officer. During the patdown, if the officer feels a weapon, he may reach beneath the surface and retrieve it. If the hard object turns out to be a container, the officer may open it if he still believes that a weapon is inside. If he finds a weapon in the container, he may have probable cause to arrest the suspect for carrying a concealed weapon.

During the patdown, if the officer feels something soft, he may not continue a tactile examination in an effort to determine whether the object is incriminating. *Minnesota v. Dickerson*, 508 U.S. 366 (1993). If the officer retrieves the soft item from beneath the surface and tries to admit it into evidence, the prosecutor may be forced to argue that there was an arrest and that the soft item was found as part of a search incident to arrest. In that situation, the prosecutor may have to prove that there was probable cause to have made an arrest of the suspect.

Stopping and Frisking Vehicles. A traffic stop requires reasonable grounds to suspect that a crime is or has been committed. It is a seizure of the passengers as well as the driver. *Brendlin v. California*, 551 U.S. 249 (2007). For a passenger, the pertinent inquiry is whether a reasonable passenger would have perceived that the police show of authority was at least partly directed at him. In a vehicle stop, without any showing that the suspect may be armed, police have the authority to order both the driver and any passengers from the vehicle to protect themselves. *Pennsylvania v. Mimms*, 434 U.S. 106 (1977); *Maryland v. Wilson*, 519 U.S. 408 (1997). The Court concluded that the intrusion on passengers was minimal, and that the motivation of a passenger to use violence to prevent detection and apprehension for a crime is great. During a vehicle stop, the driver and passengers are not free to end the encounter with the police or to move about at will. *Arizona v. Johnson*, 555 U.S. 323 (2009).

Suppose the police are determined to find some reason to stop a suspect. Are they allowed to follow the suspect's car, just waiting for him to do something illegal like running a stop sign? In *Whren v. United States*, 517 U.S. 806 (1996), although the defendants conceded that grounds existed to stop their vehicle for traffic violations, they argued that it was a pretextual stop designed to search for drugs. The Court held that the actual motivations of the police are irrelevant, as long as reasonable suspicion for a stop or probable cause for an arrest exists.

A frisk may extend beyond the suspect's person, especially during a vehicle stop. In *Michigan v. Long*, 463 U.S. 1032 (1983), when police saw Long's car swerve into a ditch, they stopped to investigate. Long appeared to be "under the influence of something" and both officers observed a large hunting knife on the floorboard of the driver's side of the car. A *Terry* frisk of Long revealed no weapons, but a vehicle frisk for weapons yielded marijuana. The Court upheld the "frisk" of the passenger compartment as reasonable, because it was limited to areas where a weapon may be placed or hidden. The frisk was permissible because the police had reasonable grounds to believe that Long was dangerous and could gain immediate control of weapons upon reentering his vehicle.

Police have attempted to justify vehicle checkpoints to check licenses and vehicle registration and to determine whether a vehicle is in proper mechanical condition. *Delaware v. Prouse*, 440 U.S. 648 (1979) criticized random stops of vehicles to accomplish those purposes, but is allowed such checkpoints which stop all incoming traffic. Using the "intrusion" v. "need" formula to determine the reasonableness of Fourth Amendment seizures and searches, the Court held that discretionary spot checks do not significantly advance the interest of ensuring that only qualified, licensed drivers are driving on American roads. Moreover, police can just as easily make a visual check of license plates on vehicles to monitor whether they are properly registered. Finally, random safety inspections do not advance safety goals, because many safety violations can be seen without stopping the vehicle.

Courts have treated sobriety checkpoints with more deference. In *Michigan Dept. of State Police v. Sitz*, 496 U.S. 444 (1990), the Court upheld the use of these checkpoints if supervisory personnel rather than officers in the field select when and where to conduct the checkpoints, the checkpoint's location is publicized in advance, police stop every approaching vehicle or stop those selected by neutral criteria (e.g., every fourth car), and the standard for detaining drivers suspected of driving while intoxicated is based on the *Terry* test of reasonable grounds.

By comparison, the Court has invalidated a checkpoint where the goal was to intercept persons using illegal drugs. *City of Indianapolis v. Edmond*, 531 U.S. 32 (2000). There, part of the Court's concern was that there was a low likelihood of apprehension compared to a sobriety checkpoint or a check for license and registration. Because law enforcement as a goal was too general, the intrusion outweighed the need for the brief stop. The Court, however, did recognize an exception for police to use a roadblock for ordinary crime control in an emergency or for an imminent terrorist attack.

In *Illinois v. Lidster*, 540 U.S. 419 (2004), the Court upheld a roadblock conducted for the purpose of gathering information about a recent hit-and-run crime. The Court distinguished its holding in *Edmond* on the basis that "special law enforcement" concerns will sometimes justify highway stops without individualized suspicion. The *Lidster* Court found that 1) the public interest was served by the seizure to assist in finding the perpetrator of a specific and known crime, 2) the checkpoint fit the specific investigative needs of police because it was set up at about the same location and time of night as the crime being investigated to increase the likelihood of getting useful information from stopped drivers, and 3) the intrusion was minimal, involving a brief wait in line, a request for information and distribution of a flyer about the past crime.

Stopping Personalty. The *Terry* analysis extends to investigative seizures of property. In *United States v. Place*, 462 U.S. 696 (1983), police detained Place's luggage as he deplaned in New York City, but they told him that he was free to leave. By acknowledging that detaining his luggage effectively detains its owner, the Court stated that it would examine such seizures more strictly than when the seizure results only in depriving the owner of a possessory interest. Even then, the seizure requires reasonable suspicion for temporary detention of personal property.

As with detentions of persons, however, a seizure of property at some point requires probable cause to continue. The relevant factors for deciding whether probable cause has replaced reasonable suspicion are 1) the diligence of the investigation, 2) the length of the seizure, and 3) information given to the suspect about the seizure. Although police suspected Place of drug involvement, the Court first criticized them because they had not called for a drug detection dog until Place's flight arrived. Second, detaining property may become excessively lengthy (ninety minutes in this case). Third, the police failed to inform Place about where they were taking the luggage and what arrangements would be made for returning the luggage if the investigation dispelled their suspicion.

POINTS TO REMEMBER

- Even though the Court has expressed a preference for warrants, it has upheld various warrantless searches and seizures under a "reasonableness" standard.

- In deciding whether a search or a seizure is "reasonable," the Court balances the "need" for the search against the "intrusion" caused thereby.

- Using the "need" versus "intrusion" test, the Court has upheld stop and frisks.

- The stop and frisk implicates the Fourth Amendment because a stop is a "seizure" and a pat down or frisk is a "search."

- A stop and frisk is permissible when a police officer reasonably believes that criminal activity is afoot and that the suspect is armed and dangerous.

- Investigative "stops" or "seizures" that do not involve a frisk require only a reasonable suspicion that the person being stopped is engaged in criminal activity.

- After a motorist is lawfully stopped, the area within the vehicle where that person could reach for weapons may be frisked.

- "Reasonable suspicion" is determined under a "totality of the circumstances" test, meaning that each case must be judged on its own facts.

- A stop must be temporary and last no longer than is necessary to effectuate its purpose.

- Stopping vehicles for driver sobriety checks are likely to be upheld when conducted under neutral criteria.

- Investigative stops of personalty are allowed under the *Terry* criteria.

I. OTHER ISSUES RELATING TO INVESTIGATIVE SEARCHES AND SEIZURES

While seizures range from an investigatory stop to an arrest, most seizures are investigative in nature and can be relatively brief. Roadside stops usually fit this description. But police also "seize" individuals for fingerprinting, lineups and interrogation purposes. These seizures are subject to differing constitutional requirements.

The first task is to determine whether a "seizure" has occurred. In *California v. Hodari D.*, 499 U.S. 621 (1991), police officers on patrol in a high crime area saw youths who panicked and ran. As they chased the youths, they came close to Hodari D., who tossed away what turned out to be cocaine. The officer tackled Hodari and handcuffed him. The Court concluded that Hodari had not been seized when he abandoned the cocaine.

To constitute an arrest, "the mere grasping or application of physical force with lawful authority, whether or not it succeeded in subduing the arrestee, was sufficient." At the time he threw away the cocaine, he had not been grasped or subjected to any physical force, but had simply been subjected to a "show of authority." There was no seizure when Hodari refused to yield to that show of authority. In the Court's view, an arrest required either "physical force" or "submission to the assertion of authority."

Hodari D.'s logic has been applied in other cases. In *Michigan v. Chesternut*, 486 U.S. 567 (1988), when Chesternut saw a patrol car, he began to run. The officers drove alongside him for a short distance, when Chesternut discarded a number of packets that were found to contain illegal narcotics. The Court concluded that Chesternut had not been seized when he threw away the narcotics: a reasonable person in Chesternut's position would not have believed that there was an attempt to capture or otherwise intrude upon his freedom of movement. "The record does not reflect that the police activated a siren or flashers; or that they commanded respondent to halt, or displayed any weapons; or that they operated the car in an aggressive manner to block respondent's course or otherwise control the direction or speed of his movement."

The Court has distinguished the *Hodari D.* and *Chesternut* situations from the slightly different situation found in *United States v. Mendenhall*, 446 U.S. 544 (1980). Two Drug Enforcement Agency (DEA) agents believed that Mendenhall's conduct was characteristic of persons illegally carrying narcotics as she disembarked from an airplane. After the agents approached her, identified themselves, and asked to see her identification and airline ticket, she produced her driver's license. Because her airline ticket was issued in a different name, the agent inquired about the discrepancy. When one agent stated that he was a federal narcotics agent, Mendenhall became very nervous. At that point, she went with the agent to the DEA office at the agent's request. The issue was whether Mendenhall had been seized or whether she went to the office voluntarily.

The Court found that there was no seizure (had she been seized, that fact would have been relevant to the question of whether her consent was voluntary). No seizure occurs when the individual "remains free to disregard the questions and walk away." The question of whether a reasonable person would have believed that she was not free to leave is asked under a "totality of the circumstances" test with the government bearing the burden of proof. Relevant factors include "the threatening presence of several officers, the display of a weapon by an officer, some physical touching of the person of the citizen, or the use of language or tone of voice indicating that compliance with the officer's request might be compelled." Without evidence of coercion, there is no seizure.

The Court concluded that Mendenhall had not been seized. The encounter occurred in a public area; the agents were not wearing uniforms, did not display weapons, and did not "summon" Mendenhall. Instead, they approached her, identified themselves, and "requested" rather than demanded to see her identification and ticket. As a result, she had no reason to believe "that she was not free to end the conversation in the concourse and proceed on her way." The fact that Mendenhall was not explicitly told that she was free to leave was not determinative.

The Court also held that the movement from the public area to the DEA office did not change the encounter to a seizure. The Court also rejected the argument that factors specific to Mendenhall suggested that the movement to the office involved a seizure: she was 22 years old, female, black, had not graduated from high school, and was being confronted by white male officers. The "totality of the evidence" suggested that Mendenhall had voluntarily agreed to accompany the DEA officers to their office.

Florida v. Royer, 460 U.S. 491 (1983), was similar to *Mendenhall*, but the Court distinguished the two cases. In *Royer*, a man was approached by the police, who asked to see his driver's license and airplane ticket, but who did not return them to him. When the officers realized that Royer was traveling under an assumed name, they asked him to go with them to the DEA office at the airport. They also removed Royer's luggage from the airplane and brought it to the office where Royer consented to a search of his suitcases. The Court held that Royer had been seized, because the officers had kept his license and plane ticket and removed his luggage from the plane.

The Court has applied *Hodari D.* and *Mendenhall* to police interrogations that take place on buses. In *Florida v. Bostick*, 501 U.S. 429 (1991), two police officers boarded a bus during a stopover. The officers picked out Bostick (a passenger), asking for permission to inspect his ticket and identification. Bostick's ticket matched his identification, and both were returned to him. The officers then explained that they were narcotics agents looking for illegal drugs, and requested permission to search Bostick's luggage. The police specifically advised Bostick that he had the right to refuse consent, and did not threaten him with a weapon. The Court concluded that Bostick had not been seized and that his consent was valid: "[When a] person is seated on a bus and has no desire to leave, the degree to which a reasonable person would feel that he or she could leave is not an accurate measure of the coercive effect of the encounter."

The Court has applied similar rules to immigration "sweeps" of factories. In *Immigration and Naturalization Service v. Delgado*, 466 U.S. 210 (1984), the INS surveyed the work force at a factory in search of illegal aliens. The agents approached employees, identified themselves, and asked questions relating to the employees' citizenship. If the employee gave an uncredible response or admitted that he was an alien, the employee was asked to produce his immigration papers. During the survey, employees continued with their work and were free to walk around within the factory. The Court rejected the employees' claim that they had been "seized" at the time of the questioning. Because they were at work, their freedom of movement was restricted "by the workers' voluntary obligations to their employers." No employees were detained unless they tried to flee or evade the agents.

Whether a seizure has occurred is important for a variety of reasons. In cases like *Mendenhall*, when a suspect has consented to a subsequent search, the existence of a "seizure" is relevant to the question of whether the consent was voluntary or coerced. If the seizure is illegal, that factor suggests coercion. In cases like *Hodari D.*, the question of whether there has been a seizure is also important. If Hodari D. had been seized when he abandoned the cocaine, the Court would have been forced to determine whether the seizure was legal or illegal. If the seizure was illegal, and discovery of the contraband was directly attributable to the seizure, the evidence might be deemed "fruit of the poisonous tree" of the illegal seizure. As a result, the evidence might be subject to exclusion.

POINTS TO REMEMBER

- A seizure occurs when the police take "physical possession" of an individual.

- A seizure can also occur when a suspect voluntarily submits to a show of police authority.

- In the show of authority situation, the beginning of a seizure can be traced to the point when a reasonable person in the suspect's position would not feel free to leave.

- The determination of whether there is a "seizure" is determined by reference to the totality of circumstances.

- When INS agents "sweep" through a factory, there may or may not be a seizure depending on how the sweep is conducted.

- When the police enter a bus to question the occupants, there may or may not be a seizure depending on how the incident is handled.

Questioning and Fingerprinting. Between an arrest and an investigative stop, there are other types of seizures. For example, in *Dunaway v. New York*, 442 U.S. 200 (1979), the Court held that, if the police want to pick up a suspect and take him to the station for questioning, they must have probable cause. The Court regarded this type of seizure as tantamount to an arrest. In *Davis v. Mississippi*, 394 U.S. 721 (1969), the Court held that probable cause is also required when the police want to pick up a suspect and take him to the station for fingerprinting. However, in *Hayes v. Florida*, 470 U.S. 811 (1985), the Court suggested in dicta, that when fingerprinting is done in the field, reasonable suspicion of criminal activity might justify that brief detention.

Requests for Identification. In *Hiibel v. Sixth Judicial District Court*, 542 U.S. 177 (2004), the Court held that the police could demand identification from a suspect, and upheld an officer's decision to arrest for a statutory refusal to comply with the demand. The Court relied on the *Terry* balancing test, concluding that an "officer's reasonable suspicion that a person may be involved in criminal activity permits the officer to stop the person for a brief time and take additional steps to investigate further." Questioning a suspect "may help clear a suspect and allow the police to concentrate their efforts elsewhere."

POINTS TO REMEMBER

- A suspect may not be forced to go to the police station for questioning or fingerprinting absent probable cause.

- However, if the fingerprinting is done in the field rather than at the station, it might be justified based on a "reasonable suspicion."

- The police may not stop individuals to demand identification absent a reasonable suspicion of criminal activity.

Temporary Detentions While Seeking or Executing a Warrant. In *Illinois v. McArthur*, 531 U.S. 326 (2001), the Court held that the police could temporarily detain a man while seeking a warrant to search his home. A woman told police that her husband had dope hidden under the couch in their home. After the husband refused to consent to a search, an officer remained at the home and prevented the man from re-entering his home unaccompanied by a police officer. At trial, McArthur moved to suppress the pipe, box, and marijuana found during the later search. The Court balanced the "privacy-related and law-enforcement-related concerns" and held that the police acted properly in temporarily seizing McArthur. The Court emphasized that the contraband would be destroyed before they could obtain a warrant, and that the police imposed only a limited restraint by preventing McArthur from re-entering his home while a search warrant was sought. The search did not occur until after the warrant was obtained.

In *Michigan v. Summers*, 452 U.S. 692 (1981), the occupant of a house was detained while a search warrant for the house was being executed. The Court held that the warrant made the occupant sufficiently suspect to justify his temporary seizure. The "limited intrusion on the personal security" of the person detained was justified "by such substantial law enforcement interests" that the seizure could be made on articulable suspicion not amounting to probable cause. In *Los Angeles County v. Rettele*, 550 U.S. 609 (2007), the Court held that the police acted reasonably when, during the execution of a search warrant, they found two unclothed people in bed and required them to stand naked briefly before permitting them to dress.

Special Situations. Sometimes, when the police execute a warrant, they find others present on the scene, or they fear the presence of others. In *Maryland v. Buie*, 494 U.S. 325 (1990), the police arrested Buie as he emerged from the basement of his home, and an officer went to the basement to make sure that no one else was there. In the basement, the officer found a red running suit in plain view that implicated Buie. The Court held that the officer acted properly in entering the basement. The police are entitled "in such circumstances to take reasonable steps to ensure their safety after, and while making, the arrest," and that this "interest is sufficient to outweigh the intrusion such procedures may entail."

Incident to the arrest, the police can automatically "look in closets and other spaces immediately adjoining the place of arrest from which an attack could be immediately launched." To search further beyond those spaces, there must "be articulable facts which, taken together with the rational inferences from those facts, would warrant a reasonably prudent officer in believing that the area to be swept harbors an individual posing a danger to those on the arrest scene." The protective sweep is a cursory inspection for persons, and should last "no longer than is necessary to dispel the reasonable suspicion of danger and in any event no longer than it takes to complete the arrest and depart the premises."

POINTS TO REMEMBER

- While a warrant is being sought, the police may temporarily detain the occupant of a home to prevent him from destroying evidence inside the home.

- When the police make a lawful search of a house, they may detain occupants of the house who are on site.

- When the police arrest an individual at home, they can conduct a limited protective sweep for other persons.

- The police can ask the driver and passengers of a lawfully stopped vehicle to exit the vehicle.

Probationers and Parolees. Even after their release from prison, inmates who become probationers and parolees are subject to special rules. In *Griffin v. Wisconsin,* 483 U.S. 868 (1987), the Court held that a State's operation of its probation system presented a "special need" for the "exercise of supervision to assure that [probation] restrictions are in fact observed." As a result, warrantless searches of probationers were deemed to be reasonable.

In *United States v. Knights*, 534 U.S. 112 (2001), the Court held that warrantless searches of a probationer might be permissible. Knights' condition required him to submit to a "search at anytime, with or without a search warrant, warrant of arrest or reasonable cause by any probation officer or law enforcement officer." An arson investigation revealed that Knights was involved. A police officer, who was aware of the condition of Knights' probation, then made a warrantless search of Knights' apartment that produced evidence incriminating Knights in the fire. The Court upheld the search.

The Court emphasized that the probation order clearly stated the condition, and "Knights was unambiguously informed of it." As a result, the condition diminished Knights' reasonable expectation of privacy. In assessing the governmental interest, the Court emphasized that "the very assumption" of probation is that the probationer "is more likely than the ordinary citizen to violate the law." As a result, the Court held "that the balance of these considerations requires no more than reasonable suspicion to conduct a search of this probationer's house."

In *Samson v. California*, 547 U.S. 843 (2006), the Court upheld a California statute providing that parolees, as a condition of their release, could be searched "at any time of the day or night, with or without a search warrant and with or without cause." Relying on *Knights*, the Court noted that "parolees have fewer expectations of privacy than probationers," and that "parole is more akin to imprisonment than probation is to imprisonment." The parole conditions were clearly expressed to Samson, who did not have an expectation of privacy that society would recognize as legitimate. In addition, the Court concluded that the State has an "overwhelming interest" in supervising parolees because "parolees . . . are more likely to commit future criminal offenses."

Border Searches. Special rules have always applied to searches conducted at or near the United States border. At the border itself, customs and immigration officials have the right to "stop" those who seek to enter the United States, and to force them to prove their right to enter (by presenting their passport and relevant immigration documents).

Customs officials have usually enjoyed the right to conduct limited searches of those who enter the United States. These searches are designed to make sure that entrants 1) are not carrying contraband, 2) do not have dutiable items that they have failed to declare, and 3) are not carrying harmful or dangerous items (e.g., agricultural products with dangerous parasites).

In *United States v. Flores–Montano*, 541 U.S. 149 (2004), the Court upheld the actions of customs officials who dismantled a gasoline tank at the United States border in a successful search for marijuana hidden in the tank. The dismantlement required a 20 to 30 minute delay to obtain a mechanic, and an additional 15 to 25 minutes to dismantle the tank. The Court upheld the search, refusing to make fine distinctions between "routine" searches and more "intrusive" searches at international borders. The Court noted the "Government's interest in preventing the entry of unwanted persons and effects is at its zenith at the international border."

Inside the United States, the rules regarding searches and seizures are somewhat more complicated and tend to parallel the ordinary search and seizure rules. Sometimes, for example, the police seek to stop a vehicle because they believe that it contains illegal aliens. In *United States v. Brignoni–Ponce*, 422 U.S. 873 (1975), the Court held that such stops could be justified by a "reasonable suspicion."

United States v. Arvizu, 534 U.S. 266 (2002) illustrates the reasonable suspicion standard. A border patrol agent was conducting a checkpoint near the Mexican border when a magnetic sensor indicated the presence of traffic consistent with smuggling on a nearby road. An officer found a vehicle that slowed dramatically when it saw the officer. The vehicle then turned at the last place that it could turn before it reached an immigration checkpoint. Radio communication revealed that the vehicle was registered to a place near the Mexican border that was "notorious for alien and narcotics smuggling." At that point, the officer stopped the vehicle, and the driver consented to a search that revealed marijuana. Based on these facts, the Court concluded that a reasonable suspicion of illegal activity existed to stop the vehicle.

Despite the general rules regarding automobile stops (requiring reasonable suspicion), the Court has established special rules for near-border roadblocks or checkpoints. *United States v. Martinez–Fuerte*, 428 U.S. 543 (1976) involved near-border checkpoints at which agents slowed all traffic "to a virtual, if not a complete, halt" at a highway roadblock, and referr[ed] vehicles chosen at the discretion of Border Patrol agents to an area for "secondary inspection." The Court upheld the checkpoints, noting that the "objective intrusion—the stop itself, the questioning, and the visual inspection—also existed in roving-patrol stops. But we view checkpoint stops in a different light because the subjective intrusion—the generating of concern or even fright on the part of lawful travelers—is appreciably less in the case of a checkpoint stop."

POINTS TO REMEMBER

- Probationers and parolees have reduced rights compared to other citizens.

- Border searches have always been treated differently than searches that occur inside the borders of the United States.

- Customs officials have an automatic right to stop individuals who seek to enter the United States, and to force those individuals to prove their right to enter.

- Customs officials also have the right to conduct limited searches at the border to make sure that the entering individual is not carrying contraband or other items that may be harmful to the United States, its economy and people.

- Immigration stops can be made inside the United States based on a reasonable suspicion that a vehicle contains aliens.

- Immigration "checkpoints" or "roadblocks" can be established within the United States close to the border.

Investigatory Seizures of Property. *Terry*'s analysis extends to investigative seizures of property. In *United States v. Place*, 462 U.S. 696 (1983), Place's behavior aroused the suspicions of police at the Miami airport. After he was allowed to depart for New York, Miami agents contacted DEA authorities in New York to relay their suspicions. In New York, two agents approached him and suggested that he was carrying narcotics. When Place refused to consent to a search of his luggage, the agents decided to seize it while they sought a warrant from a judge. The agents then subjected the bags to a "sniff test" by a trained narcotics detection dog. The dog reacted positively to one bag. Although the sniff was conducted within a 90–minute period, the agents kept the bags over a weekend, until they obtained a search warrant from a judge. In the subsequent search, they found cocaine in the bag.

Invalidating the search, the Court began by noting that containers can be seized while the police seek a warrant, because "the risk of the item's disappearance or use for its intended purpose before a warrant may be obtained outweighs the interest in possession." Especially when the police "possess specific and articulable facts warranting a reasonable belief that a traveler's luggage contains narcotics, the governmental interest in seizing the luggage briefly to pursue further investigation is substantial."

Some brief seizures are so minimally intrusive that they can be justified based "only on specific articulable facts that the property contains contraband or evidence of a crime." Based on a reasonable conclusion that a traveler's luggage contains narcotics, the police can briefly detain the luggage for investigative purposes, provided that the detention is limited in scope. A luggage "seizure can effectively restrain the person," because he may disrupt his travel plans to remain with the luggage or to arrange for its return.

Applying these rules, the Court concluded that the seizure of Place's luggage went too far. "The length of the detention of respondent's luggage alone precludes the conclusion that the seizure was reasonable in the absence of probable cause." The 90–minute detention of Place's luggage was too long, especially given that the agents had advance notice of Place's arrival and could have prepared for the additional investigation. The additional step of holding the bags over the weekend was also unreasonable.

The Court has upheld the seizure of mailed packages. In *United States v. Van Leeuwen*, 397 U.S. 249 (1970), respondent mailed two 12–pound packages at a post office near the Canadian border. One package was addressed to a post office box in California, and the other to a post office box in Tennessee. Respondent declared that they contained coins. Each package was sent by registered mail and insured for $10,000, a type of mailing that did not subject them to discretionary inspection.

When the postal clerk told a policeman that he was suspicious of the packages, the policeman noticed that the return address on the packages was a vacant housing area, and that the license plates of respondent's car were Canadian. A customs official obtained a search warrant, and the packages were opened and inspected. The Court upheld the seizure, noting: "No interest protected by the Fourth Amendment was invaded by forwarding the packages the following day rather than the day when they were deposited. The significant Fourth Amendment interest was in the privacy of this first-class mail; and that privacy was not disturbed or invaded until the approval of the judge was obtained." On the facts, a 29–hour delay between the mailings and the service of the warrant was reasonable.

POINTS TO REMEMBER

- Despite the warrant preference, containers can be seized based on probable cause while the police seek a warrant.

- This temporary seizure is permissible because "the risk of the item's disappearance or use for its intended purpose before a warrant may be obtained outweighs the interest in possession."

- Based on a reasonable conclusion that a traveler's luggage contains narcotics, the police can briefly detain the luggage for investigative purposes, "provided that the investigative detention is properly limited in scope."

- Although a canine sniff does not qualify as a search, it can intrude on the suspect's possessory interest in his luggage as well as his liberty interest in proceeding with his itinerary.

- A 90–minute detention of luggage to effectuate a canine sniff is excessive when the police have ample advance notice and could have arranged the sniff more efficiently.

- When customs officials have reason to believe that mailed packages contain contraband, they can cause a limited delay (e.g., one day) in the mailing of a package to give them time to obtain a warrant.

J. EXIGENT CIRCUMSTANCES

The police can conduct a warrantless search when "exigent circumstances" exist. Many of the already discussed Fourth Amendment warrantless search exceptions involve exigent situations when there is insufficient time to obtain a warrant (e.g., search incident to arrest, vehicle searches). Courts have devised a separate category for exigent circumstances in fact patterns which occur less frequently.

The exigent circumstances exception applies to cases where there is a concern about imminent destruction of evidence, risk of danger to police or others, or hot pursuit of fleeing suspects. Probable cause that an emergency situation exists will justify entry into private premises, and an ensuing search may last only as long as the exigency exists. *Flippo v. West Virginia*, 528 U.S. 11 (1999). For example, in a hot pursuit case, the exigency ends when the suspect is captured, i.e., without other justification, the police may not continue to search the premises after the suspect is taken to the police station.

The exigency for entry into the premises determines the scope of the subsequent search. For example, in hot pursuit of a person suspected of a crime of violence, the police may search for weapons as they are seeking the suspect. *Warden v. Hayden*, 387 U.S. 294 (1967).

In *Brigham City v. Stuart*, 547 U.S. 398 (2006), police officers responded to a call regarding a loud party at a residence at 3:00 a.m. On arriving, they heard shouting from inside, proceeded to investigate, and saw through a screen door an altercation in the kitchen. At this point, an officer opened the screen door and announced his presence. Nobody noticed. When the officer entered, the argument ceased as the occupants became aware that the police were on the scene. The officers arrested respondents and charged them with contributing to the delinquency of a minor, disorderly conduct, and intoxication.

The Court upheld the entry into the house, holding that the exigent circumstances exception includes a need to enter "to assist persons who are seriously injured or threatened with such injury." The officers "had an objectively reasonable basis for believing both that the injured adult might need help and that the violence in the kitchen was just beginning." The Fourth Amendment did not require the police to delay until someone was unconscious, semiconscious, or in an even worse condition before entering.

In *Warden v. Hayden*, 387 U.S. 294 (1967), following an armed robbery, police received a description of the robbers and followed them to a nearby house. A search revealed Hayden in a bedroom. In other parts of the house, officers found weapons and clothing used in the robbery. The Court held that the warrantless search of the entire house was valid. "Speed here was essential, and only a thorough search of the house for persons and weapons could have insured that Hayden was the only man present and that the police had control of all weapons which could be used against them or to effect an escape."

In *United States v. Santana*, 427 U.S. 38 (1976), after an undercover drug buy, the police went to Santana's home to arrest her. They found her standing in the doorway with a brown paper bag in her hand. When Santana retreated into the vestibule of her house, the officers followed through the open door and caught her. The Court upheld the entry into the house, applying the "hot pursuit" exception. "Once Santana saw the police, there was . . . a realistic expectation that any delay would result in destruction of evidence."

In *Kentucky v. King*, 131 S.Ct. 1849 (2011), the Court held that law enforcement officers may rely on the exigent circumstances exception even when they had a role in creating the exigency, as long as they did not engage in, or threaten to engage in, conduct that violates the Fourth Amendment.

In some cases, the Court has held that the circumstances were not sufficiently exigent to justify a warrantless entry. For example, in *Minnesota v. Olson*, 495 U.S. 91 (1990), the morning after an armed robbery that resulted in the death of a gas station attendant, a woman called the police and said that Olson admitted his participation in the robbery to two other women. When the police learned that Olson had gone to the home of the two women, police surrounded the home. Without seeking permission and with weapons drawn, the police entered and found Olson hiding in a closet. The Court found insufficient exigent circumstances to justify the warrantless entry into the home: 1) Olson was the driver of the getaway car, not the one who pulled the trigger; 2) the murder weapon was already recovered; and 3) no showing existed that either of the women was in danger or that Olson could escape.

Welsh v. Wisconsin, 466 U.S. 740 (1984) is another example when the exigent circumstances exception did not apply. Police received eyewitness reports that Welsh had been driving under the influence of alcohol, and went to Welsh's home to investigate. When Welsh's stepdaughter answered the door, the police entered and proceeded to Welsh's bedroom where they found him lying in bed. The Court concluded that the police acted improperly since they were unable to show that exigent circumstances existed. The Court found that there was no hot pursuit or continuing threat to "public safety," because Welsh had abandoned his car and returned home. The only need for immediate action was that the police wanted to test Welsh's blood-alcohol level before the level dissipated. The State's interest in the evidence was minimal given that the State had chosen to classify the offense as "noncriminal," i.e., a conviction carried no jail time.

Other exigent circumstances cases have dealt with police attempts to gather evidence from the body of a suspect that is likely to disappear absent prompt or immediate action. For example, in *Cupp v. Murphy*, 412 U.S. 291 (1973), Murphy's wife died by strangulation at her home. During questioning, the police noticed a dark spot on Murphy's finger. Suspecting that the spot might be dried blood, the police took a sample without a warrant. Tests revealed that the samples included traces from the victim's skin and blood. The Court upheld the search, "considering the existence of probable cause, the very limited intrusion undertaken incident to the station house detention, and the ready destructibility of the evidence."

In *Rochin v. California*, 342 U.S. 165 (1952), the police believed that Rochin was selling narcotics, and went to his home where they found two capsules which might have been narcotics. When the officers inquired about the capsules, Rochin immediately swallowed them. Rochin was handcuffed and taken to a hospital where the police instructed doctors to "pump" his stomach. The procedure caused Rochin to vomit and the police recovered the capsules which were found to contain morphine. Concluding that the police had violated Rochin's rights, the Court relied upon the Due Process Clause in ruling that the officers' conduct had shocked the conscience of the court.

Rochin was followed by *Schmerber v. California*, 384 U.S. 757 (1966) where Schmerber was arrested at a hospital while receiving treatment for injuries suffered in an automobile accident. A police officer, who believed that Schmerber's intoxication caused the accident, directed a physician to take a blood sample from him. The Court upheld the blood sample extraction even though it involved an intrusion into Schmerber's body. The Court noted that the officer had probable cause to arrest Schmerber, and upheld the search on the basis that there was an "emergency" which would have led to the destruction of evidence. The test used was: 1) highly effective in determining whether an individual is intoxicated, 2) commonly used in routine physical examinations, 3) extracted a minimum amount of blood, 4) involves virtually no risk, trauma, or pain, and 5) was performed in a reasonable manner "by a physician in a hospital environment according to accepted medical practices."

POINTS TO REMEMBER

- The police can dispense with a warrant when they are faced with "exigent circumstances."

- The police must have probable cause that exigent circumstances justify their entry/search, and the exigency for entry into a building determines the scope of a subsequent search.

- The justification to search ends when the exigency no longer exists.

- Even though the police arrest a suspect outside his home, the police may not enter and search the home without a warrant absent some indication that evidence inside the house is about to be destroyed.

- Generally, the justification for this type of extraction focuses on evidence that will be lost if the police do not act quickly.

- Assuming that the procedure used presents little risk to the suspect, and is conducted under appropriate medical conditions, the police may be permitted to make a warrantless extraction of a blood sample from a person whom they reasonably believe was driving under the influence of alcohol.

Special Needs Searches. A traditional warrant/probable cause analysis is unnecessary for a category of searches based on "special needs." Courts evaluate whether the public interest in support of the warrantless search is a special need that is beyond the normal need for law enforcement. Courts balance the state's interest justifying the search against the intrusion upon privacy caused by the search. Special needs searches have been upheld in distinct contexts such as drug testing for employees and for public school students.

For example, *Skinner v. Railway Labor Executives' Association*, 489 U.S. 602 (1989), involved a challenge to federal regulations mandating blood and urine tests of railroad employees involved in "major" train accidents, and authorizing breath and urine tests of employees who violate certain safety rules. The Court upheld the regulations, emphasizing: 1) the governmental interest "in ensuring the safety of the traveling public and of the employees themselves"; 2) the need to make sure that restrictions on drug and alcohol use are being observed; and 3) the need to act quickly to take samples after an accident.

The intrusion on privacy was limited, because the employees worked "in an industry that is regulated pervasively to ensure safety, a goal dependent, in substantial part, on the health and fitness of covered employees." The Court found that the tests were not intrusive, could be conducted safely outside a hospital environment "with a minimum of inconvenience or embarrassment," and "reveal the level of alcohol in the employee's bloodstream and nothing more."

The Court held that drug testing could be required even in the absence of a reasonable suspicion, because the employees' jobs involved them in "duties fraught with such risks of injury to others that even a momentary lapse of attention can have disastrous consequences." In addition, the testing provided "invaluable information about the causes of major accidents."

Special Rules for School-age Children. The Court has applied special rules to searches of school-age children. In *New Jersey v. T.L.O.*, 469 U.S. 325 (1985), the Court upheld a limited search of a high school student. A teacher found two girls smoking in a lavatory and took both girls to the assistant principal, who demanded to see her purse where he found cigarettes as well as rolling papers, marijuana and a large number of one-dollar bills. At that point, T.L.O. confessed to the crime of selling marijuana. The Court upheld the search, balancing the child's interest in privacy against "the substantial interest of teachers and administrators in maintaining discipline in the classroom and on school grounds."

Noting that public schools had been the scene of drug use and violent crimes, the Court held that the "school setting requires some easing of the restrictions to which searches by public authorities are ordinarily subject." The Court held that searches should be evaluated under a two-part test which ultimately focused on the "reasonableness" of the school's action: 1) the search must be "justified at its inception," i.e., a school official must have "reasonable grounds" to think that a search would yield evidence of legal or school rule violations; and 2) the search must be "reasonably related to the objectives of the search and not excessively intrusive in light of the age and sex of the student and the nature of the infraction."

Applying these criteria, the Court upheld the assistant principal's action. Since a teacher had reported that he saw T.L.O. smoking in a lavatory, he had reason to believe that she was carrying cigarettes in her purse. Although the search extended to a zippered compartment in the purse, the Court held that he acted reasonably because he had already found rolling papers and marijuana. In another case, the Court found that school officials had reasonable suspicion to search the student's backpack and outer clothing for drugs, but it held that they did not have sufficient suspicion to conduct a strip search of her underwear. *Safford Unified School District #1 v. Redding*, 557 U.S. 364 (2009).

Vernonia School District v. Acton, 515 U.S. 646 (1995) upheld suspicionless drug-testing of high school athletes, because of their reduced expectation of privacy when they participate in a school activity and a documented drug problem among athletes in the district. The Court emphasized that the testing occurred in a "public school environment where the State is responsible for maintaining discipline, health and safety."

Board of Education of Independent School District No. 92 of Pottawatomie County v. Earls, 536 U.S. 822 (2002) extended the *Acton* case in two ways to drug testing for all middle and high school students involved in competitive extracurricular activities. The policy of drug-testing applied to students participating in all extracurricular activities, rather than athletes only. There was no documented problem of drug abuse among the students in the school district. The Court stated that drug testing for all students was preferable to a standard of "individualized reasonable suspicion of wrongdoing," which would place various burdens on schools and might subject them to lawsuits, thereby making the overall program of drug detection less effective.

Again applying a balancing test examining the governmental interest and the intrusion on privacy, the Court upheld the constitutionality of the policy, which was aimed at promoting health and safety of all students by detecting and preventing drug use. The students had a diminished expectation of privacy and the urine samples were not collected in an intrusive manner; the faculty monitor waited outside the room to collect the sample and the collection method constituted a "negligible" intrusion. The test results were 1) maintained in a file separate from students' other educational records, 2) released to school personnel only on a "need to know" basis, and 3) were never the basis for school discipline and never turned over to the police.

The Court struck down a hospital's policy of drug testing pregnant mothers suspected of cocaine use in *Ferguson v. City of Charleston*, 532 U.S. 67 (2001). Unlike the earlier cases, the Court held that these tests were not "special needs" searches because their "central and indispensable feature" was to promote law enforcement goals. The results of this drug testing were turned over to the police without the knowledge or consent of the tested women so that they could be prosecuted for child neglect and/or drug offenses. The Court distinguished the earlier drug-testing cases because those policies protected against dissemination of the test results to third parties like the police, and the special need in those cases was "divorced from the State's general interest in law enforcement."

POINTS TO REMEMBER

- Special needs searches balance the state interest justifying the search against the intrusion on the person's privacy.

- Drug testing of public employees has been upheld to determine the cause of accidents.

- School officials may search public school students only on a showing of "reasonable grounds for suspecting that the search [would] turn up evidence that the student has violated or is violating either the law or the rules of the school."

- Suspicionless drug testing of students in extracurricular activities is permissible.

- The Court struck down drug testing programs for pregnant women when the results were turned over to law enforcement for prosecution.

WARRANTLESS SEARCH AND
SEIZURE CHECKLIST

I.   Warrantless Searches and Seizures. Warrantless searches are disfavored and are *"per se* unreasonable subject only to a few specifically established and well-delineated exceptions." *Katz v. United States*.

A.   **Plain View Exception**. What are the requirements of the plain view exception to the warrant requirement?

>   1.   There are two requirements: a) the police are in a place where they have the right to be (as when they are conducting a lawful search), pursuant to a warrant or a warrantless search; and b) police may seize an item when its incriminating character is "immediately apparent." The following cases are examples of the Court's application of the plain view exception.

>   2.   *Coolidge v. New Hampshire*, 403 U.S. 443 (1971). The police seized defendant's car because they thought that it might contain microscopic fibers that would implicate him in a crime. The seizure of the car was invalid because the incriminating character of the car (containing the fibers) was not immediately apparent.

>   3.   *Arizona v. Hicks*, 480 U.S. 321 (1987). Police moved stereo components to observe the serial numbers, which initially were not "immediately apparent."

>   4.   *Minnesota v. Dickerson*, 508 U.S. 366 (1993). A police officer frisked defendant and felt a small "lump" in his nylon jacket. The contraband was not in plain view, because the officer did not know the "lump" was contraband until he manipulated it.

B.   **Search Incident to Legal Arrest**. When the police make a legal arrest, they have the right to make a search incident to that arrest.

>   1.   **What constitutes a "legal" arrest?** A custodial arrest occurs when the police take a suspect into custody in order to bring charges. *United States v. Watson*, 423 U.S. 411 (1976).

a. ***Payton v. New York***, 445 U.S. 573 (1980). Absent exigent circumstances, police cannot arrest a person at his home without an arrest warrant.

b. ***Steagald v. United States***, 451 U.S. 204 (1981). A law enforcement officer may not search for the subject of an arrest warrant in the home of a third party without first obtaining a *search* warrant.

2. **The Scope of a Search Incident to Arrest**. Once a legal arrest occurs, police are allowed to search the arrestee and the area within her immediate control, contemporaneous with the arrest. ***Chimel v. California***, 395 U.S. 752 (1969).

a. ***United States v. Robinson***, 414 U.S. 218 (1973). The exception applies regardless of either the type of crime for which the arrest is made or whether the police can prove that the arrestee is carrying a weapon or contraband.

b. For purposes of safety or evidentiary concerns, police may search the passenger compartment of a vehicle incident to a recent occupant's arrest only if the arrestee is within reaching distance of the passenger compartment at the time of the search or it is reasonable to believe the vehicle contains evidence of the offense of arrest. ***Arizona v. Gant***, 556 U.S. 332 (2009). The search extends to items found in containers within the passenger compartment, e.g., the glove compartment.

c. The search incident to legal arrest must be conducted relatively contemporaneously with the arrest, i.e., it cannot be too remote in time or place to have been made as incidental to the arrest.

C. **Booking Searches**. The booking exception is part of the routine administrative procedure at a police station house incident to booking and jailing the suspect.

1. *Illinois v. Lafayette*, 462 U.S. 640 (1983). Under the booking exception, jail officials can remove both contraband and valuables to prevent personal items from being stolen, protect police against false claims of theft, and prevent the arrestee from introducing contraband into the jail population.

2. *United States v. Edwards*, 415 U.S. 800 (1974). Courts loosely apply temporal limitations in this context. The search may occur after the arrest when the accused arrives at the place of detention.

D. **Automobile Exception**

1. When there is probable cause to search the automobile, the ready mobility of a vehicle and the reduced expectation of privacy in a vehicle justifies an immediate warrantless search before it and its occupants become unavailable.

2. Most decisions have loosely applied the contemporaneousness requirement, i.e., if the automobile could be searched on the street, the search later could occur at the police station. *Chambers v. Maroney*, 399 U.S. 42 (1970).

3. The search may be of every part of the vehicle and its contents that may conceal the object of the search, e.g., containers, trunk, door side panels. *United States v. Ross*, 456 U.S. 798 (1982); *California v. Acevedo*, 500 U.S. 565 (1991).

E. **Inventory Exception**. The inventory exception is justified by the need "to protect an owner's property while it is in the custody of the police, to insure against claims of lost, stolen, or vandalized property, and to guard the police from danger." *South Dakota v. Opperman*, 428 U.S. 364 (1976). The requirements for conducting an inventory search are:

1. Inventory searches are permitted as long as the sole motive is not for criminal investigation.

2. The vehicle must have been legally impounded. Not only may the police search the passenger compartment, they can also search the trunk and closed containers.

3. Courts will sometimes require that inventory searches be conducted pursuant to departmental regulations. *Florida v. Wells*, 495 U.S. 1 (1990). Police officers can exercise discretion in applying the regulations, provided that the "discretion is exercised according to standard criteria."

F. **Consent**

1. **Voluntary Consent**. Consent searches are permissible, but the State must prove "that the consent was, in fact, freely and voluntarily given." Consent does not exist when the suspect was "coerced." *Schneckloth v. Bustamonte*, 412 U.S. 218 (1973).

   a. A "totality of the circumstances" test is applied to determine whether a person's consent to search was voluntarily given, using a variety of factors peculiar to the suspect (e.g., if the suspect is not very intelligent), *and* factors that suggest coercion (e.g., police guns were drawn, police demanded the right to search).

   b. The issue of voluntariness is a question of fact and it is to be determined from all the circumstances.

   c. The scope of consent extends to closed containers, if it is reasonable for the police to conclude that the general consent to search included consent to search containers. *Florida v. Jimeno*, 500 U.S. 248 (1991).

   d. Consent may be negated by police misrepresentations of authority and right. *Bumper v. State of North Carolina*, 391 U.S. 543 (1968).

2. **Third Party Consent**. When a third party consents to a search of property, a court must decide not only whether the consent was voluntarily given, but also whether the third party could consent to the search. *United States v. Matlock*, 415 U.S. 164 (1974).

   a. A third party can consent if she has "common authority" over the area.

b. Even if a third party does not possess "common authority" over the area, the police are entitled to believe that the person had "apparent authority" to consent based on the facts before them. *Illinois v. Rodriguez*, 497 U.S. 177 (1990).

c. *Georgia v. Randolph*, 547 U.S. 103 (2006) held that a person's consent to search did not validate the search when another person objects, unless there is some "recognized hierarchy" within a household (e.g., parent and child or barracks housing military personnel of different grades).

G. Administrative Inspections

1. The Fourth Amendment applies to administrative inspections. *Camara v. Municipal Court*, 387 U.S. 523 (1967). The validity of an administrative search is determined by balancing the governmental interest against the private interest.

2. "Administrative" probable cause permits inspection of all places in a particular area. The broader scope of administrative probable cause can be based on an assessment of "conditions in the area as a whole, not on [the officer's] knowledge of conditions in each particular building."

3. Warrantless administrative inspections are constitutionally permissible. A warrant is not required in "emergency situations."

4. There is an administrative search exception to the warrant requirement for certain "closely regulated" businesses, but certain criteria must be met.

   a. The business must have "such a history of government oversight that no reasonable expectation of privacy could exist for a proprietor over the stock of such an enterprise." *Marshall v. Barlow's, Inc.*, 436 U.S. 307 (1978).

   b. The regulatory statute must provide notice about the search, a properly defined scope, and limit the discretion of the inspecting officers by time, place, and scope. *New York v. Burger*, 482 U.S. 691 (1987).

H. Stop and Frisk

1. A stop is a temporary seizure of a person short of an arrest, and is proper when a police officer has reasonable grounds to believe that criminal activity may be afoot. *Terry v. Ohio*, 392 U.S. 1 (1968).

2. The constitutional standard for an "investigative stop" is "reasonable suspicion" (less than probable cause) that the defendant is involved in criminal activity.

3. A frisk is a "protective search for weapons" of the suspect's outer clothing. If the police officer feels something beneath the clothing that feels like a weapon, she can reach beneath the clothing to retrieve the object.

4. In addition to suspecting that an individual is engaged in criminal activity, the officer must also have reason to believe that the suspect is "armed and dangerous."

5. "Reasonable suspicion" is determined using a totality of the circumstances standard, i.e., a particularized and objective basis for suspecting the particular person of criminal activity. The "reasonable suspicion" standard involves less proof of wrongdoing than a preponderance of the evidence.

6. Police can rely on an anonymous tip in developing "reasonable suspicion." "Reasonable suspicion" depends on both the "quantity and quality" of the evidence. *Alabama v. White*, 496 U.S. 325 (1990).

7. Reasonable suspicion cases.

    a. *Illinois v. Wardlow*, 528 U.S. 119 (2000). Flight from an officer is suggestive of wrongdoing.

    b. *Florida v. J.L.*, 529 U.S. 266 (2000); *Sibron v. New York*, 392 U.S. 40 (1968). Police action must be based on objective criteria rather than simply a "hunch."

8. Stop and frisk people cases.

    a. *Florida v. Royer*, 460 U.S. 491 (1983). A seizure of the suspect occurred because airport officers kept the suspect's driver's license and plane ticket and removed his luggage from the plane.

    b. *United States v. Sharpe*, 470 U.S. 675 (1985). Police must diligently pursue the investigation to confirm or dispel their suspicions quickly.

    c. *Adams v. Williams*, 407 U.S. 143 (1972). An officer may skip the frisk of outer clothing and reach into the car to remove a fully loaded revolver from the driver's waistband, which was the place indicated by the informant.

    d. Relevant factors are: the length and intrusiveness of the seizure and the time reasonably needed to effectuate the purpose of the seizure.

9. Stop and frisk vehicle cases.

    a. *Pennsylvania v. Mimms*, 434 U.S. 106 (1977); *Maryland v. Wilson*, 519 U.S. 408 (1997). Police can order a driver and passenger(s) of a lawfully stopped car to exit the vehicle.

    b. *Michigan v. Long*, 463 U.S. 1032 (1983). An armed suspect may be "dangerous" based on the circumstances. After a stop of a vehicle, the police may frisk the area where the occupant is sitting if she reasonably believes that the occupant is dangerous and may gain immediate control of weapons.

    c. *Michigan Department of State Police v. Sitz*, 496 U.S. 444 (1990). Roadblocks or traffic checkpoints, where all vehicles are stopped, may be used to look for drunk drivers or expired licenses and registrations, because of the strong governmental interest in preventing drunk driving, and the slight intrusion caused by the brief stops.

      d. *City of Indianapolis v. Edmond*, 531 U.S. 32 (2000). A general crime control traffic checkpoint is invalid.

      e. *Illinois v. Lidster*, 540 U.S. 419 (2004). An information-seeking roadblock is permissible when the stop is brief and the criminal investigation is for a known crime that involved a death nearby.

10. Stopping personalty cases. *United States v. Place*, 462 U.S. 696 (1983); *United States v. Van Leeuwen*, 397 U.S. 249 (1970). The *Terry* analysis extends to investigative seizures of property. Such an intrusion on possessory interests can vary "both in its nature and extent," ranging from an "on the spot" inquiry (as with the use of a dog to sniff the luggage) to the relinquishment of custody and control.

I. Other Issues Relating to Investigative Searches and Seizures

1. A "seizure" occurs when police grasp or apply physical force with lawful authority, whether or not it succeeds in subduing the arrestee. *California v. Hodari D.*, 499 U.S. 621 (1991); *United States v. Mendenhall*, 446 U.S. 544 (1980).

2. The test for deciding the validity of an investigative seizure is whether a reasonable person would have believed that she was not free to leave. The inquiry made under a "totality of the circumstances" test with the government bearing the burden of proof.

3. Relevant factors include "the threatening presence of several officers, the display of a weapon by an officer, some physical touching of the person of the citizen, or the use of language or tone of voice indicating that compliance with the officer's request might be compelled." Absent some evidence of coercion, there is no seizure.

4. The Supreme Court has applied its standards in several cases.

      a. *Florida v. Royer*, 460 U.S. 491 (1983). A seizure of the suspect occurred because airport officers kept the suspect's driver's license and plane ticket and removed his luggage from the plane.

    b. ***Florida v. Bostick***, 501 U.S. 429 (1991). No seizure occurred when two police officers boarded a bus during a stopover and asked for permission to inspect a passenger's ticket and identification.

    c. ***Immigration and Naturalization Service v. Delgado***, 466 U.S. 210 (1984). In search of illegal aliens, INS surveyed the work force at a factory. No seizure occurred when agents approached employees, identified themselves, and asked questions relating to citizenship.

5. The consequences of a finding that a seizure by the police has occurred carries special importance.

    a. For example, in *Mendenhall*, when a suspect has consented to a subsequent search, the prior existence of a "seizure" is relevant to the question of whether consent was voluntary or coerced. If the seizure is illegal, that factor suggests involuntary consent.

    b. In *Hodari D.*, if the suspect had been seized when he abandoned the drugs, the Court would have had to decide whether the seizure was illegal.

6. **Questioning and Fingerprinting**

    a. ***Dunaway v. New York***, 442 U.S. 200 (1979). Police must have probable cause to pick up a suspect and take her to the station for questioning, because this type of seizure is tantamount to an arrest.

    b. ***Davis v. Mississippi***, 394 U.S. 721 (1969). Probable cause is also required when police pick up a suspect and take her to the station for fingerprinting.

7. **Requests for Identification**. The police may demand identification from a suspect, and arrest her for refusing

to comply with the demand. *Hiibel v. Sixth Judicial District Court*, 542 U.S. 177 (2004).

8. **Scope and Length of Investigative Seizures**. Limits on the length of an investigative seizure must be related to the nature of the seizure.

   a. Relevant factors are: the length and intrusiveness of the seizure and the time reasonably needed to effectuate the purpose of the seizure.

   b. Police must diligently pursue the investigation to confirm or dispel their suspicions quickly. *United States v. Sharpe*, 470 U.S. 675 (1985).

9. **Special Situations**. The following cases show how the Court has balanced the nature of the governmental interest against the intrusion into an individual's privacy for investigative seizures.

   a. *Illinois v. McArthur*, 531 U.S. 326 (2001). While seeking a warrant to search a home, police can temporarily detain a person to prevent her from re-entering to destroy suspected contraband.

   b. *Michigan v. Summers*, 452 U.S. 692 (1981). The occupant of a house can be detained while a search warrant for the house is being executed.

   c. *Maryland v. Buie*, 494 U.S. 325 (1990). Incident to an arrest, the police may without probable cause or reasonable suspicion, look in closets and other spaces immediately adjoining the place of arrest from which an attack could be immediately launched. To conduct a further, protective cursory sweep for persons, police need reasonable suspicion.

   d. *Pennsylvania v. Mimms*, 434 U.S. 106 (1977); *Maryland v. Wilson*, 519 U.S. 408 (1997). Police can order a driver and passenger(s) of a lawfully stopped car to exit the vehicle.

   e. *Michigan Department of State Police v. Sitz*, 496 U.S. 444 (1990). Roadblocks or traffic checkpoints may be used to look for drunk drivers or expired licenses and registrations, where all vehicles are stopped, because of the strong governmental interest in preventing drunk driving, and the slight intrusion caused by the brief stops.

f. *City of Indianapolis v. Edmond*, 531 U.S. 32 (2000). A general crime control traffic checkpoint is invalid.

g. *Illinois v. Lidster*, 540 U.S. 419 (2004). An information-seeking roadblock is permissible, when the stop is brief and the criminal investigation is for a known crime that involved a death nearby.

h. *Griffin v. Wisconsin*, 483 U.S. 868 (1987); *United States v. Knights*, 534 U.S. 112 (2001); *Samson v. California*, 547 U.S. 843 (2006). Operation of a State probation or parole system presents a "special need" that justifies warrantless searches of probationers.

i. *United States v. Flores–Montano*, 541 U.S. 149 (2004). At the border itself, customs and immigration officials can "stop" those who seek to enter the United States and force them to prove their right to enter (by presenting their passport and relevant immigration documents).

j. *United States v. Brignoni–Ponce*, 422 U.S. 873 (1975); *United States v. Arvizu*, 534 U.S. 266 (2002). Inside the United States, the rules regarding searches and seizures parallel the ordinary search and seizure rules. Stopping a vehicle because police believe that it contains illegal aliens requires reasonable suspicion.

k. *United States v. Martinez–Fuerte*, 428 U.S. 543 (1976). Special rules apply for near-border roadblocks or checkpoints. Near-border checkpoints have been upheld where agents referred vehicles at their discretion to an area for secondary inspection.

l. ***United States v. Place***, 462 U.S. 696 (1983); ***United States v. Van Leeuwen***, 397 U.S. 249 (1970). *Terry*'s analysis extends to investigative seizures of property. Such an intrusion on possessory interests can vary "both in its nature and extent," ranging from an "on the spot" inquiry (as with the use of a dog to sniff the luggage) to the relinquishment of custody and control.

m. Some brief seizures are so minimally intrusive that they can be justified based "only on specific articulable facts that the property contains contraband or evidence of a crime."

n. Based on a reasonable conclusion that property contains contraband, police can briefly detain the property for investigative purposes if the detention is limited in scope.

J. Exigent Circumstances

1. The nature of the exigent circumstances exception includes the existence of probable cause that there is a need to enter "to assist persons who are seriously injured or threatened with such injury." The Fourth Amendment does not require police to delay until someone is injured. ***Brigham City v. Stuart***, 547 U.S. 398 (2006). The case law recognizes several types of exigent circumstances. Law enforcement officers may rely on the exigent circumstances exception even when they had a role in creating the exigency, as long as they did not engage in, or threaten to engage in, conduct that violates the Fourth Amendment.

2. "**Hot pursuit.**" When does the hot pursuit exception apply?

   a. ***Warden v. Hayden***, 387 U.S. 294 (1967). Following an armed robbery, police followed the robbers to a nearby house. A search revealed Hayden in a bedroom. In other parts of the house, officers found weapons and clothing used in the robbery. The Court held that the warrantless search of the entire house was valid.

b. ***Minnesota v. Olson***, 495 U.S. 91 (1990). The morning after a robbery, police entered a residence to look for Olson. At the time of the entry, no exigent circumstances justified a warrantless entry into a residence because Olson was merely the driver of the getaway car (not the shooter), the murder weapon already was recovered, and there was no showing that anyone was in danger or that Olson could escape.

3. **Gathering evidence from suspect's body**. What limits apply to the gathering evidence exception?

a. ***Cupp v. Murphy***, 412 U.S. 291 (1973). After Murphy's wife's death, he refused to provide a sample of a dark spot on his finger and tried to remove the spot. Police took the dried blood sample without a warrant. The Court upheld the search, "considering the existence of probable cause, the very limited intrusion undertaken incident to the station house detention, and the ready destructibility of the evidence."

b. ***Rochin v. California***, 342 U.S. 165 (1952). The police pumped defendant's stomach after he swallowed capsules. Concluding that the police had violated Rochin's rights, the police conduct had shocked the conscience of the Court.

c. ***Schmerber v. California***, 384 U.S. 757 (1966). The Court upheld a blood sample extraction to prevent the loss of evidence in a drunk driving case, because there was probable cause that the test would yield evidence, and the procedure used was effective and rarely painful.

4. **Special needs cases.** *Skinner v. Railway Labor Executives' Association*, 489 U.S. 602 (1989) challenged federal regulations mandating blood and urine tests of railroad employees who were involved in "major" train accidents or violated safety rules. The Court found that the governmental interest "in ensuring the safety of the traveling public and of the employees themselves" outweighed the minimal intrusiveness of the tests which could be conducted "with a minimum of inconvenience or embarrassment." The drug testing could be required even in the absence of reasonable suspicion.

5. **Special rules for school-age children.** Special rules apply to searches of school-age children. *New Jersey v. T.L.O.*, 469 U.S. 325 (1985) upheld a limited search of a high school student. The Court held that searches should be evaluated under a two-part test focusing on the "reasonableness" of the school's action.

   a. The search must be "justified at its inception," i.e., a school official must have "reasonable grounds" to think that a search would yield evidence of legal or school rule violations.

   b. The search also must be "reasonably related to the objectives of the search and not excessively intrusive in light of the age and sex of the student and the nature of the infraction."

   c. *Vernonia School Dist. 47J v. Acton*, 515 U.S. 646 (1995) upheld suspicionless drug testing of school athletes, using a fact-specific balancing of the children's Fourth Amendment rights and legitimate governmental interests relating to preventing, deterring and detecting drug use. *Board of Education of Independent School District v. Earls*, 536 U.S. 822 (2002) upheld drug tests for all middle and high school students participating in competitive extracurricular activities. The samples were not collected in an intrusive way. The test results were confidential

and could not be turned over to the police or
lead to disciplinary or academic consequences.

6. **Drug tests for pregnant women**. In *Ferguson v. City of
    Charleston*, 532 U.S. 67 (2001), the Court struck down
    cocaine drug testing for pregnant women, again applying
    its balancing test and finding that the purpose of the tests
    was "indistinguishable from the general interest in crime
    control."

IV. Burden of proof. Warrantless arrests, searches and seizures are
presumed to be illegal. *Schneckloth v. Bustamonte*, 412 U.S. 218 (1973).
The burden is on the prosecution to prove that the intrusion is
justified under some exception to the warrant requirement. *Vale v.
Louisiana*, 399 U.S. 30 (1970).

ILLUSTRATIVE PROBLEMS

■ PROBLEM 5.1 PLAIN VIEW ■

David Burns told Officer Sharp that someone, whom he suspected
to be the defendant, stole a tool box from his pickup truck while it
was parked outside a bar. Sharp and Burns then went to the
defendant's house and knocked on the door. While standing on the
front porch waiting for the door to be answered, the two men
looked through the front window and observed a tool box, which
Burns identified as his, on the kitchen floor. When the defendant
answered the door, Sharp immediately entered the house, proceeded to the kitchen, and seized the box. When the defendant
moves to suppress the box, how should a court rule? If the plain
view exception cannot justify Sharp's conduct, can any other
exception?

Analysis

Plain view justifies warrantless seizures from a place the officer has
a right to be, but it does not justify warrantless searches or entries.

The viewing through the window from the front porch would not be considered a search. Because the observation of the tool box was legal, the officer would be able to testify to what she observed. But the tool box itself would have to be suppressed unless the officer had some basis for a warrantless entry, e.g., exigent circumstances. Plain view cannot justify the officer going inside the house.

■ PROBLEM 5.2 AUTOMOBILE EXCEPTION AND CONTAINERS ■

An unidentified female called the Atlanta police dispatcher and claimed that she had driven two females, Vesely and Higgs, from Ohio to Atlanta. She also reported that the two females were currently on their way to the Greyhound bus station, where they intended to retrieve two suitcases filled with drugs from lockers 17 and 20 and transport them to Savannah. The caller detailed the appearances of both women and one of the suitcases.

In response to the call, police officers went to the station platform where the bus for Savannah was waiting. After the luggage was brought out some time later, the bus driver loaded it into the luggage compartment under the bus. The driver then permitted the passengers to board the bus. When the driver started to back the bus out of its parking space, the officers signaled the driver to stop, boarded the bus, arrested and handcuffed the two women, and directed the driver to retrieve the suitcases. The officers then opened the suitcases, finding crack cocaine. The defendants file a motion to suppress. How should the motion be decided?

Analysis

The first issue is whether the informant's tip provided probable cause. The caller reports personal knowledge, but there is no information about her credibility. The corroboration by the police may be enough to establish credibility. So, here the strength in the basis of knowledge prong may compensate for a deficiency in the credibility prong.

Assuming that there is probable cause, the suitcases are part of a vehicle. The automobile exception applies to containers in the vehicle whether the police have probable cause to search the vehicle generally or only probable cause to search the vehicle for a particular container. It does not matter that the police's probable cause went only to the suitcases, and not to the rest of the bus. The warrant protection that the suitcases enjoyed in the station was lost when they became part of the bus.

■ PROBLEM 5.3 INVENTORY SEARCH ■

As the defendant walked into a hospital emergency room, police officers lawfully arrested her for a shooting incident that had occurred some months before. The defendant then asked the police to park and close the windows of her car, which she had left partially blocking the ambulance approach to the emergency room. An officer responded, however, that the police would take the car to the City Garage for safekeeping. After they had done so, the police discovered stolen goods in an inventory search that complied with the department's written and detailed guidelines. How should a court decide the defendant's motion to suppress?

Analysis

Inventories of lawfully impounded vehicles are permitted to protect the owner's property, to protect the police from suits (false and true) over lost or damaged property, and to protect the police or the public from danger. In conducting an inventory, the officers must be following a standardized procedure. That procedure need not eliminate all police discretion, but the discretion must be exercised in light of standardized criteria and on the basis of something other than suspicion of wrongdoing.

To inventory a car, police must have a right to possess the car. This defendant's car was not lawfully parked but was partially

blocking the ambulance approach to the emergency room. Therefore, the police did not have the option of simply leaving the car
alone. While the purpose of the search here may have related to the
criminal investigation, moving the car and conducting an inventory
search also related to concerns about traffic access to the emergency
room entrance. The inventory search was proper.

■ PROBLEM 5.4 CONSENT ■

On August 11 at the Cincinnati International Airport, Officer
Eades and four other members of a drug interdiction squad
observed Rector with two other persons exit the bus which had just
arrived from New York City. The squad then "deployed." Eades
approached Rector while another officer approached one of the
other men. Both officers faced the bus; both interviewees faced the
bus station exit. Officer Nowka stood as a backup about five feet
behind the two interviewees, thus forming a triangle with the two
interview pairs. The other two officers caught up with and questioned the third individual nearer to the bus station exit, but at a
point still visible to Rector.

Following his usual routine, Eades introduced himself and
asked whether he could see Rector's ticket. When Rector complied,
Eades asked if Rector was carrying drugs. When Rector answered
that he was not, Eades asked if he could search Rector's tote bag.
Rector answered that he had no problem with that. In the pocket
of a swimming suit inside the bag, Eades found cocaine.

Rector's suppression hearing revealed these additional facts.
Rector, who was born in Jamaica, was a twenty-year-old electrical
engineering student at Brooklyn College. At the time of the search,
he had been in the United States five years. Eades estimated that in
his three years on the interdiction squad, he had conducted about
1,500 interviews like this one, and in approximately two-thirds of
these he had asked for consent to search. Eades also claimed that no
person had ever walked away from him on his initial contact and
only eleven had refused consent to search. Eades said that squad
members wear plain clothes, speak in a conversational tone, and do

not block an interviewee's path. Eades also estimated that about twelve percent of interviews result in an arrest.

Analysis

The totality of circumstances is used to assess the voluntariness of consent. The defendant was a 20–year old Jamaican, who had been in the United States only five years. On the other hand, he was a student at Brooklyn College. The procedures used by the interdiction squad were obviously designed for maximum effectiveness: only 11 people out of 1,000 refused consent. This alone does not make the consent involuntary. The squad's "deployment" helped to create an impression that the men had no choice. Although the men were never told they had a choice, this is just one factor to consider. On the other hand, the officer said that the officers spoke in a conversational tone, and they did not block the subject's path. They used words of request rather than command. The consent appears to be voluntary.

■ PROBLEM 5.5 STOP AND FRISK ■

On September 23, at approximately 1:00 p.m., two police officers responded to a "burglary in process" call. At the designated address, the officers discovered that the rear door to a first floor apartment had been forced open. After a fruitless search for clues, the officers left the apartment. Outside they noticed a man walking down an alley behind the building. When the man observed the officers, he began running in the direction he had been walking. The officers pursued in their vehicle. After temporarily losing the man, they rediscovered him walking a couple of blocks away. Stopping their vehicle, the officers called for the man to approach them, which he did. One officer asked the man his name and then immediately conducted a "patdown." Finding a knife, the officers arrested the man and more fully searched his person. This search produced a number of items taken from the burglarized apartment. How should a court rule on a motion to suppress the evidence? Did a seizure occur before the patdown? If the officers had sufficient cause for a seizure, did they also have sufficient cause for a "frisk"?

Analysis

The first issue is whether there was reasonable suspicion. A crime had definitely been committed. The officers, upon seeing the defendant flee, had to make a quick decision whether to stop him. Moreover, burglary is one of those crimes for which the offender is typically caught in the act, shortly thereafter, or not at all. In short, the officers saw the defendant in close proximity to a recently committed burglary, and the defendant ran when he saw the officers.

Even if there was reasonable suspicion to justify a stop of the defendant for questioning, the issue of whether there was reasonable suspicion that the defendant was armed and dangerous is a closer question. If there was reasonable suspicion that the defendant had committed a daytime burglary, it is necessary to decide whether there was reasonable suspicion to frisk, arising solely from the nature of the crime, i.e., that the defendant was armed and dangerous. There is a possibility that the defendant had a burglar's tool, such as a crowbar, on his person which could be used as a weapon.

■ PROBLEM 5.6 ROADBLOCKS ■

At 10:00 p.m., Kentucky State Police troopers Lodge and Kincaid received a radio dispatch indicating that two women, one with a shotgun, had robbed a motel in Bowling Green, Kentucky, within the past seven minutes. Based on statements from witnesses, the dispatch further reported that the robbers were two black women, both about five feet tall, who had fled in a car traveling toward the northwest. At the time of the dispatch, the officers were located on State Road 18, four miles east of U.S. Highway 231, and fifteen miles northwest of the robbery. Knowing Highway 231 to be a major link-up between Highway 52 and Interstate 65 (the most direct route to Nashville), the officers immediately proceeded to the intersection of Highways 18 and 231. Their hope was to intercept the robbers traveling northbound on Highway 231. As Officer Lodge later testified, "We knew from the time element that the individuals we were looking for had time to be at this location at about this time."

The officers established a roadblock at the intersection. They then stopped two cars, which they immediately released after observing that the occupants were white. After stopping a third car, driven by a black female, Officer Lodge asked to see a driver's license. Officer Kincaid in the meantime looked into the car with his flashlight and observed another black female lying on the rear floor with a shotgun in open view. The officers then arrested the women, and a further search of the car uncovered items taken in the robbery. What result when the defendants move to suppress the shotgun and the robbery proceeds?

Analysis

There was no individualized cause for the stop. Roadblock stops can be upheld only by dispensing with the requirement of individualized cause. Supreme Court cases have upheld fixed checkpoint stops. The annoyance from being stopped is reduced by the fixed location of the checkpoint, the fact that motorists were given advance notice, and the fact that everyone was subject to the procedure. This roadblock is not at a fixed place, the motorists have no advance notice, and the field officers have total discretion both in setting up the roadblock and in conducting it. Courts weigh the degree of intrusion against the law enforcement need for the procedure. The need to catch armed robbers is important. The time factor also is important. If the robbers get away, it will be much harder to solve the crime. If the use of the roadblock was permissible, there's no problem with letting the white drivers go through. The robbers were described as black. There's also no problem with the officer looking into the car with his flashlight. Enhancing the senses by use of flashlight is not a search.

■ PROBLEM 5.7 EXIGENT CIRCUMSTANCES ■

At 2:00 a.m. on April 16, someone in the Brown Hotel reported a serious fight to the police. The police arrived within minutes and found a person lying on the floor with a fatal gunshot wound. The desk clerk advised the officers that Silvers had gone upstairs with a gun, apparently wounded. The officers and clerk went to Silvers' room, knocked on the door, and received no answer. At the officers' request, the clerk unlocked the door. Inside, the officers observed a blood-stained shirt on the bed. After looking under the bed and in the closet and bathroom, they concluded that Silvers was not in the room. Continuing to search the room, the officers opened a suitcase that was in the closet and discovered $12,000 under some clothing. Silvers was arrested after bank employees subsequently identified the money as stolen. After Silvers moves to suppress the money, how should the court decide the motion?

Analysis

The basic ground for excusing the warrant requirement is the existence of exigent circumstances making a warrant impractical. The warrantless entry should not cause a problem. The officers can argue either hot pursuit of a fleeing felon or that they reasonably believed that emergency medical assistance might have been necessary. Either way, posting a guard and securing a warrant would have been impractical. Because the defendant went to his room with a gun, it was reasonable for the police to search for weapons as long as there was a possibility that he was in the room. The difficulty arises because the police continued to search the room after concluding the defendant wasn't there.

The police can argue that they had probable cause to look for the defendant's gun or evidence of his whereabouts. If probable cause existed, there was no emergency need to find the gun once they secured the room. However, if it was reasonable to believe that the room might provide a clue as to where the defendant had gone, there was not time to get a warrant. On the other hand, perhaps a court could decide that the police could have sealed off the room and obtained a warrant.

CHAPTER 6

Police Interrogations & Confessions

*M*iranda v. Arizona, 384 U.S. 436 (1966), held that Fifth Amendment "*Miranda* warnings" must be given to all persons prior to custodial interrogation. The Supreme Court has relied on other doctrinal sources for judicial regulation of police interrogation, creating rules based on: 1) Fourteenth Amendment Due Process, 2) the Sixth Amendment right to counsel, and 3) the Court's supervisory power over the federal courts.

A. THE *MCNABB–MALLORY* RULE

The Supreme Court's regulation of the admissibility of confessions in federal courts is based on its supervisory power over all federal courts. In *McNabb v. United States*, 318 U.S. 332 (1943), the Court created an exclusionary rule for confessions obtained during the improper detention of arrestees not taken promptly to a federal judicial officer after arrest.

Congress incorporated the substance of *McNabb* into Rule 5(a) of the Federal Rules of Criminal Procedure in 1946, requiring that arrested persons must be presented to a judicial officer "without unnecessary delay." A confession obtained during a period of unnecessary delay is inadmissible. *Mallory v. United States*, 354 U.S. 449 (1957) warned against pre-appearance questioning that "lends itself, even if not so designed, to eliciting damaging statements." The six-hour delay in *Mallory* was held to be unnecessary, because a magistrate was available for two hours in the same building where the defendant was questioned.

The *McNabb–Mallory* rule never was incorporated into Due Process doctrine and applied to the States, despite repeated requests by State defendants during the years between *McNabb* and *Miranda*. Under the *McNabb–Mallory* rule as revised by 18 U.S.C. § 3501(c), if a confession is voluntary and was obtained within six hours of arrest, it is admissible and the weight to be given the confession is left to the jury. If the confession occurred before the initial appearance and beyond six hours and if the court decides that the delay was unreasonable or unnecessary, the confession is to be suppressed. *Corley v. United States*, 556 U.S. 303 (2009).

B.   THE FIFTH AMENDMENT AND *MIRANDA*

Miranda v. Arizona, 384 U.S. 436 (1966) found *incommunicado* interrogation "at odds with" the Fifth Amendment privilege against self-incrimination. Unless "adequate protective devices" were used to relieve the coercion "inherent in custodial surroundings, no statement obtained from a defendant can truly be the product of his free choice." *Miranda* articulated the protection of a defendant's "free will" to protect the privilege, and created a Fifth Amendment right to counsel in order to protect a defendant's access to the privilege during the interrogation process.

The Court adopted several Fifth Amendment safeguards:

[An interrogated person in custody] must be warned prior to any questioning that he has the right to remain silent, that anything he says can be used against him in a court of law, that he has the right to the presence of an attorney, and that if he cannot afford an attorney one will be appointed for him prior to any questioning if he so desires. Opportunity to exercise these rights must be afforded to him throughout the interrogation. After such warnings have been given, and such opportunity afforded him, the individual may knowingly and intelligently waive these rights and agree to answer questions or make a statement. But unless and until such warnings and waiver are demonstrated by the prosecution at trial, no evidence obtained as a result of interrogation can be used against him.

The Court also required police to honor the defendant's invocations of the Fifth Amendment rights to silence or counsel.

If the individual indicates in any manner, at any time prior to or during questioning, that he wishes to remain silent, the interrogation must cease. [If] the individual states that he wants an attorney, the interrogation must cease until an attorney is present. At that time, the individual must have an opportunity to confer with the attorney and to have him present during any subsequent questioning. If the individual cannot obtain an attorney and he indicates that he wants one before speaking to police, they must respect his decision to remain silent. [If] authorities conclude that they will not provide counsel during a reasonable period of time in which investigation in the field is carried out, they may refrain from doing so without violating the person's Fifth Amendment privilege so long as they do not question him during that time.

The inadmissibility of confessions obtained in violation of these rules extends to all statements made during custodial interrogation; "no distinction" may be drawn between inculpatory statements and statements alleged to be merely "exculpatory."

Two findings were at the core of the *Miranda* Court's reasoning. First, all custodial interrogation creates a "potentiality for compulsion," a conclusion based on the Court's review of police manual instructions for interrogation techniques which promoted an "atmosphere of domination" by police interrogators. Second, the "human dignity" value of the Fifth Amendment could be protected only if new rules were created to limit the inherent coercion of interrogation so that confessions may be "truly [the] product of free choice." A "full opportunity to exercise the privilege" could be provided if the accused was "adequately and effectively apprised of his rights and the exercise of those rights . . . fully honored."

Miranda did not provide for police recitation of all rights potentially useful for a criminal defendant prior to custodial interrogation. For example, 1) there is no right to be informed that if a defendant invokes silence or counsel rights, a cut-off of questioning will follow; 2) a lawyer does not have to be "present at all times to advise prisoners;" 3) there is no right to contact people outside the interrogation room; and 4) there is no right to defense counsel's access to a client during interrogation. None of these techniques of psychological "domination" is a *Miranda* violation *per se*.

State courts and legislatures are free to create different standards to protect the privilege, as long as they are "equally effective." The Court has not recognized any alternate rules as adequate *Miranda* substitutes, and has invalidated a Congressional attempt to overrule *Miranda* by legislation. See *Dickerson v. United States*, 530 U.S. 428 (2000).

However, the Court has created significant exceptions to *Miranda*. For example, the rules do not apply to 1) questioning conducted by undercover police agents, *Illinois v. Perkins*, 496 U.S. 292 (1990); 2) "routine booking questions," *Pennsylvania v. Muniz*, 496 U.S. 582 (1990); or 3) police questioning about a weapon under the "public safety exception," *New York v. Quarles*, 467 U.S. 649 (1984). In addition, statements taken in violation of *Miranda* may be used to impeach the defendant if she chooses to testify and the statement was not obtained in violation of Due Process. *Harris v. New York*, 401 U.S. 222 (1971).

1. *Miranda* Custody

Miranda does not require an officer to give *Miranda* warnings to everyone approached for information concerning a crime. *Miranda* applies only to "custodial interrogation," which is defined as "questioning initiated by law enforcement officers after a person has been taken into custody or otherwise deprived of his freedom of action in any significant way." If the defendant is "in custody" on one charge, *Miranda* is still required even if questioning is about another charge. *Mathis v. United States*, 391 U.S. 1 (1968).

The Court uses an objective standard to determine custody;

"the only relevant inquiry is how a reasonable [person] in the suspect's situation would have understood [the] situation." *Stansbury v. California*, 511 U.S. 318, 324 (1994). An individual defendant's idiosyncratic reaction to an encounter with police will not dictate a finding of custody. More importantly, a police officer's opinion about the custodial status of the interrogated person is irrelevant to the custody inquiry, as long as this opinion is not revealed to that person.

In deciding custody issues, the Court has said that a trial judge should examine "whether the relevant environment presents the same inherently coercive pressures as the type of station house questioning at issue in *Miranda*." *Howes v. Fields*, 132 S.Ct. 1181 (2012). In *Howes*, a prison inmate was not entitled to *Miranda* warnings, because he was not in custody while being questioned by sheriff's deputies in a prison conference room. The court distinguished between the inherently coercive situation where a citizen is taken from familiar surroundings and interrogated in a police station and one involving prisoners being taken from one controlled environment to another.

Appellate courts use a multi-factor test to determine whether a reasonable person would feel free to leave or terminate an interrogation. Factors include the purpose of the questioning, whether the place of questioning was hostile or coercive, the length of the questioning, whether defendant was informed that questioning was voluntary or he was free to leave, whether he was restrained during questioning, and whether defendant initiated the contact with the police.

In *J.D.B. v. North Carolina*, 131 S.Ct. 2394 (2011), the Court addressed the relevance of the suspect's age in deciding whether she is in custody for *Miranda* purposes. Emphasizing the objective nature of the inquiry, the Court posed two questions: 1) what were the circumstances surrounding the interrogation, and 2) under those circumstances, would a reasonable person have felt at liberty to terminate the interrogation and leave? "A reasonable child subjected to police questioning will sometimes feel pressured to submit when a reasonable adult would feel free to go." However, the Court went on to say that age is insignificant when the defendant is a teenager close to the age of majority. If the suspect is almost the age of majority and/or savvy enough to invoke her rights after her arrest, she likely is not a frightened adolescent. Other relevant factors relating to age would be the suspect's criminal past and her prospects for rehabilitation.

Some post-*Miranda* cases held that custody could exist outside the station house. For example, in *Orozco v. Texas*, 394 U.S. 324 (1969), the defendant was held to be in custody in his own home when he was awakened in his bedroom at 4:00 a.m. by four police officers. He was not informed that he was under arrest, but he was questioned about his presence at the scene of a homicide and about the location of his gun. However, in *Beckwith v. United States*, 425 U.S. 341 (1976), a defendant was interviewed at his home for three hours by IRS agents. His claim that he was in custody failed because he had consented to the interview and had been warned about the consequences of his answers and his right to consult an attorney.

While a person at home may be regarded as being in "custody," *Miranda* warnings do not have to be administered to imprisoned defendants. In *Maryland v. Shatzer*, 130 S.Ct. 1213 (2010), the Court observed, "Without minimizing the harsh realities of incarceration, . . . lawful imprisonment imposed upon conviction of a crime does not create the coercive pressures identified in *Miranda*." In contrast to their time in a small interrogation room removed from other inmates, inmates in the general prison population are in "their accustomed surroundings and daily routine."

Not every encounter between a defendant and a police officer qualifies as "custodial." "General on-the-scene questioning as to facts surrounding a crime or other general questioning of citizens in the fact-finding process is not affected by our holding. [In] such situations the compelling atmosphere inherent in the process of in-custody interrogation is not necessarily present." *Miranda*.

Certain situations are non-custodial *per se*, absent unusual circumstances. For example, in *Minnesota v. Murphy*, 465 U.S. 420 (1984), a probationer's interview with a probation officer was held to be a non-custodial event. The obligations of probationers to report to their probation officers and to be truthful with them "in all matters," upon penalty of probation revocation, do not establish sufficient restraint.

The Court provided further guidance concerning non-custodial situations in *Berkemer v. McCarty*, 468 U.S. 420 (1984), by determining that the typical "traffic stop" does not qualify as "custody." The Court explained that a temporary detention for purposes of receiving a traffic citation does not compare to the "police-dominated" atmosphere of a station house interrogation. In the typical traffic stop, a driver expects to be detained only briefly and to be questioned by no more than one or two police officers in the comparative safety of the public eye. However, the Court did recognize that some traffic stops may not fit the typical non-custodial pattern, necessitating *Miranda* warnings.

2. *Miranda* Interrogation

A suspect does not have to be advised of her *Miranda* warnings upon her arrest, so long as she is advised prior to the commencement of interrogation. Volunteered statements are admissible even if the defendant is in custody when the statement was made and no *Miranda* warnings had been given. "There is no requirement that police stop a person who enters a police station and states that he wishes to confess to a crime, or a person who calls the police to offer a confession or any other statement he desires to make." *Miranda v. Arizona*, 384 U.S. at 478.

The *Miranda* definition of "interrogation" was a crucial concept for determining police compliance with the *Miranda* duties: 1) to give warnings before interrogating persons in custody, 2) to refrain from interrogating after warnings in the absence of waiver, and 3) to refrain from interrogating after an invocation of rights. *Rhode Island v. Innis*, 446 U.S. 291 (1980) established a test for assessing whether a particular police comment or action would qualify as "interrogation."

Miranda safeguards "come into play whenever a person in custody is subjected to either express questioning or its functional equivalent," defined as any words or actions on the part of the police (other than those normally attendant to arrest and custody) that the police should know are reasonably likely to elicit an incriminating response from the suspect. The latter portion of this definition focuses primarily upon the perceptions of the suspect, rather than the intent of the police.

In this respect, the *Innis* definition of interrogation is consistent with the *Stansbury* definition of custody, because both rules avoid focusing on police intent or state of mind.

Innis was arrested for armed robbery, and was also suspected of a shotgun murder five days earlier. He was placed in the rear seat of a police car, and three police officers traveled with him. Innis overheard two of the officers talking to each other about how they should "continue to search for the weapon" because "a school for handicapped children [was] located nearby," and because "God forbid" that a little girl might "pick up the gun, maybe kill herself." Innis then immediately stated that he would show the officers the location of the gun, and led them to that location.

The *Innis* majority emphasized several aspects of the police dialogue that justified its conclusion that interrogation did not occur: 1) the police conversation was "brief" not "evocative;" 2) it was not directed to Innis but merely overheard by him; 3) the police had no knowledge of any "peculiar" susceptibility of Innis to an appeal for the safety of handicapped children, and they knew of no disorientation or upset suffered by Innis at the time of arrest; and 4) the incriminating response of the defendant was "unforeseeable."

Three important *Miranda* exceptions allow police to engage in conduct that would constitute "interrogation" under *Innis* without honoring the duty to give *Miranda* warnings: 1) routine booking questions, 2) interrogators who are not known to the suspect as law enforcement officers, and 3) public safety. The common doctrinal thread for these exceptions is the Court's recognition of a particular police need to gather information that might not be provided by an arrestee if the warnings were given.

The origin of the "routine booking question" exception is the *Innis* Court's recognition that any questions "normally attendant to arrest and custody" should not count as "interrogation" under *Miranda. Pennsylvania v. Muniz*, 496 U.S. 582 (1990). This exception allows police to gather the biographical data needed to complete the booking process and arrange for pretrial services. The rationale is that the answers to questions about a defendant's name, address, age, and like subjects are "reasonably related to administrative . . . concerns" and are unrelated to the quest for incriminating statements.

In *Illinois v. Perkins*, 496 U.S. 292 (1990), the Court created a second interrogation exception in its ruling that *Miranda* warnings are not required if a person "is unaware that [she] is speaking to a law enforcement officer." This exception allows police to use undercover agents to pose as prison inmates in order to obtain incriminating statements from an unsuspecting defendant. The *Perkins* interrogation did not "implicate the concerns underlying *Miranda*," which relate to the risks of self-incrimination that are inherent in a coercive, "police-dominated atmosphere."

The "public safety exception" in *New York v. Quarles*, 467 U.S. 649 (1984), allows police to ask an arrestee a question about the location of a weapon that the arrestee may have abandoned or hidden in a public area near the scene of arrest. These questions may be asked without first providing *Miranda* warnings that could prompt the arrestee to refuse to disclose any information about the weapon. In *Quarles*, police officers had reliable information that the arrestee had recently discarded a gun somewhere in the supermarket where they arrested him. The police asked "only the question necessary to locate the missing gun" before providing the defendant with *Miranda* warnings. If a question about a weapon was "reasonably prompted by a concern for public safety" under the circumstances of the arrest, the arrestee's answer to the question is admissible evidence, as well as any weapon that is located as a result of the questioning.

3. Adequate *Miranda* Warnings

a. Incomplete or Misleading Warnings

The Court has established guidelines for the types of tolerable ambiguity in the *Miranda* warnings. In *California v. Prysock*, 453 U.S. 355 (1981), the police officer's language was as follows: "You have the right to talk to a lawyer before you are questioned, have him present with you while you are being questioned, and all during the questioning. Do you understand this? . . . You also, being a juvenile, you have the right to have your parents present, which they are. Do you understand this? . . . You have the right to have a lawyer appointed to represent you at no cost to yourself. Do you understand this?"

The defendant argued that the warnings failed to connect the right to consult counsel before questioning with the right to appointed counsel. The defendant did not realize that the "lawyer appointed to represent" him "at no cost" would be appointed before any questioning began. The defendant assumed instead that any "appointed lawyer" would be appointed after the interrogation, presumably by a judge at some proceeding in the future. The Court ruled that separate references to the right to consult counsel before questioning and the abstract right to appointed counsel sufficiently conveyed the meaning of the *Miranda* rights.

What saved the *Prysock* warnings was the clarity with which the right to consult counsel was attached to the time period "prior to and during interrogation." The defendant was expected to infer that the description of the right to "appointed counsel" referred to the earlier description of the right to consult counsel before questioning. The ambiguity in the warnings was not significant.

The *Prysock* Court did recognize, however, that the "right-to-counsel" warnings would be constitutionally inadequate if they expressly suggested "any limitation on the right to the presence of appointed counsel" that was different from the "rights to a lawyer in general." Specifically, "if the reference to the right to appointed counsel was linked with some future point in time after the police interrogation," the text of the warning would "not fully advise the suspect of his right to appointed counsel before" an interrogation. *Prysock* also settled that *verbatim* recitation of the *Miranda* warnings is unnecessary.

In *Duckworth v. Eagan*, 492 U.S. 195 (1989), the police told the suspect that he had a right to an attorney during interrogation and the right to an appointed attorney. In addition though, police also told him that an attorney would be appointed for him if and when he went to court. The Court again found that the warning was sufficient because it "simply anticipated" a question the suspect might be expected to ask after receiving *Miranda* warnings, i.e., when will he obtain an attorney.

In *Florida v. Powell*, 130 S.Ct. 1195 (2010), the Court stated that "the four warnings *Miranda* requires are invariable, but this Court has not dictated the words in which the essential information must be conveyed." For example, when police officers arrested Powell they warned him about his "right to talk to a lawyer before answering any . . . questions." They also told him that he had "the right to use of these [*Miranda*] rights at any time [he] want[ed] during th[e] interview." The Supreme Court upheld those warnings, which did not "entirely omi[t] any required information" and because they "reasonably conveyed Powell's right to have an attorney present not only at the outset of interrogation but at all times."

The prosecution must prove that the warnings were given, but no particular form of proof is necessary to show that the warnings were given. The receipt of the warnings is the first step for government arguments for a valid *Miranda* waiver.

b. Ineffective "Midstream" Warnings

Missouri v. Seibert, 542 U.S. 600 (2004) held that when police "question first and warn later," warnings that are given "midstream" between two interrogations that are "close in time and similar in content" do not "reasonably convey" the *Miranda* rights as required by *Duckworth*. Such warnings are likely to mislead the interrogated person about "the nature of his rights and the consequences of abandoning them." "[A] suspect would hardly think he had a genuine right to remain silent, let alone persist in so believing once the police began to lead him over the same ground again."

Seibert noted that midstream warnings may be adequate in some circumstances, such as those in *Oregon v. Elstad*, 470 U.S. 298 (1985), where police made a "good faith" mistake in failing to give warnings before a single comment by an officer prompted an unwarned admission by Elstad during his arrest in his home. The warnings given later at the station were "adequate," according to *Seibert*, because the station house interrogation was deemed to be a "new and distinct experience" for Elstad, and thus his station house confession was admissible.

Bobby v. Dixon, 132 S.Ct. 26 (2011) clarified *Seibert*'s scope: it applies only when different periods of interrogation form one continuous whole. The use of *Miranda* warnings at subsequent periods is sufficient to offset the failure to do so at an earlier period of questioning. In *Dixon*, four hours passed between his

> unwarned interrogation and his receipt of *Miranda* rights, during which time he traveled from the police station to a separate jail and back again; claimed to have spoken to his lawyer; and learned that police were talking to his accomplice and had found [the victim's] body. Things had changed. Under *Seibert*, this significant break in time and dramatic change in circumstances created "a new and distinct experi- ence," ensuring that Dixon's prior, unwarned interrogation did not undermine the effectiveness of the Miranda warnings he received before confessing to . . . murder.

Dixon's facts also lacked the two-step interrogation technique that undermined the *Miranda* warnings in *Seibert*. In *Dixon*, there was no earlier confession to repeat because Dixon initially gave no confession. After receiving the *Miranda* warnings, "Dixon contra- dicted his prior unwarned statements" by confessing to murder. Thus, the police did not use an earlier admission to induce a later waiver. "Dixon declared his desire to tell police what happened to Hammer before the second interrogation session even began."

4. Waiver of *Miranda* Rights

The prosecution must prove that an arrestee waived her *Miranda* rights in order for any statement obtained during custodial interrogation to be admitted at trial. The *Miranda* opinion provided only one example of a hypothetical case where a waiver could be found, an express statement that an arrestee "is willing" to talk and "does not want an attorney" that is followed closely by an incriminating statement.

Miranda requires that waivers must be "voluntary, knowing and intelligent." The State must prove waiver by a preponderance of the evidence. *Colorado v. Connelly*, 479 U.S. 157 (1986). A waiver may be implied through oral statements and conduct, and does not have to be in writing. *North Carolina v. Butler*, 441 U.S. 369 (1979). A waiver may be inferred from the fact that the suspect eventually makes statements to the police. *Berghuis v. Thompkins*, 130 S.Ct. 2250 (2010). Finally, a valid waiver must include proof that an arrestee understood the *Miranda* warnings, and therefore a court may not rely on a presumption that such an understanding exists. *Tague v. Louisiana*, 444 U.S. 469 (1980). To satisfy the *Tague* burden, police sometimes administer the *Miranda* warnings and ask whether the arrestee understands her rights, thereafter seeking a written acknowledgment of the suspect's understanding.

In *Moran v. Burbine*, 475 U.S. 412 (1986), the Court summarized post-*Miranda* principles defining voluntary, knowing and intelligent waivers. "Only if the 'totality of the circumstances surrounding the interrogation' reveals both an uncoerced choice and the requisite level of comprehension may a court properly conclude that the *Miranda* rights have been waived."

The first key component of a waiver is its "voluntary" quality. A defendant needs to demonstrate that coercive police conduct caused her waiver to be the product of intimidation, coercion, or deception under *Moran*. A totality of the circumstances test is used: "the duration and conditions of detention, . . . the manifest attitude of the police toward [the defendant], [the] physical and mental state [of the defendant], [and] the diverse pressures which sap or sustain [the defendant's] powers of resistance and self-control." *Colorado v. Spring*, 479 U.S. 564 (1987).

The Court has been unsympathetic to claims that police silence constitutes a form of coercion. In *Colorado v. Spring*, police failed to tell the defendant, before his waiver, that they planned to ask him questions about an old murder crime as well as about the unrelated crime for which he had been arrested. The Court decided that, because the defendant had been affirmatively warned that anything he said could be used against him, he should have inferred that he was giving the police an unlimited waiver for interrogation about all his crimes. The *Spring* Court reserved the issue of whether sufficient "coercion" invalidates a waiver if police affirmatively misrepresent the scope of the interrogation.

In another waiver ruling, the Court found that a mentally ill defendant can voluntarily waive his *Miranda* rights when there is no police overreaching. *Colorado v. Connelly*, 479 U.S. 157 (1986). The defendant approached an off-duty police officer and confessed to murder. The officer responded by reciting the *Miranda* warnings, which were repeated by an officer summoned to question him. The defendant told them that he had been a patient in mental hospitals, but he showed no signs of mental illness during interrogation. During his interview with appointed counsel the next day, the defendant stated that auditory hallucinations led him to confess.

The second component of a valid waiver is its "knowing and intelligent" quality. In *Spring*, the Court rejected defendant's argument that more information about the subject of the interrogation was necessary for a knowing waiver. The Court concluded that the *Miranda* warnings supplied all the information necessary for a "knowing and intelligent" waiver. Moreover, an "extension of *Miranda* would spawn numerous problems of interpretation because any number of factors could affect a suspect's decision to waive *Miranda* rights."

In *Connecticut v. Barrett*, 479 U.S. 523 (1987), Barrett told police after three sets of warnings that he would talk to them, but would not make a written statement without a lawyer. He then made oral admissions without police asking him for a written statement. The defendant repeatedly had said that he understood his rights and testified about knowing that he did not have to talk without a lawyer present. That the defendant's conduct appeared "illogical" did not prevent police from obtaining a valid waiver. The defendant "made clear his intentions, and they were honored by police." Barrett's "conditional waiver" of the right to silence was held to be voluntary, knowing and intelligent.

5. Invocation of *Miranda* Rights

Under *Miranda*, police officers must honor an arrestee's invocations of the right to silence, the right to counsel, or both, by "cutting off" the interrogation. Post–*Miranda* cases have resolved three questions about a suspect's invocation of rights: 1) an invocation of counsel is different from an invocation of silence; police are barred from initiating discussions and seeking waiver after the former but not after the latter invocation; 2) police may seek a waiver after either type of invocation when the arrestee initiates a generalized discussion about the investigation with the police; and 3) an invocation of either silence or of counsel must be unambiguous. If an arrestee's invocation does not satisfy these standards, police may ignore the invocation and continue to interrogate.

a. Unambiguous Invocation of Rights

The invocation of the right to silence by a suspect must be explicit and unambiguous. *Berghuis v. Thompkins*, 130 S.Ct. 2250 (2010) applied the "unambiguous invocation" requirement from *Davis v. United States*, 512 U.S. 452 (1994) to invocations of the right to counsel. An adequate invocation occurs when a reasonable police officer in the circumstances would understand the statement to be a request not to talk to the police (e.g., the suspect says to the police, "Leave me alone").

Davis v. United States, 512 U.S. 452 (1994) determined that an adequate invocation occurs when "a reasonable police officer in the circumstances would understand the statement to be a request for an attorney." An officer can ignore an invocation that is "ambiguous or equivocal in that a reasonable officer in light of the circumstances would have understood only that the suspect *might* be invoking the right to counsel." Requiring an "unambiguous" invocation ensures that police officers will not "be forced to make difficult judgment calls" about ambiguous invocations, and not be faced with "the threat of suppression if they guess wrong."

Davis had waived his rights and answered questions for an hour and a half before saying, "Maybe I should talk to a lawyer." Asked to clarify his request, Davis said that he was "not asking for a lawyer" and added, "No, I don't want a lawyer." The *Davis* Court held that the initial "maybe" request for counsel did not "meet the requisite level of clarity," the *Edwards* right therefore did not attach, and the police did not have to stop questioning. *Davis* also rejected the imposition of a law enforcement "duty to clarify" an ambiguous invocation.

When a defendant's invocation interrupts the police officer before all the warnings are administered, the officer should stop the interrogation as soon as the invocation is uttered. *Smith v. Illinois*, 469 U.S. 91 (1984). The rationale for this rejection is that police should not be allowed to ignore unambiguous invocations "as if the defendant had requested nothing," in the hope that later statements might create some retrospective ambiguity in the invocation.

b. Right to Silence

Michigan v. Mosley, 423 U.S. 96 (1975) held that an invocation of silence does not permanently end the interrogation if the police "scrupulously honor" the invocation. Mosley told police that he did not want to answer questions about the robberies for which he was arrested. Two hours later, a different police officer told him that he was investigating a murder. After receiving a second set of warnings during questioning in another part of the station house, Mosley waived his rights and made incriminating statements.

The *Mosley* Court began its analysis by noting the text of the governing *Miranda* rule and its policy justifications.

Once warnings have been given, the subsequent procedure is clear. If the individual indicates in any manner, at any time prior to or during questioning that he wishes to remain silent, the interrogation must cease. At this point he has shown that he intends to exercise his Fifth Amendment privilege; any statement taken after the person invokes his privilege cannot be other than the product of compulsion, subtle or otherwise."

The *Mosley* Court viewed this passage as leaving open the question whether, and under what circumstances, "a resumption of questioning is permissible."

The *Mosley* Court declared that "a blanket prohibition" against questioning after invocation of the right to silence would inhibit police investigations and prevent suspects from making "informed and intelligent assessments" of their interests. Moreover, a resumption of questioning after a time lapse permits the suspect to retain "control" over the timing, subject and duration of an interrogation, in order to counteract "the coercive pressures of the custodial setting."

Mosley's invocation of the right to silence was "scrupulously honored," which the Court explained as a combination of several factors: the invocation appeared to be limited to the robbery crimes, the subject of questioning was an "unrelated" crime, a two-hour time lapse occurred before the re-interrogation, the defendant received a second set of *Miranda* warnings, and the second interrogation was conducted by a different police officer. The Court has not explained the scope of the multi-factor holding since *Mosley*.

c. Right to Counsel

If the suspect in custody invokes his right to counsel instead of his right to silence, different rules apply. The invocation of silence shows that the suspect does not want to talk, while the invocation of counsel is an indication by the suspect that he feels incapable of speaking to the police on his own. Because of the Court's concern that a suspect asserting his right to counsel is not as likely to change his mind for reasons other than police pressure, the Court accords the police less flexibility, i.e., after the invocation, the police cannot interrogate the suspect unless he initiated the contact.

In *Edwards v. Arizona*, 451 U.S. 477 (1981), the Court refused re-interrogation of the defendant following an invocation of the right to counsel. *Miranda* had stated, "If the individual states that he wants an attorney, the interrogation must cease until an attorney is present." The Court accepted *Miranda*'s blanket prohibition against questioning after invocation of the right to counsel. The defendant in *Edwards* had declared, "I want an attorney before making a deal." The police had cut off questioning but then returned the next morning, telling the defendant he "had to" talk to them. The Court determined that the *Edwards* waiver was invalid because the police initiated the second interrogation. The only proper scenario for police seeking a waiver was where the *arrestee* "initiates further communication, exchanges, or conversations with the police" after invocation of the right to counsel.

In distinguishing *Edwards* from *Mosley*, *Edwards* cited *Mosley*'s recognition of the different "procedural safeguards" that were "triggered" by the two different invocations. Because the defendant in *Edwards* had "expressed his desire to deal with the police only through counsel," he should not be "subject to further interrogation by the authorities until counsel has been made available to him." However, the *Edwards* opinion did not speak directly to the question whether the ban on re-interrogation after the invocation of counsel should apply to a re-interrogation concerning a different crime.

In *Arizona v. Roberson*, 486 U.S. 675 (1988), the Court ruled that *Edwards* bars re-interrogation about different crimes. The *Roberson* Court relied on several rationales to justify its use of the *Edwards* rule to govern re-interrogations on all subjects: 1) a bright line-rule barring all re-interrogations after invocation of counsel would be easy for police, prosecutors, and lower courts to interpret and apply, and 2) any invocation of counsel seeks the advice of counsel concerning questioning about any crime.

The Court's final extension of *Edwards* came in a case where re-interrogation followed the defendant's consultation with counsel. In *Minnick v. Mississippi*, 498 U.S. 146 (1990), the defendant invoked his right to counsel after his arrest in California for a crime in Mississippi, and the arresting FBI agents allowed him to meet with counsel several times. Although his lawyer told him not to talk to anyone or to sign any waivers, Minnick was told that he "had" to talk to the Mississippi sheriff. His conversation with the sheriff led to a discussion of the crime. *Minnick* held that the *Edwards* rule bars re-interrogation of any kind unless counsel is present. As in *Roberson*, the *Minnick* Court valued the "clarity and certainty" of a "bright-line rule" application of *Edwards*. Only the presence of counsel after invocation provided adequate protection of the Fifth Amendment right to counsel.

Edwards specifically noted that the ban on re-interrogation after the invocation of counsel does not apply if the defendant "initiates further communication, exchanges, or conversations with the police." The rationale is that the defendant "initiates" a discussion, then she has demonstrated a lack of desire to deal with the police only through counsel. The Court soon decided that initiation is not *per se* proof of a waiver. Assuming that a post-invocation "initiation" has occurred, the police must seek a valid waiver under the totality of the circumstances. *Oregon v. Bradshaw*, 462 U.S. 1039 (1983).

The definition of "initiation" split the *Bradshaw* Court. All agreed that questions "relating to routine incidents of the custodial relationship," such as a request for a drink of water or requests to use the telephone, were "bare inquiries" that do not qualify as an "initiation." For the plurality, though, an "initiation" occurs whenever an arrestee engages in a "generalized discussion" of the investigation. For the dissenters, an "initiation" should be found only when an arrestee communicates explicitly about "the subject matter of the criminal investigation" in a way that invites "further interrogation."

Shortly after he invoked his right to counsel, while being transferred from the police station to the jail, Bradshaw asked the escorting officer, "Well, what is going to happen to me now?" Instead of immediately answering the question, the police gave an incomplete version of the *Miranda* warnings. The *Bradshaw* plurality held that the police officer had not violated *Edwards* by resuming the waiver-seeking process. While acknowledging that the defendant's question was "ambiguous," the police officer's response showed that the officer understood the question as "relating generally to the investigation." The officer's conduct in seeking a waiver was valid under *Edwards*.

In *Maryland v. Shatzer*, 130 S.Ct. 1213 (2010), the Supreme Court held that *if* a suspect is released from custody after invoking his right to counsel, the *Edwards* prohibition on police questioning lasts for fourteen days. The Court reasoned that a suspect will not feel pressured if questioned again after a substantial period of time during which he is free. This amount of time is enough "for the suspect to get reacclimated to his normal life, to consult with friends and counsel, and to shake off any residual coercive effects of his prior custody."

Summarizing the effect of *Shatzer*, the *Edwards* rules remain in effect until the suspect is released from jail and before the end of the fourteen days of release. After the fourteen-day period, the police may resume questioning without the suspect re-initiating the conversation.

6. Uses of *Miranda*–Defective Evidence

a. When Defective Evidence Leads Police to Other Evidence

If the police violate the *Miranda* rules and obtain a statement during custodial interrogation, that statement will be inadmissible. In *Oregon v. Elstad*, 470 U.S. 298 (1985), however, the Court rejected the need to use the Fourth Amendment "fruit of the poisonous tree" doctrine in the *Miranda* context. See Chapter 8. The Court in *Elstad* decided that the failure to give warnings before obtaining an initial confession does not invalidate a second confession, obtained after warnings, as the inadmissible fruit of the *Miranda* violation. Although *Elstad* permits the police ordinarily to remedy an initial failure to warn by subsequently giving the warnings, *Missouri v. Seibert*, 542 U.S. 600 (2004) qualified *Elstad* by holding that "midstream" warnings may be inadequate to convey *Miranda* rights in some circumstances. See the topic of Adequate *Miranda* Warnings, *supra*.

The rejection of the *Wong Sun* "fruits" doctrine in the *Miranda* context was justified, because the exclusion of all non-attenuated fruits of *Miranda* violations is unnecessary to provide adequate deterrence of violations by police officers. For example, the Court held in *United States v. Patane*, 542 U.S. 630 (2004), that if police discover physical evidence based on information provided in a defendant's unwarned statement, that evidence is admissible as long as the statement was not procured by "actual coercion."

b.   *Impeachment Based on Defective Statements or Silence During Interrogation*

The "impeachment exception" to *Miranda* was established in *Harris v. New York*, 401 U.S. 222 (1971). The Court ruled that an unwarned statement was admissible during cross-examination to impeach the credibility of the defendant's testimony if the statement was not obtained in violation of Due Process, i.e., if it was given voluntarily. Exclusion of *Miranda*-defective statements from the prosecution's case-in-chief is sufficient deterrence of *Miranda* violations by police. Impeachment also is necessary to prevent the *Miranda* doctrine from being used as a "shield" for the commission of perjury by defendants who could contradict their statements to police without those statements being used to impeach them.

Doyle v. Ohio, 426 U.S. 610 (1976) recognized that the exercise of the "right to remain silent" in the *Miranda* warnings would be penalized at trial if a prosecutor were allowed to ask a defendant during cross-examination why she refrained, after being arrested and receiving warnings, from telling the police information that she has communicated to the jury at trial. Thus, questions about a defendant's silence or comments about her silence during closing argument may constitute Due Process violations. However, *Doyle* is inapplicable to questioning at trial about pre-arrest silence or post-arrest silence before warnings are delivered. *Jenkins v. Anderson*, 447 U.S. 231 (1980); *Fletcher v. Weir*, 455 U.S. 603 (1982). Sometimes, when defense counsel objects to a *Doyle* violation, it may satisfy Due Process for the trial judge to caution the jury to disregard the impermissible question by the prosecutor. *Greer v. Miller*, 483 U.S. 756 (1987).

C. SIXTH AMENDMENT RIGHT TO COUNSEL

The Sixth Amendment right to counsel attaches upon the commencement of adversary judicial proceedings. In *Rothgery v. Gillespie County*, 554 U.S. 191 (2008), the Court identified a short list of events that qualify a "adversary judicial proceedings," including initial appearance, formal charge, preliminary hearing, indictment or information. Once adversary proceedings are instituted, law enforcement officials or their agents may not interrogate the accused in the absence of counsel, unless the accused has validly waived that right.

In *Massiah v. United States*, 377 U.S. 201 (1964), the Supreme Court held that an indicted defendant's surreptitious questioning by an undercover police agent violated the Sixth Amendment right to counsel. Years later, the Court declared that *Massiah* clearly established "that once adversary proceedings have commenced against an individual, he has a right to legal representation when the government interrogates him." *Brewer v. Williams*, 430 U.S. 387 (1977).

The *Massiah* Court relied on three arguments to support its holding. First, lack of access to counsel during questioning "might deny a defendant 'effective representation by counsel at the only stage when legal aid and advice would help him.'" Second, counsel's investigation and preparation are "vitally important," and defendants are therefore "as much entitled to [the] aid of counsel during that period as at the trial itself." Finally, if the Sixth Amendment right to consult counsel were to be meaningful, "it must apply to indirect and surreptitious interrogations as well as those conducted in the jailhouse."

After *Miranda*, the Court did not rely on *Massiah*'s Sixth Amendment right to counsel doctrine in a confession case until *Brewer v. Williams*. *Brewer v. Williams* held that police violated the Sixth Amendment right of an arraigned defendant in custody when an officer deliberately elicited incriminating statements from him without a waiver. The *Brewer* Court issued multiple rulings concerning the scope of *Massiah* and its ramifications: 1) *Massiah* bans the deliberate elicitation of statements by undercover police agents; 2) to conduct questioning, the police must obtain a Sixth Amendment waiver; and 3) if police officers do not obtain such a waiver, they may not engage in "deliberate elicitation" of incriminating statements. "Elicitation" includes both express questioning and other kinds of police statements that are "tantamount to interrogation." The *Massiah* waiver standard is the same as the waiver standard established in *Johnson v. Zerbst*, 304 U.S. 458 (1938): "an intentional relinquishment or abandonment of a known right or privilege."

On the advice of his Des Moines lawyer, Williams surrendered to police and was arraigned on an abduction charge in Davenport, while two officers traveled by car from Des Moines to retrieve Williams and escort him back for "booking" in Des Moines. Williams was suspected of murdering the victim of an abduction. His lawyer obtained the agreement of police officials that they would not question him in transit, and he would be allowed to consult with the lawyer in Des Moines before questioning. Williams received *Miranda* warnings from the Davenport police, the Davenport judge, and the Des Moines detective. Both of his lawyers also warned him against making any statements.

Soon after the police car left Davenport, the detective delivered the so-called "Christian burial speech." He told Williams that he expected that they would be driving past the area where the victim's body was hidden, and that Williams might be unable to find it because "[t]hey are predicting several inches of snow for tonight. . . . " The detective reminded Williams that "you yourself are the only person that knows where this little girl's body is." The detective opined "that the parents of this little girl should be entitled to a Christian burial for the little girl who was snatched away from them on Christmas Eve and murdered." Finally the detective said, "I do not want you to answer me. I don't want to discuss it any further. Just think about it as we're riding down the road." After thinking about it for 100 miles, Williams made incriminating statements and ultimately led the police to the body.

The violation of a *Massiah* right would require three elements: the attachment of the *Massiah* right to counsel, the failure of police to obtain a waiver of *Massiah* rights, and finally, the prohibited act of "deliberate elicitation" (equivalent to improper "interrogation") by police that produced incriminating statements. First, the Sixth Amendment right to counsel attached to Williams because the Davenport arraignment qualified as the commencement of "adversarial judicial proceedings." Second, the detective engaged in "deliberate elicitation" by making the "Christian burial speech," which was viewed as "tantamount to interrogation." *Brewer* implicitly recognized that express questioning was unnecessary for a finding of "deliberate elicitation." Third, there was no affirmative evidence of waiver before the "Christian burial speech" was delivered. Instead, Williams stated several times that he would talk to police after seeing his lawyer in Des Moines. Evidence also negated waiver, namely the defendant's "consistent reliance on the advice of counsel in dealing with the authorities," and his "express and implicit assertions of his right to counsel."

Later cases have clarified several issues unresolved by *Brewer.* First, the waiver standards for *Miranda* and *Massiah* rights are so similar that the *Miranda* warnings serve as an adequate method for informing a defendant of *Massiah* rights. *Patterson v. Illinois*, 487 U.S. 285 (1988).

Second, the *Massiah* right attaches at the initiation of "adversary judicial proceedings" but requires an invocation of that right. The police must "cut off" questioning when a defendant actually requests a lawyer or otherwise asserts his Sixth Amendment right to counsel. *Montejo v. Louisiana*, 556 U.S. 778 (2009). Montejo's statement was admissible because he never asserted his right to counsel. For a defendant who never asserted the right to counsel's presence, police may seek a waiver of counsel from her after giving her *Miranda* warnings which are sufficient to waive the Sixth Amendment right to counsel. The Court in *Montejo* approvingly cited *Patterson* on this issue. Any questioning by police after the suspect invokes the right to counsel is limited to crimes *other* than the charged offense to which the Sixth Amendment has attached. *McNeil v. Wisconsin*, 501 U.S. 171 (1991).

Third, although *Rhode Island v. Innis*, 446 U.S. 291 (1980) observed that the concepts of "deliberate elicitation" under the

Sixth Amendment and "interrogation" under the Fifth Amendment are "not necessarily interchangeable, since the policies underlying the two constitutional protections are quite distinct," the Court has not identified any differences between *Miranda* "interrogation" and "deliberate elicitation" under *Massiah* where defendants are questioned by police.

Fourth, statements taken in violation of *Massiah* may be used to impeach the defendant if she chooses to testify, as long as the statement was not obtained in violation of Due Process. *Kansas v. Ventris*, 556 U.S. 586 (2009).

The chief distinction between the Fifth and Sixth Amendments relates to the treatment of persons who are questioned by undercover police agents. The *Perkins* exception to *Miranda* allows the "interrogation" by undercover agents of persons in custody. *Massiah* does not allow the "deliberate elicitation" of incriminating statements by undercover agents from persons who possess Sixth Amendment rights, regardless of whether the suspect is incarcerated at the time of questioning.

1. Deliberate Elicitation

"Deliberate elicitation" exists when an undercover informant-cellmate is not a "passive listener" and joins as an active participant in conversations with the defendant despite instructions to the informant "not to initiate any conversation with [the defendant]" about the crime. *United States v. Henry*, 447 U.S. 264 (1980). By contrast, the Court held that "deliberate elicitation" did not occur in *Kuhlmann v. Wilson*, 477 U.S. 436 (1986), when a police informant was placed in the defendant's cell and merely listened to a defendant's statements, without making comments to stimulate incriminating conversations. This behavior does not resemble police interrogation and is not barred by the Sixth Amendment.

The *Kuhlmann* record showed that the informant made one remark that deviated from the role of "passive listener." The trial judge found that the informant followed his instructions to ask no "questions with respect to the crime," and that the defendant's incriminating statements were "spontaneous and unsolicited." *Ku-*

hlmann decided that the defendant failed to prove that "the police and their informant took some action, beyond merely listening, that was designed deliberately to elicit incriminating remarks."

Maine v. Moulton, 474 U.S. 159 (1985) affirmed an important limitation of *Massiah* that statements obtained through "deliberate elicitation" by undercover agents are admissible at a trial on offenses *other* than the crime to which the Sixth Amendment right already has attached. The *Moulton* majority described this scope limitation as a "sensible solution" to the problem of the government's need to continue to investigate "the suspected criminal activities" of indicted defendants. *Moulton* also clarified the scope of *Massiah*'s prohibition of "deliberate elicitation" by holding that it applies to situations where the defendant initiates a meeting with an undercover police agent as well as to situations where the agent initiates a meeting with the defendant.

2. Waiver

The waiver standards for *Miranda* and *Massiah* rights are so similar that the *Miranda* warnings serve as an adequate method for informing a defendant of *Massiah* rights. In *Patterson v. Illinois*, 487 U.S. 285 (1988), the Court interpreted the "key inquiry" in both "formulations" of waiver to be whether "the accused, who waived his Sixth Amendment rights during postindictment questioning, [was] made sufficiently aware of his right to have counsel present during the questioning, and of the possible consequences of a decision to forgo the aid of counsel?"

The defendant in *Patterson* had received *Miranda* warnings after arrest and had not invoked the Fifth Amendment right to counsel. After being informed of his indictment and given another set of *Miranda* warnings, he signed a waiver and made statements that were held to be admissible. His post-indictment *Miranda* warnings adequately informed him of both his *Miranda* and *Massiah* rights, and his *Miranda* waiver adequately established a *Massiah* waiver as well.

The Court determined that the third and fourth *Miranda* "right-to-counsel" warnings satisfied the first component of the

Patterson waiver formulation, to make the defendant "sufficiently aware of his right to have counsel present during the questioning." *Patterson* also determined that the second *Miranda* warning about the consequences of waiving the privilege described implicitly "the possible consequences of a decision to forgo the aid of counsel." The *Patterson* majority expected that a *Massiah* defendant could draw suitable inferences about the possible consequences of going without counsel during questioning.

3. Invocations

When police question a defendant after the initiation of "adversary judicial proceedings," she may invoke her Sixth Amendment right to counsel. The legal consequences of that invocation depend on whether the suspect is in custody when the invocation occurs. *Montejo v. Louisiana*, 556 U.S. 778 (2009). Regardless of whether a suspect has requested or obtained a lawyer, the police may question and seek a waiver from any suspect who is not in custody. "When a defendant is not in custody, he is in control, and need only shut his door or walk away to avoid police badgering." *Id.*

However, if the suspect is in custody and the police have informed him of his *Miranda* rights, a suspect who assets his right to counsel is protected by the *Edwards v. Arizona* rules discussed previously under "Invocation of *Miranda* Rights". If the suspect re-initiates contact with the police following the invocation, the police may seek a waiver and question him.

The invocation of the Sixth Amendment right to counsel applies only to the offenses that have been charged. (The Fifth Amendment rule in *Arizona v. Roberson*, 486 U.S. 675 (1988) prohibits the questioning of arrestees for *any* crime, once the *Miranda* right to counsel is invoked.) The Court refused to extend *Roberson* to the Sixth Amendment context in *McNeil v. Wisconsin*, 501 U.S. 171 (1991). Because the Sixth Amendment right to counsel is "offense-specific," the invocation of the *Massiah* right to counsel cannot bar questioning for crimes to which the Sixth Amendment has not yet attached.

Police may continue to question a defendant who invokes the Sixth Amendment right to counsel about offenses that have not been charged, as long as those uncharged offenses do not constitute the "same offense." *Texas v. Cobb*, 532 U.S. 162 (2001). Reaffirming the concept that the Sixth Amendment right to counsel is "offense specific," the Court formally adopted the definition of "offense" from the Double Jeopardy context, i.e., "where the same act or transaction constitutes a violation of two distinct statutory provisions, the test to be applied to determine whether there are two offenses or only one, is whether each provision requires proof of a fact which the other does not."

To summarize: As with the Fifth Amendment doctrine under *Miranda*, a defendant may invoke her right to counsel under the Sixth Amendment. The invocation must be unequivocal and the defendant must reinitiate communications with her police interrogators in order to waive her rights. However, there are differences between Sixth and Fifth Amendment invocations of the right to counsel. First, a Sixth Amendment invocation may occur even prior to *Miranda* warnings. Second, *McNeil* indicates that the consequences of a Sixth Amendment invocation require that the police may nevertheless continue questioning the suspect about uncharged offenses.

A *Massiah* defendant in custody will be provided with *Miranda* warnings that do double duty as *Massiah* warnings under *Patterson v. Illinois*, 487 U.S. 285 (1988). If a *Massiah* defendant invokes the right to counsel in response to such warnings, both *Miranda* and *Massiah* rights to cut off police questioning will arise. The *Miranda* right will provide the defendant with the *Roberson* protection of a "cut off" of questioning about all crimes, while the *Massiah* right will provide the redundant *Edwards* protection of a "cut off" of questioning about only the charged crime. However, if a defendant fails to invoke the right to counsel in response to the warnings, then neither *Miranda* nor *Massiah* "cut off" rights will arise. Only if she is in custody and affirmatively has invoked the *Massiah* right to counsel, will the *Massiah* right provide her with the *Edwards* "cut off" right.

D. DUE PROCESS

Before the decisions in *Miranda* and *Massiah*, the admissibility of a defendant's statement was tested by determining whether it was "voluntary." If the statement was not voluntary, then its admission into evidence was barred by the Due Process Clause of the Fourteenth Amendment. In order to be admissible in evidence today, a statement of the defendant must not only comply with the requirements of the Fifth and Sixth Amendments, but it must also be voluntary so as to satisfy Due Process.

Part of the reason for Due Process's vitality is that the Fifth and Sixth Amendment doctrines contain gaps that can be filled only by reference to Due Process rules. For example, *Miranda* does not apply to undercover investigations, to impeachment evidence, or to defendants who have waived their *Miranda* rights. *Massiah* is relevant only when a defendant has been charged with crimes to which the Sixth Amendment right has attached. The most significant Due Process decisions in the post-*Miranda* era involve defendants who fall between these cracks of the Fifth and Sixth Amendment doctrines.

The concept of voluntariness bars any statement which was not the product of the defendant's free will as a result of police overreaching. A statement is not admissible if it fails to meet any of the objectives of the voluntariness test. The objectives of the voluntariness test are to bar statements which: (1) may not be true, (2) were obtained by offensive police practices, or (3) were obtained under circumstances where the defendant's free will was significantly impaired.

The standard of voluntariness is also important with respect to the requirements of *Miranda*. A *Miranda* violation may make a statement inadmissible, but only in the prosecution's case-in-chief. However, the prosecution may never make use of an involuntary confession. If a confession is involuntary, the confession cannot even be used for impeachment or cross-examination, which might not be the case with evidence gained from a *Miranda* violation.

Brown v. Mississippi, 297 U.S. 278 (1936) was the Court's first decision holding that the State court admission into evidence of an involuntary confession violated Due Process. *Brown* held that the police interrogation "method" of physical torture caused any confession to be "involuntary." The Court reasoned that the use of such coerced confessions at trial "offends some principle of justice so rooted in the traditions and conscience of our people as to be ranked fundamental."

Over time, the Court expanded the definition of coercion to include physical and psychological treatment that fell short of the police brutality in *Brown*. The Court expanded the definition of coercion in *Ashcraft v. Tennessee*, 322 U.S. 143 (1944), where the defendant was interrogated *incommunicado* for thirty-six hours, without sleep or rest, by relays of officials. The *Ashcraft* confession was found to be involuntary *per se* because of an "inherently coercive" interrogation.

The early cases looked at voluntariness issues in three ways to express concern about: 1) confessions of doubtful reliability, 2) confessions obtained with dubious police practices, even if reliability was not a concern (due to corroborating evidence), and 3) confessions where the defendant's free choice was significantly impaired even if the police did not use offensive tactics. *Colorado v. Connelly*, 479 U.S. 157 (1986) altered the judicial approach to these issues. First, the Court stated that the issue of reliability is governed by the jurisdiction's evidentiary rules rather than by the Due Process Clause. Second, the Court held that, while the defendant's free choice is relevant, its importance depends on the police having engaged in overreaching the suspect.

In the post-*Miranda* era, the Court affirmed its pre-*Miranda* Due Process rules and also revealed the influence of *Miranda* jurisprudence on Due Process analysis. Affirmations of old holdings appear in *Arizona v. Fulminante*, 499 U.S. 279 (1991), which applied the totality of the circumstances approach to hold that a "credible threat of violence" was a Due Process violation. *Mincey v. Arizona*, 437 U.S. 385 (1978). New Due Process holdings appear in *Mincey*, where the Court ruled that police cannot take advantage of coercion created by external forces, and in *Colorado v. Connelly*, 479 U.S. 157 (1986), which held that some police "overreaching" is needed for a finding of coercion. In *Mincey*, the Court treated *Miranda* violations as coercive elements in the Due Process totality of the circumstances. In *Connelly*, police compliance with *Miranda* influenced the Court to find that the police did not take advantage of a mentally ill defendant's inner compulsion to confess.

The Court followed a traditional case-by-case approach to reach its finding of involuntariness in *Mincey v. Arizona*, where a police officer questioned a wounded arrestee for three hours while he was hospitalized in intensive care. The officer took advantage of Mincey's physical trauma by interrogating him in his vulnerable state and also repeatedly violated *Miranda* by ignoring Mincey's three invocations of his right to counsel. The evidence of involuntariness consisted of police "relentlessness," of *Miranda* violations, and of Mincey's condition. Building from earlier cases, a defendant's personal vulnerabilities thus continued to be a foundation for a Due Process violation.

Colorado v. Connelly concluded that "coercive police activity is a necessary predicate to the finding that a confession is not 'voluntary.' " Even if a defendant's free will is "overborne" by his mental illness, this does not make his confession involuntary in the absence of police coercion. The *Connelly* police knew only that the defendant had been a patient in several mental hospitals in the past, and knew nothing of the auditory hallucinations that led him to confess; his symptoms of mental illness were manifested only the day after his confession during an interview with appointed counsel. At the time of his unsolicited confession, the defendant was given *Miranda* warnings, and "appeared to understand fully the nature of his acts" when he waived his rights. By contrast, if police had politely questioned Connelly knowing that he was insane, they would have exploited a situation even though they did not create it.

Arizona v. Fulminante viewed the defendant's situation as a match for *Payne v. Arkansas*, 356 U.S. 560 (1958), where a sheriff promised protection to an inmate from the angry mob outside the jailhouse door in exchange for his confession. The equivalent of the "angry mob" in *Fulminante* was the group of inmates who had threatened the defendant with violence because of rumors that he had killed a child. The informant-inmate played the role of sheriff, bargaining for Fulminante's confession with a promise to provide protection from the other inmates. This promise carried weight, in the Court's view, because the informant-inmate was pretending to be an organized crime figure. The *Fulminante* majority treated this promise as a "credible threat of violence" and viewed the defendant's situation as a frightening one, because failure to confess to the informant could have resulted in attacks by the threatening inmates. Affirming the totality-of-the-circumstances analysis, the Court treated the defendant's individual frailties as relevant to its finding that the confession was involuntary.

As noted in *Fulminante*, direct or implied promises by the police must be evaluated as part of the totality of the circumstances. The promise must have been "sufficiently compelling to overbear the suspect's will in light of . . . circumstances." The Court has found Due Process violations when the police threatened to take the suspect's wife into custody if he did not confess, *Rogers v. Richmond*, 365 U.S. 534 (1961), and when the suspect was told that she could lose her welfare payments and custody of her children if she did not confess, *Lynumn v. Illinois*, 372 U.S. 528 (1963).

Lower court cases are split when police tell the suspect that his cooperation would fare better in subsequent proceedings. If the suspect initiated the conversation about leniency as a precondition, courts are less likely to find a subsequent confession to be involuntary. Moreover, courts are less likely to tolerate a misrepresentation of the law (e.g., a false promise that the trial judge would grant immunity to the defendant) than a misrepresentation of fact (e.g., falsely stating that the shooting victim is still alive).

Assuming that police have engaged in overreaching conduct, courts also consider the particular characteristics of the suspect in order to evaluate his ability to resist the coercive police pressure. The common factors present in both traditional voluntariness and *Miranda* waiver cases include the defendant's: 1) age, *Fare v. Michael C.*, 442 U.S. 707 (1979), *Gallegos v. Colorado*, 370 U.S. 49 (1962); 2) intelligence, *Culombe v. Connecticut*, 367 U.S. 568 (1961); 3) education, see *id.*; 4) criminal experience, *Haynes v. Washington*, 373 U.S.

503 (1963); 5) mental condition, *Colorado v. Connelly*; 6) intoxication on alcohol or drugs, *Townsend v. Sain*, 372 U.S. 293 (1963); 7) physical injury and coercion, *Brown v. Mississippi*, *Payne v. Arkansas*; 8) threats to others, see *Lynumn v. Illinois*, 372 U.S. 528 (1963); and 9) length of interrogation and number of interrogators, *Reck v. Pate*, 367 U.S. 433 (1961), *Ashcraft v. Tennessee*.

POLICE INTERROGATION AND CONFESSIONS CHECKLIST

I. The *McNabb–Mallory* Rule

A. The legal basis for Supreme Court regulation of the admissibility of confessions in federal courts is based on the Court's supervisory power over all federal courts.

B. Under *McNabb v. United States*, 318 U.S. 332 (1943) confessions are excluded when they were obtained during the period of unnecessary delay when arrestees are not taken promptly to a federal judicial officer.

    1. Congress incorporated *McNabb* into Rule 5(a) of the Federal Rules of Criminal Procedure in 1946, requiring that arrested persons be presented to a judicial officer "without unnecessary delay."

    2. *Mallory v. United States*, 354 U.S. 449, 453 (1957) held that a six-hour delay in taking an arrestee before a judge was an unnecessary delay, because a magistrate was available in the same building where the defendant was questioned for two hours.

C. As revised by 18 U.S.C. § 3501(c), if a confession occurred before the initial appearance, beyond six hours after arrest and if the court decides that the delay was unreasonable or unnecessary, the confession is to be suppressed. *Corley v. United States*, 556 U.S. 303 (2009).

II. The Fifth Amendment and *Miranda*

A. Warnings required under *Miranda v. Arizona*, 384 U.S. 436, 479 (1966):

1. The required warnings for an interrogated person in custody are that:

   a. The suspect has the right to remain silent,

   b. Anything he says can be used against him in a court of law,

   c. He has the right to the presence of an attorney, and

   d. If he cannot afford an attorney, one will be appointed for him prior to any questioning if he so desires.

2. After the warnings, a suspect knowingly and intelligently may waive these rights and agree to answer questions or make a statement.

3. The purpose of the warnings is to address the inherently coercive nature of custodial interrogation.

4. These warnings are not the exclusive method for police to deal with suspects prior to interrogation.

   a. The Court invited creation of other, "equally effective" standards to protect a person's Fifth Amendment rights, i.e., State courts and legislatures are free to create different standards to protect the privilege. However, the Court has not recognized any alternate rules as adequate *Miranda* substitutes.

   b. The Court even invalidated a Congressional attempt to overrule *Miranda* by legislation with a statutory "voluntariness" standard. ***Dickerson v. United States***, 530 U.S. 428 (2000).

5. Significant exceptions to *Miranda*:

   a. It does not apply to questioning conducted by undercover police agents. ***Illinois v. Perkins***, 496 U.S. 292 (1990).

   b. It does not apply to "routine booking questions." ***Pennsylvania v. Muniz***, 496 U.S. 582 (1990).

c.   It does not apply to police questioning about a weapon under the "public safety exception." ***New York v. Quarles***, 467 U.S. 649 (1984).

    d.   Statements taken in violation of *Miranda* may be used to impeach the defendant if she chooses to testify, and if the statement was not obtained in violation of Due Process. ***Harris v. New York***, 401 U.S. 222 (1971).

B. Custody under *Miranda*. "Custodial interrogation" triggers the duty to give *Miranda* warnings.

    1.   The relevant inquiry for custody under *Miranda* is how a reasonable person in the suspect's shoes would have understood the situation. ***Stansbury v. California***, 511 U.S. 318 (1994).

        a.   The inquiry requires case-by-case scrutiny of the circumstances surrounding an interrogation. The following cases exemplify the Court's approach to the custody issue.

        b.   ***Oregon v. Mathiason***, 429 U.S. 492 (1977) relied on several factors for deciding the issue of custody: whether the defendant's presence was "voluntary;" whether he was told that he was not under arrest; and after making incriminating statements, whether he was released as promised.

        c.   In ***Orozco v. Texas***, 394 U.S. 324 (1969), the defendant was held to be in custody in his own home when he was awakened in his bedroom at 4:00 a.m. by four police officers.

        d.   Certain situations are non-custodial *per se*, absent unusual circumstances. For example, ***Berkemer v. McCarty***, 468 U.S. 420 (1984) determined that the typical "traffic stop" does not qualify as "custody."

        e.   In ***J.D.B. v. North Carolina***, 131 S.Ct. 2394 (2011), the Court addressed the relevance of the suspect's age in deciding the custody issue. The Court asked whether, under the circumstances of the interrogation, a reasonable child would have felt at liberty to terminate the interrogation and leave?

f. *Miranda* warnings do not have to be administered to imprisoned defendants. **Maryland v. Shatzer**, 130 S.Ct. 1213 (2010). Contrasted with an inmate in a small interrogation room removed from other inmates, inmates in the general prison population are not under the coercive pressures described in *Miranda*.

2. Lower courts have identified relevant factors for custody: purpose of the investigation, location and length of the interrogation, the person's awareness of her freedom to leave the scene, any form of physical restraint, use of coercive interrogation methods.

C. **Interrogation under *Miranda***

1. The relevant inquiry for interrogation under *Miranda* is whether "any words or actions on the part of the police (other than those normally attendant to arrest and custody) that the police should know are reasonably likely to elicit an incriminating response from the suspect." **Rhode Island v. Innis**, 446 U.S. 291 (1980). The latter part of the definition focuses on the suspect's perception rather than the intent of the police.

2. There are Court exceptions which allow the police to engage in "interrogation" without the duty to give *Miranda* warnings. Three exceptions recognize a particular police need to gather information that might not be provided by an arrestee if the warnings were given.

a. The "routine booking question" exception in **Pennsylvania v. Muniz**, 496 U.S. 582 (1990) allows police to gather biographical data needed to complete the booking process and arrange for pretrial services.

b. **Illinois v. Perkins**, 496 U.S. 292 (1990) created a

second interrogation exception for situations where a person "is unaware that [she] is speaking to a law enforcement officer," allowing police to use undercover agents to pose as prison inmates to obtain incriminating statements.

c. The "public safety exception" in **New York v. Quarles**, 467 U.S. 649 (1984) allows police to ask an arrestee a question about the location of a weapon that the arrestee may have abandoned or hidden in a public area near the scene of arrest.

D. **Adequate Warnings**

1. **Incomplete or Misleading Warnings**. When the warnings are not recited *verbatim* as described in *Miranda*, the Court tolerates some ambiguity. The "totality" of the warnings must adequately convey the meaning of the *Miranda* rights. **Duckworth v. Eagan**, 492 U.S. 195 (1989).

2. **Ineffective "Midstream" Warnings**. Warnings that are given "midstream" between two interrogations that are "close in time and similar in content" do not "reasonably convey" the *Miranda* rights. **Missouri v. Seibert**, 542 U.S. 600 (2004).

E. **Waiver of *Miranda* Rights**

1. The prosecution must prove by a preponderance of the evidence that an arrestee waived her *Miranda* rights for any statement obtained during interrogation to be admitted at trial. **Colorado v. Connelly**, 479 U.S. 157 (1986).

2. The standard for a *Miranda* waiver is that it must be "voluntary, knowing and intelligent," looking at the totality of the circumstances. **Moran v. Burbine**, 475 U.S. 412 (1986).

3. A waiver may be implied through oral statements and conduct, rather than being in writing. **North Carolina v. Butler**, 441 U.S. 369 (1979).

4. A defendant may give a "conditional" waiver, (e.g., agreeing to speak orally but not signing a written confession). ***Connecticut v. Barrett***, 479 U.S. 523 (1987).

F. **Invocation of *Miranda* Rights**

1. **Unambiguous Invocation of Rights**

   a. The invocation of the right to silence by a suspect in custody must be explicit and unambiguous. ***Berghuis v. Thompkins***, 130 S.Ct. 2250 (2010) applied the requirement for an invocation of the right to counsel from ***Davis v. United States***, 512 U.S. 452 (1994) to invocations of the right to silence.

   b. Police can ignore an ambiguous or equivocal invocation that a reasonable officer under the circumstances would have understood as ambiguous. ***Id.***

2. **Silence**

   a. An invocation of silence by the suspect does not permanently end the interrogation, if the police "scrupulously honor" the invocation at a later interrogation session. ***Michigan v. Mosley***, 423 U.S. 96 (1975).

   b. When a court decides whether the suspect's rights were scrupulously honored after invoking the right to silence, courts look at several factors: the new interrogation session concerned a different crime, the time lapse between sessions, police gave a second set of *Miranda* warnings, and a different officer conducted the second interrogation session.

3. **Counsel**

   a. After a suspect invokes her right to counsel, police should stop the interrogation as soon as the invocation is uttered. ***Smith v. Illinois***, 469 U.S. 91 (1984).

b. After a defendant invokes her right to counsel, police cannot resume interrogation about any crime until after the suspect re-initiates the conversation. *Arizona v. Roberson*, 486 U.S. 675 (1988); *Edwards v. Arizona*, 451 U.S. 477 (1981).

c. *If* a suspect is released from custody after invoking his right to counsel, the *Edwards* prohibition on police questioning lasts for fourteen days. After the fourteen-day period, the police may resume questioning without the suspect re-initiating the conversation. *Maryland v. Shatzer*, 130 S.Ct. 1213 (2010).

d. Re-interrogation is barred unless counsel is present. *Minnick v. Mississippi*, 498 U.S. 146 (1990).

e. After the suspect re-initiates further conversation, police can seek a valid waiver under the totality of the circumstances. *Oregon v. Bradshaw*, 462 U.S. 1039 (1983).

f. A re-initiation of further conversations occurs whenever an arrestee engages in a "generalized discussion" about the investigation. *Id.*

G. **Uses of *Miranda*–Defective Evidence**

1. Evidence obtained after a defect in the *Miranda* procedure may be excluded from the suspect's trial. The Fourth Amendment "fruit of the poisonous tree" doctrine may not apply in the *Miranda* context. *Oregon v. Elstad*, 470 U.S. 298 (1985).

2. If police discover physical evidence based on information in a defendant's unwarned statement, that evidence is admissible as long as the statement was not procured by "actual coercion." *United States v. Patane*, 542 U.S. 630 (2004).

3. A *Miranda*-defective confession may be used to impeach a defendant. An unwarned, *voluntary* statement is admis-

sible during cross-examination to impeach the credibility of the defendant's testimony. *Harris v. New York*, 401 U.S. 222 (1971).

4. Questions about a defendant's silence or comments about her silence during closing argument violate Due Process. *Doyle v. Ohio*, 426 U.S. 610 (1976). However, *Doyle* is inapplicable either to pre-arrest silence or to post-arrest silence before warnings are delivered. *Jenkins v. Anderson*, 447 U.S. 231 (1980); *Fletcher v. Weir*, 455 U.S. 603 (1982).

III. Sixth Amendment Right to Counsel

A. The Sixth Amendment right to counsel prevents police from deliberately eliciting incriminating statements from a defendant at or after the start of adversary judicial proceedings against her, i.e. initial appearance, formal charge, preliminary hearing, indictment or information. *Rothgery v. Gillespie County*, 554 U.S. 191 (2008).

1. If adversary proceedings have not begun, the Sixth Amendment is not applicable.

2. If adversary proceedings have begun against the person, unconstitutionally obtained confessions about the charged offenses (as well as any greater or lesser offenses of those charges) are inadmissible.

3. The right to counsel does not require a Sixth Amendment invocation.

4. The deliberate elicitation of statements, even by under-cover police agents, is banned.

5. To conduct questioning, police must obtain a Sixth Amendment waiver.

6. If police officers do not obtain such a waiver, they may not engage in "deliberate elicitation" of incriminating statements.

7. "Elicitation" includes both express questioning and other kinds of police statements that are "tantamount to interrogation."

8. Statements taken in violation of *Massiah* may be used to impeach the defendant if she chooses to testify, as long as the statement was obtained voluntarily under Due Process standards. ***Kansas v. Ventris***, 556 U.S. 586 (2009).

B. **Deliberate Elicitation**

1. "Deliberate elicitation" focuses on the subjective motivation of the police officer, while "interrogation" focuses on the suspect's response.

2. While recognizing conceptual differences in ***Rhode Island v. Innis*** between the terms' meanings, the Court has not identified significant differences between *Miranda* "interrogation" and "deliberate elicitation" under the Sixth Amendment when defendants are questioned by police.

3. "Deliberate elicitation" exists in the undercover informant-cellmate context when the informant is an active participant (rather than a passive listener) in conversations with the defendant. ***United States v. Henry***, 447 U.S. 264 (1980).

   a. "Deliberate elicitation" does not occur when a police informant is placed in the defendant's cell as a passive listener. ***Kuhlmann v. Wilson***, 477 U.S. 436 (1986).

   b. Statements obtained through "deliberate elicitation" by undercover agents are admissible at a trial on offenses other than the crime to which the Sixth Amendment right has attached. ***Maine v. Moulton***, 474 U.S. 159 (1985).

C. **Waiver of Rights and Invocation of Rights**

1. **Waiver.** The Sixth Amendment standard for waiver is the same as the standard for Fifth Amendment waiver. Because the waiver standards for *Miranda* and Sixth Amendment rights are so similar, the *Miranda* warnings serve as an adequate method for establishing an indicted defendant's knowing and voluntary waiver of her Sixth Amendment rights. ***Patterson v. Illinois***, 487 U.S. 285

(1988). The waiver standard requires "an intentional relinquishment or abandonment of a known right or privilege."

2. **When no waiver is necessary**

    a.   An undercover agent does not have to obtain a waiver from a defendant before operating as a passive listener about crimes with which the defendant is charged.

    b.   An undercover agent likewise does not need to obtain a waiver before "deliberately eliciting" statements from a defendant about crimes other than those with which she is charged.

3. **Invocation.** The Sixth Amendment always requires an invocation of counsel to "cut off" police questioning. An actual request for counsel during questioning is necessary to trigger the protection of the *Edwards* right to a "cut off" questioning. ***Montejo v. Louisiana***, 556 U.S. 778 (2009).

    a.   If the defendant has counsel after the Sixth Amendment attaches, but does not request counsel, the police can seek a waiver and question her. ***Patterson v. Illinois***; ***Texas v. Cobb***, 532 U.S. 162 (2001).

    b.   If the defendant requests counsel after the Sixth Amendment attaches, police cannot seek a waiver and deliberately elicit statements until counsel is present, unless the defendant initiates communications with them. See ***Edwards v. Arizona***, 451 U.S. 477 (1981).

    c.   However, police may seek a waiver from a defendant who requests her right to counsel, as long as the "deliberate elicitation" of statements is limited to crimes other than the charged offense to which the Sixth Amendment has attached. ***McNeil v. Wisconsin***, 501 U.S. 171 (1991).

IV. Due Process

A. Due Process doctrine has a role in the constitutional analysis of police interrogation, because Fifth and Sixth Amendment doctrines each contain gaps.

    1. The Fifth Amendment does not apply to undercover investigations, to impeachment evidence, or to defendants who have waived the *Miranda* rights.

    2. The Sixth Amendment is relevant only when a defendant has been charged with crimes to which the Sixth Amendment right has attached.

B. **Pre–*Miranda* Due Process**

    1. ***Brown v. Mississippi***, 297 U.S. 278 (1936) held that the police interrogation "method" of physical torture caused any confession to be "involuntary."

    2. The Court expanded "coercion" to include physical and psychological treatment. In ***Ashcraft v. Tennessee***, 322 U.S. 143 (1944), because defendant was interrogated *incommunicado* for thirty-six hours, without sleep or rest, by relays of officials, the confession was involuntary *per se* because of an "inherently coercive" interrogation.

    3. Several judicial approaches evolved for evaluating allegations of Due Process violations.

        a. One focused on coercive methods such as threats of violence, promises of incentives, and/or use of false statements.

        b. Another focused on the defendant's susceptibility to police coercion, the police conduct, the surrounding circumstances, and the defendant's character and life experiences.

        c. The third focused on the nature of *incommunicado* interrogation rather than the defendant's peculiar vulnerability.

    4. The Court never created specific Due Process requirements for police conduct during interrogations, instead creating a case-by-case approach.

C. Post–*Miranda* Due Process

1. The Court has retained the case-by-case approach. Police disregard of *Miranda* requirements is relevant to the totality of the circumstances for Due Process inquiries. See ***Mincey v. Arizona***, 437 U.S. 385 (1978) (ignoring multiple invocations of right to counsel was coercive).

2. The Court also relied on *Miranda* policy concerns to reinterpret Due Process theory. See ***Colorado v. Connelly***, 479 U.S. 157 (1986) (giving *Miranda* warnings mitigated coercion).

3. The modern Due Process test for evaluating the admissibility of a confession is that "coercive police activity is a necessary predicate to a finding of involuntariness." If a defendant's free will is "overborne" by his mental illness, his confession is voluntary in the absence of police coercion.

4. The Court still treats the defendant's individual frailties as relevant to its finding that a confession was involuntary. ***Arizona v. Fulminante***, 499 U.S. 279 (1991) (credible threat of violence violated Due Process).

5. The common factors used by courts in both traditional voluntariness as well as *Miranda* waiver cases are the defendant's:

    a. age,

    b. intelligence,

    c. education,

    d. criminal experience,

    e. mental condition,

    f. intoxication on alcohol or drugs,

    g. physical injury and coercion,

    h. threats to others,

    i. length of interrogation and number of interrogators, and

> j. other circumstances, (e.g., "false friend" technique).

V. Burden of Proof

A. Because of the coercive nature of custodial interrogation, the prosecution has the burden of proving the voluntariness of custodial statements by a preponderance of the evidence. *Jackson v. Denno*, 378 U.S. 368 (1964).

B. If an involuntary confession is erroneously admitted into evidence, the prosecution must prove to an appellate court that its admission was "harmless beyond a reasonable doubt" under *Chapman v. California*, 386 U.S. 18 (1967). *Arizona v. Fulminante*.

ILLUSTRATIVE PROBLEMS

■ PROBLEM 6.1 *MIRANDA* CUSTODY ■

Because the FBI suspected Pervis Griffith of involvement in a recent bank robbery, two FBI agents went to Griffith's home at 7:00 p.m. and were admitted by Griffith's stepfather, who owned the home. Griffith was not home, but his stepfather permitted the agents to wait for him in the living room. When they heard Griffith approach a little over an hour later, the agents moved to the hall near the front door. As soon as Griffith entered, the agents identified themselves, indicated that they were investigating a bank robbery, and said that they needed to speak with him. Griffith immediately said, "The gun wasn't loaded."

After explaining to his parents that they needed to talk in private, the agents asked Griffith to step into the dining room. Griffith's parents then went upstairs. The agents did not draw their guns, handcuff Griffith, or place him under formal arrest, but they also did not inform him that he was not under arrest or that he was free to leave without speaking to them. During the two-hour interview, Griffith twice asked to obtain cigarettes from elsewhere in the house. One of the agents escorted Griffith each time he went to get cigarettes. After Griffith implicated himself and another individual in the robbery, the agents arrested him, transported him to their office, and for the first time gave him *Miranda* warnings. How should a court rule on Griffith's motion to suppress his statements in the hallway and the dining room?

Analysis

The issue here is whether a reasonable person in Griffith's shoes would have felt that his freedom of action was curtailed to a degree associated with formal arrest. The FBI did not advise Griffith that he was free to go or to ask them to leave. They accompanied him when he twice went for cigarettes. They initiated the interview; indeed Griffith didn't even admit them to the house. The FBI dominated the scene, having taken control of the scene and having told his parents that they needed to talk to Griffith in private. Finally, Griffith was arrested after the interview. These factors outweigh the fact that the interview occurred in the familiar setting of the defendant's home. Griffith would reasonably associate the police conduct with the restraints imposed by formal arrest. Thus, he was in custody during the interview, he should have been warned at the start of the interview, and his incriminating statements should be suppressed.

■ PROBLEM 6.2 *MIRANDA* INTERROGATION ■

Police arrested the defendant for the murder of a young man and the rape and stabbing of the man's female companion. At the police station, a detective introduced himself and stated, "I just want to tell you where we stand." The detective then stated that the police had arrested the defendant's accomplice, which was true, and that the surviving victim had identified the defendant from a photograph, which was false. The defendant then said, "I can't keep this to myself any longer. I'll tell you what happened." The detective then read the defendant his *Miranda* rights, and the defendant agreed to talk without a lawyer.

What result on the defendant's subsequent motion to suppress his confession?

Analysis

Interrogation is either direct questioning or words or conduct on the part of the police that the police should know are reasonably likely to elicit an incriminating response. The latter part of the test focuses upon the perception of the defendant rather than the intent of the police, but since the police cannot be held accountable for the unforeseeable consequences of their actions, only that conduct that they should know is likely to elicit a response is interrogation.

The issue is whether the detective should have known that his words, uttered without *Miranda* warnings, were reasonably likely to elicit an incriminating response. It is important to learn whether the defendant was already upset when the officer intended to try to elicit a response. In other words, the court must decide whether the police statements were likely to encourage the defendant to make some spontaneous incriminating remark, i.e., did they call for or elicit an incriminating response.

■ PROBLEM 6.3 INVOCATION OF AND WAIVER OF *MIRANDA* RIGHTS ■

Police arrested Michael Trapp in connection with a robbery and kidnaping. At the station, Detective Gazaway gave Trapp *Miranda* warnings, and Trapp replied that he understood his rights and that he would not answer questions. Gazaway immediately terminated the discussion, but he remained in the room with Trapp tending to other work. A minute or so later, Trapp asked, "How did you find out where I would be?" Gazaway responded that he could not talk about the investigation because Trapp had originally refused to discuss the matter. Gazaway added that he could talk to Trapp only if Trapp voluntarily requested that he do so. Trapp then said he would discuss his role in the crimes as long as he did not have to implicate anyone else.

After calling another officer to join them, Gazaway recited that Trapp had both received his rights and acknowledged that he understood them, that Trapp had exercised his right to remain silent, and that only moments later Trapp had voluntarily requested to talk to Gazaway as long as he was not asked to implicate others. Trapp confirmed the accuracy of Gazaway's recitation and said he was willing to talk. The other officer then left the room, and in response to Gazaway's questions, Trapp made incriminating statements, which he now wants to suppress. Did Trapp invoke his rights, did the police scrupulously honor those rights, and did Trapp waive his rights?

Analysis

When the police initiate a second attempt at interrogation after a suspect invokes his right to silence, a fresh set of *Miranda* warnings may be necessary to conclude that the police scrupulously honored the suspect's right to cut off questioning. There is also the issue of whether Trapp initiated the conversation with the police. The question, "How did you find out where I would be?," seems to qualify. In fact, Gazaway did not take the defendant's statement as an invitation for further discussion but instead said he couldn't talk to Gazaway unless Gazaway voluntarily requested him to. This statement may suffice as an adequate substitute for any requirement that Trapp be rewarned.

There remains the question of waiver, because not only must the police scrupulously honor Trapp's rights, but also Trapp must validly waive his rights. The defendant had just been warned of his rights, and he agreed to talk only after being told, in effect, that he didn't have to. Waiver seems adequate.

■ PROBLEM 6.4 SIXTH AMENDMENT RIGHT TO COUNSEL ■

Epstein broke into the Feed and Seed Store in February and stole seven leather-studded spiked dog collars. A month later, she broke into the Pet Shop and stole a pet python snake and lamp to keep the snake warm. Entry into both shops was gained by throwing a rock through the glass front door. In April, she was arrested for the Pet Shop break-in and was arraigned the following day and remanded to the jail. In May, detective Murphy took Epstein from the jail to the detective bureau for questioning about other burglaries that had occurred in the city. At that time, Epstein had not been arrested on the Feed and Seed burglary. Before he began to question Epstein, Murphy did not know that Epstein had an attorney on the Pet Shop charge. During the interview, Epstein waived her *Miranda* rights and confessed to the Feed and Seed burglary. She was indicted and counsel was appointed on that charge.

Epstein has filed a motion to suppress the Feed and Seed confession. How should the court rule?

Analysis

The issue is whether the police can question Epstein about an offense that has not been charged but is factually related to the current charge. Police can question and seek a waiver of *Miranda* rights for an unrelated crime, because the Sixth Amendment is offense-specific. The police cannot question a suspect for a "same offense" as an already charged crime.

Epstein was already arraigned on the Pet Shop burglary, and could not be questioned without counsel present, but she could be questioned about the Feed and Seed burglary, which is a separate and distinct offense, committed at a different time and location and against a different victim. The common facet of a rock being thrown through the front door in each burglary has no legal effect.

With different victims, each burglary required proof of a fact that
the other does not. Thus, they were not the same offense, and the
police could question Epstein about the Feed and Seed burglary
without counsel present. Assuming that the warnings and the
waiver were proper, the Feed and Seed confession is admissible.

■ PROBLEM 6.5 DUE PROCESS ■

At 3:00 a.m., police detectives arrested Jose Amaya, a Spanish-
speaking, undocumented alien from El Salvador with an I.Q. of 75,
for murder. The detectives observed blood stains on his clothing.
They provided him with a blanket and took all of his clothes, and
placed him alone in a room with a bench where he slept. Nine
hours later, after he was offered food and while he still covered only
with a blanket, the detectives advised Amaya of his *Miranda* rights
in Spanish. Unable to write, Amaya placed his mark on a waiver of
rights form. In response to questioning, Amaya denied knowing
the victim. Further questions forced him to admit that the denial
was a lie, but he continued to maintain his innocence regarding the
murder. One detective then said untruthfully that two witnesses
had seen him run from the victim's truck. When Amaya denied his
guilt, the detective urged him to tell the truth. A few moments later,
he confessed.

Analysis

The Court has concluded that to have a due process problem with
a confession, there must be a causal link between coercive police
activity and the defendant's confession. The issue here is whether
the defendant's will was overborne by the police. Under the totality
of circumstances approach, the court will look at the action of the
officers in leaving the defendant for nine hours clad only in a
blanket, the defendant's background as a Spanish-speaking person,
the defendant's low I.Q., the lie about the two witnesses, and the
detective's urging the defendant to tell the truth.

It can be argued that the police took the defendant's clothes
for a valid reason, that there were no promises made to him, and

that a lie standing alone does not render the confession involuntary, i.e., his will was not overborne by it. Under the current due process test, a defendant's confession is not involuntary due to his cultural background. Amaya would have difficulty showing that coercive police conduct rather than internal compulsion induced his confession.

POINTS TO REMEMBER

- *Miranda* protections include the right to receive warnings during custodial interrogation, the right not to be interrogated without making a "voluntary, knowing and intelligent" waiver, and the right to have police cut off questioning if the rights to silence, to counsel, or to both are invoked.

- "Custody" exists during a formal arrest or when a reasonable person in the suspect's shoes would have understood the situation.

- "Interrogation" occurs when police reasonably should know that their words or conduct are likely to elicit an incriminating response.

- Police may not initiate questioning or seek a waiver from a person who has invoked the right to counsel, until the arrestee initiates a generalized discussion of the investigation with the police after such invocation.

- Police may initiate questioning about a different crime and seek a waiver from an arrestee who has invoked only the right to silence, as long as police "scrupulously honor" the invocation, provide new *Miranda* warnings, and allow some significant period of time to pass before initiating contact.

- Police do not need to warn an arrestee about the following matters:

  — The subject matter of the questioning;

  — The fact that a lawyer wishes to speak to the arrestee and provide assistance during the interrogation;

  — The fact that a prior interrogation by police may be inadmissible at trial because of a *Miranda* violation.

- If police use an undercover agent to "deliberately elicit" statements from a defendant who has been charged with a crime to which the Sixth Amendment has attached, any statements obtained are not admissible at the trial on the charged offense.

- An undercover agent does not "deliberately elicit" statements by merely listening to a charged defendant.

- Police may seek a Sixth Amendment waiver from a defendant who has been charged with a crime to which the Sixth Amendment has attached, but they may not "deliberately elicit" statements from the defendant in the absence of the waiver.

- Police may use *Miranda* warnings to notify a defendant of the Sixth Amendment right to counsel, and may obtain a *Miranda* waiver to serve as an adequate waiver of Sixth Amendment rights.

- A defendant may invoke the Sixth Amendment right to counsel by asking for the assistance of counsel. Such an invocation bars any subsequent police questioning about the charged offense but not questioning about other offenses.

- A confession is deemed to be involuntary and inadmissible according to Due Process requirements when it is procured by means of coercion, and there must be some government "overreaching" for a finding of coercion to be made.

- A "totality of the circumstances" approach is used to measure the voluntariness of a confession, and relevant variables include the police conduct, the surrounding circumstances, and the characteristics and experiences of the defendant.

- Police do not violate Due Process by obtaining the confession of a mentally ill arrestee, if they are not aware of the mental illness and if they comply with *Miranda*.

CHAPTER 7

Identification Procedures

A. INTRODUCTION

An eyewitness to a crime may be asked to testify that, prior to trial, she has identified the defendant as the perpetrator of the crime. The event at which such an identification was made is frequently called a "pretrial confrontation." In addition, a police officer who was present at the pretrial confrontation may be asked to testify at trial about the pretrial identification made by the eyewitness. Such testimony about the pretrial identification is called the "proof of the fact of an out-of-court identification." In addition, the eyewitness may be asked to identify the defendant in the presence of the jury. Such testimony is called an "in-court identification."

The dangers inherent in pretrial confrontations have been noted in *United States v. Wade*, 388 U.S. 218 (1967):

The vagaries of eyewitness identification are well-known; the annals of criminal law are rife with instances of mistaken identification. . . .

A major factor contributing to the high incidence of miscarriage of justice from mistaken identification has been the degree of suggestion inherent in the manner in which the prosecution presents the suspect to witnesses for pretrial identification. . . . Suggestion can be created intentionally or unintentionally in many subtle ways. . . .

Moreover, "[i]t is a matter of common experience that, once a witness has picked out the accused at the line-up, he is not likely to go back on his word later on, so that in practice the issue of identity may (in the absence of other relevant evidence) for all practical purposes be determined there and then, before the trial."

There are three possible and distinct challenges to an out-of-court identification. First, the identification may be challenged on the basis of the Sixth Amendment right to counsel rule requiring that defense counsel be present at the pretrial confrontation. Second, the out-of-court identification may be challenged on the basis of Fourteenth Amendment Due Process, which excludes a pretrial confrontation between the defendant and the eyewitness that is so impermissibly suggestive as to give rise to a very substantial likelihood of misidentification.

If the defendant is successful in either of these two challenges, then proof of the out-of-court identification is not admissible in the prosecution's case-in-chief. Furthermore, if there were a Sixth Amendment violation, an in-court identification by the eyewitness will not be permitted by the court unless the prosecution has proven by clear and convincing evidence that the in-court identification is not tainted by the out-of-court identification. Similarly, a Fourteenth Amendment violation which meets the Due Process test will also exclude an in-court identification, but the prosecution is not permitted to "rehabilitate" the identification.

A third possible challenge is that the identification is the fruit of an earlier illegality, such as an illegal arrest, search or confession. Similar to a Sixth Amendment violation, the in-court identification will be permitted only if intervening events served to remove the prior "taint."

B.   SIXTH AMENDMENT RIGHT TO COUNSEL

If adversary judicial criminal proceedings have already been initiated against the defendant, the defendant is entitled to have a lawyer present at any State-sponsored pretrial confrontation with an eyewitness. The reason for this rule is two-fold: (1) to enable the defense at trial to challenge the credibility of the witness' in-court identification, and (2) to eliminate unfair pretrial confrontations resulting in identifications of persons as the perpetrators of crime when, in fact, they are not. *Kirby v. Illinois*, 406 U.S. 682 (1972).

When defense counsel can show that the pretrial confrontation required the presence of defense counsel because adversary judicial criminal proceedings had begun but defense counsel had not been present, then any proof that an identification was made of the defendant at that pretrial confrontation is not admissible. *United States v. Wade*. Even if the confrontation was fairly conducted, the out-of-court identification must still be excluded. This is a *per se* exclusionary rule in that no proof of an out-of-court identification may be presented to the jury. *Gilbert v. California*, 388 U.S. 263 (1967). Specifically, neither the eyewitness who made the identification nor persons who were present when the eyewitness made the identification may testify before the jury that an out-of-court identification was made. It is possible, however, that the witness may still be able to identify the defendant in court.

The type of pretrial identification where the right to counsel applies includes any lineup, showup, walk-in or other type of identification process where the defendant is required to submit to a corporal identification. *Moore v. Illinois*, 429 U.S. 1061 (1977).

There is no right to have counsel present, however, when an eyewitness is shown a photographic display which includes a photo of the defendant, even where the photographic display is shown to the eyewitness after the defendant has been indicted. *United States v. Ash*, 413 U.S. 300 (1973).

When Do "Adversary Judicial Criminal Proceedings" Begin? In *Rothgery v. Gillespie County*, 554 U.S. 191 (2008), the Court identified a short list of events that qualify as "adversary judicial proceedings," including initial appearance, formal charge, preliminary hearing, indictment or information. The defendant's initial appearance triggers the attachment of the right to counsel because at such a proceeding the "government's commitment to prosecute

is sufficiently concrete" and the "accusation [there] prompts arraignment and restriction on the accused's liberty to facilitate the
prosecution." In *Moore v. Illinois*, 429 U.S. 1061 (1977), an identification of an unindicted and unrepresented defendant at a preliminary hearing was held to violate the defendant's Sixth Amendment right to counsel.

Waiver of Right to Counsel. The accused may waive the right
to have counsel present at a pretrial confrontation. The waiver
must be knowing, voluntary, and probably will be deemed more
effective if it is written.

Exclusion of Proof of In-court Identification. Once the court
determines that there was a Sixth Amendment violation in the
pretrial confrontation, the confrontation is excluded from
evidence. At this point, the "fruit of the poisonous tree" doctrine of
Wong Sun v. United States, 371 U.S. 471 (1963) becomes applicable to
the in-court identification. See Chapter 8.

The court will not permit the eyewitness to make even an
in-court identification unless the prosecution can demonstrate by
"clear and convincing evidence" that the in-court identification will
be based on the eyewitness' observations of the defendant at the
crime scene and not at the pretrial confrontation. *United States v.
Wade*. Essentially, the prosecution must prove the witness's identification has an independent origin. Certain factors should be
considered by the court in deciding whether to permit the eyewitnesses to make an in-court identification. These factors are the
same as those set forth in *Neil v. Biggers*, discussed below.

Role of Counsel at Lineup. While the defendant has the right
to counsel at a pretrial lineup after a formal charge, the role of
counsel is unclear. The majority opinion in *United States v. Wade*
implies that, at best, defense counsel might point out unfair aspects
of the lineup to the police, and suggest corrective measures. *Wade*
also stresses that counsel's presence puts her in a position to decide
whether it is tactically wise to bring out the details of the lineup
identification in order to cast doubt on an in-court identification.

C. DUE PROCESS

A second challenge to an out-of-court identification is based on the Due Process clause of the Fourteenth Amendment which is separate and distinct from the Sixth Amendment approach. A Due Process violation may exist even where the pretrial confrontation took place before adversary judicial criminal proceedings began, and it may also exist even though defense counsel was present at the pretrial confrontation. If the pretrial confrontation violated Due Process, then proof that the defendant was identified at the pretrial confrontation is not admissible in evidence nor may the witness identify the defendant at trial. This is a *per se* exclusionary rule.

The Fourteenth Amendment challenge arises from the decision of the Supreme Court in *Stovall v. Denno*, 388 U.S. 293 (1967). The Court held that a pretrial confrontation violates the Due Process Clause if it is "unnecessarily suggestive and conducive to irreparable mistaken identification." To decide whether there was a Due Process violation, the Supreme Court held that the "totality of the circumstances" had to be considered. Showups (in which the eyewitness is shown a single suspect) were condemned in *Stovall*. In the companion case of *United States v. Wade*, the Court stated that a suggestive physical lineup would occur when

> all in the lineup but the suspect were known to the identifying witness, [when] the other participants in a lineup were grossly dissimilar in appearance to the suspect, [when] only the suspect was required to wear distinctive clothing which the culprit allegedly wore, [when] the witness is told by the police that they have caught the culprit after which the defendant is brought before the witness alone or is viewed in jail, [when] the suspect is pointed out before or during a lineup, and [when] the participants in the lineup are asked to try on an article of clothing which fits only the suspect.

Because both showups and unfair lineup procedures seemed to constitute Due Process violations, defense counsel were sometimes able to convince trial judges to suppress out-of-court identifications on Due Process grounds. Then in 1972, the United States

Supreme Court, in its decision in *Neil v. Biggers*, 409 U.S. 188 (1972) changed the test for determining whether a pretrial confrontation violated Due Process.

In *Neil*, the Court held that even though a showup may have been suggestive, the in-court and out-of-court identifications are still admissible where there was "no substantial likelihood of misidentification." *Id.* at 201. An out-of-court identification was held not to violate Due Process if under the totality of the circumstances the identification was reliable.

Whereas the emphasis in *Stovall* was on the suggestiveness of the confrontation, *Neil* focused on the reliability of the identification itself.

> We turn, then, to the central question, whether under the "totality of the circumstances" the identification was reliable even though the confrontation procedure was suggestive. As indicated by our cases, the factors to be considered in evaluating the likelihood of misidentification include the opportunity of the witness to view the criminal at the time of the crime, the witness' degree of attention, the accuracy of the witness' prior description of the criminal, the level of certainty demonstrated by the witness at the confrontation, and the length of time between the crime and the confrontation. *Id.* at 199–200.

Manson v. Brathwaite, 432 U.S. 98 (1977) announced that the *Neil* test was to be used in determining whether a pretrial confrontation violated Due Process when the identification took place *after* the date of the *Stovall* decision.

The Due Process Relationship between Suggestiveness and Reliability. As *Stovall*, *Neil*, and *Manson* indicate, the suggestiveness of an identification procedure by itself does not require suppression of eyewitness evidence, even if the suggestiveness increases the risk of mistaken identification. Suggestiveness becomes problematic only when it is unnecessary, which in turn requires an analysis of all the reliability factors. A preliminary judicial inquiry into the reliability of an eyewitness identification is mandated *only* when the identification was procured under unnecessarily suggestive circumstances arranged by law enforcement. *Perry v. New Hampshire*, 132 S.Ct. 716 (2012).

The *Perry* Court used the *Stovall* facts to explain the application of its new test: there was no due process violation even though the defendant was the only person presented to the victim for identification in a show-up in the victim's hospital room and even though the defendant was presented wearing handcuffs, because the suggestive show-up used was necessary: the victim was the only eyewitness and it was not certain that she would survive long enough for the identification to be conducted under less suggestive conditions.

Perry also described alternative devices to test reliability, regardless of whether law enforcement has engaged in improper activity: expert testimony, "counsel at postindictment lineups, vigorous cross-examination, protective rules of evidence [FRE 403], and jury instructions on both the fallibility of eyewitness identification and the requirement that guilt be proved beyond a reasonable doubt."

There is a two-part test to determine whether trial testimony about an *out-of-court* identification violates Due Process. The first part of the test is whether the pretrial identification procedure was unnecessarily suggestive. If it was not, then proof about the out-of-court identification is admissible at trial. However, if the pretrial confrontation was unnecessarily suggestive, the second part of the test requires the trial court to assess whether that suggestiveness created a very substantial likelihood of misidentification at trial. In other words, was the suggestiveness outweighed by the reliability of the identification, based on the aforementioned five *Neil* factors, discussed *infra*? Expert eyewitness identification testimony is admissible on problems like cross-racial identification, identification after long delays or under stress, and psychological phenomena.

For an *in-court* identification by a witness at trial, if the suggestiveness of the pretrial confrontation outweighed the reliability of that identification, a trial court must ask itself whether the out-of-court identification was so unnecessarily suggestive as to create a very substantial likelihood of *irreparable* misidentification by the witness in the trial court, using the same *Neil* five factors, discussed *infra*.

Lack of State Action. One of the purposes of the Due Process approach to identifications is to deter improper police behavior so that police would fear that their actions would lead to the exclusion of identifications as unreliable. Private confrontations, therefore, do not give rise to the same considerations as police-initiated identifications. Consequently, the suggestibility of confrontations is not a legitimate issue where there is no State action involved.

Showup Identification. A "showup" is a one-on-one presentation of the suspect to the eyewitness. An identification based upon a showup is constitutionally acceptable if under the totality of circumstances it does not present a substantial likelihood of irreparable misidentification. For example, in *Stovall*, a hospital room showup of a suspect to a witness for identification was justified by the risk that the witness might not otherwise have an opportunity to make a proper identification, so long as the totality of circumstances did not suggest a substantial risk of misidentification. Even a station house showup may be upheld under the totality of the circumstances.

Photograph Identification. Photographic lineups are used when the suspect is not yet in custody. Even when a suspect is in custody, a physical identification may not be conducted because corporeal lineups are usually difficult to manage. It is sometimes difficult to find persons of the same race, age, height and weight who are willing to participate in a lineup. Furthermore, facilities to conduct a corporeal lineup are not always available. For these reasons, it is far easier for the police to conduct a photographic lineup.

Lineups with photos are of several types. The first is the single photo of a suspect which is shown to a witness. The second type of photo lineup is like a physical lineup where the police have a suspect in mind and display her photograph with several additional photos of similar-looking people. The third use of photographs is the so-called "mug book" view. Here, the police have no firm suspect in mind and show a victim a book of many mug shots with the hope that the culprit is among the photos. The most circumspect identification is where a single photo is presented. Where this occurs, courts assume suggestiveness and then inquire as to the totality of circumstances to see if the identification was otherwise reliable. *Manson v. Brathwaite*.

Physical Lineup. A physical lineup consists of presenting the defendant and several other similar-looking persons to the witness for identification. This is to be distinguished from the showup, where only the defendant is presented. In determining the validity of a lineup, the question is one of unnecessary suggestiveness. If the lineup is suggestive, then the *Neil* five-factor test must be considered in determining whether an identification is reliable despite suggestiveness in the identification procedure.

To determine the possible suggestiveness of a lineup, the courts have looked to numerous factors such as the circumstances of the lineup, matters which occur prior to the lineup, and the number of lineups. See *Foster v. California*, 394 U.S. 440 (1969).

Reliability of Identification. Where the proof shows unnecessary suggestiveness in the physical or photo lineup or in the showup, the court must then inquire from the totality of the circumstances whether the resulting identification was reliable. The courts look to numerous elements included within the five-factor *Neil* test to determine reliability.

The first reliability factor is the opportunity of the witness to view the criminal at the time of the crime. Here, the courts look to the lighting conditions, the amount of time for the view, and the degree of view by the victim.

The second factor is the witness's degree of attention. Courts consider whether the witness was a victim or casual observer as well as the training of the witness. *Manson v. Brathwaite*.

The third reliability factor is the accuracy of the witness's prior description of the criminal. Somewhat related is any discrepancy between the defendant's appearance at the time of the crime and at the time of identification.

The fourth factor is the level of certainty of the witness at the confrontation. The level can run from nonexistent to virtual certainty. It is highly relevant whether the witness has previously observed other physical or photographic displays and whether the witness has picked out someone else.

The final reliability factor is the time between the crime and confrontation. This is also a variable, but the other factors appear to be given more weight.

IDENTIFICATION PROCEDURES CHECKLIST

A. **Introduction**

    1. An eyewitness to a crime may testify that, prior to trial, she has identified the defendant as the perpetrator of the crime. In addition, a police officer who was present at a pretrial confrontation may testify at trial about the pretrial identification made by the eyewitness. The eyewitness may identify the defendant in the presence of the jury, a process known as an "in-court identification."

    2. The dangers inherent in pretrial confrontations were noted in *United States v. Wade*, 388 U.S. 218 (1967). The Court especially noted the degree of suggestion in the manner in which the pretrial confrontation occurred and the fact that a witness who makes an identification is unlikely to recant the identification.

    3. There are three possible challenges to an out-of-court identification:

        a. The Sixth Amendment right to counsel rule,

        b. The Fourteenth Amendment Due Process Clause, and

c.   That the in-court identification is the fruit of an earlier illegality, such as an illegal arrest.

B. Sixth Amendment Right to Counsel

1.   A defendant is entitled to the presence of counsel at a State-sponsored pretrial confrontation with an eyewitness, if adversary judicial criminal proceedings have already been initiated against the defendant. ***Kirby v. Illinois***, 406 U.S. 682 (1972).

2.   The nature of the exclusionary rule resulting from *Kirby* is a *per se* exclusionary rule that no proof of an out-of-court identification may be presented to the jury. ***Gilbert v. California***, 388 U.S. 263 (1967).

3.   The right to counsel applies to any lineup, showup, walk-in or other type of identification parade or process where the defendant is required to submit to a corporeal identification. ***Moore v. Illinois***, 429 U.S. 1061 (1977).

4.   There is no constitutional right for a defendant to have counsel present when an eyewitness is shown a photographic display which includes a photo of the defendant, even where the photographic display is shown to the eyewitness after the defendant has been indicted. ***United States v. Ash***, 413 U.S. 300 (1973).

5.   When the right to counsel is denied at a pretrial confrontation, the witness cannot testify at trial. The court will not permit the eyewitness to make even an in-court identification unless the prosecution can demonstrate by "clear and convincing evidence" that the in-court identification will be based on the eyewitness's observations of the defendant at the scene of the crime and not at the pretrial confrontation. ***United States v. Wade***.

6.   The role of counsel remains unclear; ***United States v. Wade*** implies that, at best, defense counsel might point out unfair aspects of the lineup to the police, and suggest corrective measures.

C. **Due Process**

1. The first part of the Due Process test is: Was the pretrial identification procedure unnecessarily suggestive? If it was not, then proof of the fact of the out-of-court identification is admissible.

2. If the pretrial confrontation was unnecessarily suggestive, the second part of the test requires the court to assess the reliability of the suggestive identification, i.e., the possibility that the witness would create a very substantial likelihood of misidentification at trial, based upon the totality of the circumstances.

3. A preliminary judicial inquiry into the reliability of an eyewitness identification is mandated *only* when the identification was procured under unnecessarily suggestive circumstances *arranged by* law enforcement. *Perry v. New Hampshire*, 132 S.Ct. 716 (2012).

4. Courts apply totality of circumstances factors on the issue of reliability, per **Neil v. Biggers**, 409 U.S. 188 (1972):

    a. The opportunity of the witness to view the criminal at the time of the crime.

    b. The witness's degree of attention (e.g., whether the witness was a victim or casual observer, as well as the training of the witness).

    c. The accuracy of the witness' prior description of the criminal.

    d. The level of certainty of the witness at the confrontation.

    e. The time between the crime and confrontation.

4. Private confrontations do not give rise to the same considerations as police-initiated identifications.

5. A "showup" is a one-on-one presentation of the suspect to the eyewitness.

6. A showup is constitutionally acceptable if, under the totality of circumstances, it does not present a substantial likelihood of irreparable misidentification.

7. Courts assume suggestiveness in photographic identifications where a single photo is presented, and then inquire as to the totality of circumstances to see if the identification was otherwise reliable. **Manson v. Brathwaite**, 432 U.S. 98 (1977).

8. Court do not assume suggestiveness in lineup identifications. The impermissible suggestiveness of the lineup must first be established. If the lineup is suggestive, then the *Neil* five-factor test must be considered in determining whether an identification is reliable despite suggestiveness in the identification procedure.

D. **Burden of Proof**

1. The prosecution appears to have the burden of proving the circumstances under which a pretrial identification was made. The court must first determine whether the pretrial identification was impermissibly suggestive and, if it was, the court must then decide whether the procedure created a substantial risk of irreparable misidentification. **Simmons v. United States**, 390 U.S. 377 (1968).

2. If the pretrial identification is suppressed, the prosecution must establish by clear and convincing evidence that any in-court identification is not tainted. **Moore v. Illinois**. Even if this is established to the satisfaction of the trial court, the defendant may still challenge the identification procedures before the jury. See **Watkins v. Sowders**, 449 U.S. 341 (1981).

ILLUSTRATIVE PROBLEMS

■ PROBLEM 7.1 RIGHT TO COUNSEL ■

Police arrested the defendant for car theft after finding him in a stolen car. At an arraignment held shortly thereafter, the judge appointed counsel to represent the defendant, continued the arraignment for two weeks, and released the defendant on bail.

During the two week interval, the arresting officer notified Detective Glen that the defendant fit the description of one of two men who had recently robbed a woman in her apartment. Glen then requested that the woman attend the defendant's arraignment on the stolen car charge.

At the defendant's next court appearance, the detective and woman sat together in the courtroom. Glen instructed the woman to observe the men who were arraigned and to tell him "when you see the fellow who did it." During a twenty-minute period, the woman observed eight men of various racial groups stand up for their arraignments. When she observed the defendant, she immediately told Glen that he was one of her assailants. After the arraignment, Glen arrested the defendant for robbery, and a grand jury subsequently indicted him for that offense.

During a suppression hearing in the robbery prosecution, Glen testified that he did not inform defendant's counsel, who was present at the theft arraignment, of the planned identification. Both Glen and the woman denied that Glen called attention to the defendant at the arraignment, and the woman testified that she did not hear the defendant's name before she identified him. What result?

Analysis

The first issue is whether the Sixth Amendment right to counsel could attach to this showup. A "criminal prosecution" had commenced on the theft charge but not on the robbery charge. As discussed in the prior chapter, Sixth Amendment rights are offense specific. No right to counsel had attached.

If the defendant did have a right to counsel for the identification procedure relating to the uncharged robbery, was that right violated? This issue is easy. Counsel cannot object to unfairness or even observe unfairness if counsel doesn't know that an identification procedure is occurring. The rationale for providing counsel should lead to the conclusion that the defendant's right to counsel was violated, if he had a right to counsel at all.

■ PROBLEM 7.2 DUE PROCESS ■

Two weeks after a bank robbery, which lasted only a matter of minutes, bank tellers informed Louie Kreplach, the only customer in the bank during the robbery, that police had arrested two suspects. Some two weeks later, an FBI agent showed Kreplach a six-picture photo display that included the defendant's picture. When Kreplach identified someone other than the defendant, the agent told him his selection was wrong. Kreplach then selected the defendant's picture.

At a subsequent suppression hearing, Kreplach identified the defendant and indicated that he based his identification upon his observations during the robbery and not upon the photo display. Kreplach testified that he had observed the robbers from a distance of twenty-five feet and that the defendant had worn a straw hat and sunglasses. On cross-examination, Kreplach said that he really could not be sure that the robber had worn sunglasses. Kreplach also testified that he selected the two pictures from the photo display because the men in those pictures had prominent noses that resembled the shorter robber's nose. On cross-examination, Kreplach admitted that he had not mentioned the prominence of the robber's nose in a description previously given the FBI, even though the description sheet contained a space expressly designated for noting unusual features. What result on the motion to suppress?

Analysis

Suggestiveness of an identification procedure by itself does not require suppression of eyewitness evidence, even if the suggestiveness increases the risk of mistaken identification. The suggestiveness becomes problematic only when it is unnecessary, and this requires an analysis of all the circumstances. Even when the suggestiveness is unnecessary, however, suppression is required only if the suggestiveness creates a very substantial risk of mistaken identification. This is the primary Due Process concern. The issue, then, is whether the procedure created a very substantial likelihood of misidentification. The factors are: opportunity to view the offender, accuracy of prior descriptions, time interval, etc.

POINTS TO REMEMBER

- Although identification procedures can provide crucial evidence, they can also be unreliable.

- The problem with identification procedures is suggestiveness, which can be created both intentionally and unintentionally, and can lead to irreparable mistaken identification.

- The Sixth Amendment right to counsel applies to lineups that occur after the commencement of adversarial proceedings.

- The right to counsel does not apply to lineups that occur prior to the commencement of adversarial proceedings.

- The right to counsel does not apply to photographic identifications.

- Even when the right to counsel does apply, counsel's role is limited. Counsel does not have the right to "direct" the lineup, but only to appear, observe, and object.

- By observing, counsel can determine whether the lineup is suggestive and decide best how to challenge a resulting identification at trial.

- Whether or not the right to counsel applies, the results of an identification procedure can be challenged on Due Process grounds.

- The presence of unnecessary suggestiveness is an important factor in determining whether an identification violates Due Process.

- An identification can result from unnecessarily suggestive procedures, but can still be reliable.

- Factors that bear on reliability include the opportunity of the witness to view the criminal at the time of the crime, the witness' degree of attention, the accuracy of the witness' prior description of the criminal, the level of certainty demonstrated by the witness at the confrontation, and the length of time between the crime and the confrontation.

CHAPTER 8

Exclusionary Rule

A. SUPPRESSION OF EVIDENCE AS AN EXCLUSIONARY REMEDY

The exclusionary rule prohibits prosecutors from using evidence obtained in violation of a defendant's Fourth, *Mapp v. Ohio*, 367 U.S. 643 (1961), Fifth, *Blackburn v. Alabama*, 361 U.S. 199 (1960) or Sixth, *United States v. Wade*, 388 U.S. 218 (1967) Amendment rights. It also prohibits the use of evidence in certain circumstances in which a defendant's rights have been violated, but the violation does not rise to the level of a constitutional infringement. See *Oregon v. Elstad*, 470 U.S. 298 (1985).

The purposes served by the exclusionary rule vary according to the nature of the right which has been infringed and the kind of evidence which has been obtained. As the rule relates to pretrial identification, it is intended to protect against unduly suggestive procedures which might otherwise impugn the integrity of the factfinding process. *Foster v. California*, 394 U.S. 440 (1969).

By contrast, in the case of an illegal arrest, search or seizure, the rule may result in the exclusion of evidence which is usually reliable, so that the integrity of the factfinding process is not at stake. In *Stone v. Powell*, 428 U.S. 465 (1976), the Court held that Fourth Amendment violations are different from Fifth or Sixth Amendment violations; illegal searches and seizures do not "impugn the integrity of the fact-finding process or challenge evidence as inherently unreliable;" exclusion of illegally seized evidence is intended to deter law enforcement officers from violating the Fourth Amendment. The rule is intended to deter police misconduct and to preserve the integrity of the judicial process. *Brown v. Illinois*, 422 U.S. 590 (1975).

In the case of statements from police interrogation, the rule operates to insure the voluntariness of the statement and to prevent the use of coercive techniques, and it thus serves to promote the integrity both of the factfinding process and of the judicial process. See *id.*

The exclusionary rule does not establish a *per se* rule of exclusion forbidding the use of all illegally obtained evidence in all situations. For example, in *United States v. Calandra*, 414 U.S. 338 (1974), the Court found that extending the exclusionary rule to grand jury proceedings would substantially impede the grand jury's role while achieving only a speculative and minimal advance in deterring police misconduct. Instead, courts balance the interest of deterrence against the societal costs of suppressing probative evidence, concluding that in certain circumstances suppression is inappropriate. See *Massachusetts v. Sheppard*, 468 U.S. 981 (1984).

1. Constitutional Origins

When the Supreme Court first adopted the exclusionary rule as a constitutional remedy, it applied to *federal* criminal trials only. *Weeks v. United States*, 232 U.S. 383 (1914). In *Mapp v. Ohio*, 367 U.S. 643 (1961), three Cleveland police officers attempted to gain entrance to Mapp's residence by claiming to have obtained information from a confidential informant. Officers forced their way into the house and searched her house from top to bottom. Police found pornographic materials in her bedroom, and she was charged with and convicted of possession and control of obscene material. The *Mapp* Court held that the same exclusionary rule recognized in *Weeks* applied in State court proceedings. The Court suppressed the evidence seized by the police and reversed Mapp's conviction.

The Court found that the exclusionary rule was a constitutional requirement. Noting that "other remedies" for police misconduct, discussed below, "have been worthless and futile," the Court ruled that "all evidence obtained by searches and seizures in violation of the Constitution is, by that same authority, inadmissible in a state court."

State courts also may apply the exclusionary rule under their own State constitutions. Moreover, any legislative body can enact statutes which contain an exclusionary rule to serve as a remedy for police (or even private) violations of whatever criminal or civil prohibitions are set out in the legislation. A statutory exclusionary rule would apply as a matter of non-constitutional, statutory law.

2. Alternatives to the Exclusionary Rule

Justice (then Judge) Cardozo criticized the exclusionary rule by noting that under the constitutional exclusionary doctrine "[t]he criminal is to go free because the constable has blundered." *People v. Defore*, 150 N.E. 585 (1926). Despite criticism, the exclusionary rule survives (although without the same strong *constitutional* grounding today as when *Mapp* was decided) because a majority of the Supreme Court continues to believe that "nothing else works" to deter police misconduct. What else is there?

Public Opinion. Reliance on public opinion to correct and remedy police misconduct has proved problematic. First, "the public" is unaware of a significant percentage of cases when police misconduct occurs. Second, because the case law involves defendants who are "guilty," there is usually little public sympathy for constitutional claims.

Criminal Prosecution. Criminal prosecution of police officers who engage in constitutional misconduct as an effective remedy is generally dismissed as impractical. Prosecutors use their discretion to decide who and when (not) to prosecute. Usually, prosecutors exercise their discretion by not prosecuting police officers whose conduct might be problematic. While an occasional criminal prosecution of police officers may deter subsequent police misconduct, their infrequency dilutes the deterrence of such prosecutions.

Disciplinary Proceedings and Review Boards. Internal police review boards suffer from the difficulty of judging and sanctioning one's own peers. External police review boards are often composed of non-law enforcement members and suffer from the perceived lack of identity with the police officers whose conduct is under scrutiny. Those boards often lack statutory or legal power to put their recommendations of discipline into effect. Practically, disciplinary proceedings and review boards do not prevent law enforcement officers from engaging in unconstitutional activity or remedy the consequences of such misconduct.

Civil Actions. Civil actions for damages against law enforcement officers for alleged constitutional rights violations are insufficient or ineffective, because: 1) recovery is unlikely, given that a police officer's "good faith" typically is a complete defense; 2) the prospect of an enforceable damage recovery is unlikely against an individual officer; and 3) recovery is available against a governmental unit only to the extent that its "policy or custom, whether made by its lawmakers or by those whose edicts or acts may fairly be said to represent official policy, inflicts the injury. . . . " *Monell v. Department of Social Services of the City of New York*, 436 U.S. 658 (1978).

B. LIMITS ON THE EXCLUSIONARY RULE'S APPLICATION

1. Private Actors

The Fourth and Fifth Amendments are inapplicable to the acts of private actors. Physical evidence seized by private individuals is admissible in criminal proceedings, even if the conduct is otherwise the same as if it were undertaken by law enforcement officers. *Burdeau v. McDowell*, 256 U.S. 465 (1921). The exclusionary rule applies to the actions of private individuals who are acting with (or as) the agents of governmental actors.

2. Non–Criminal Proceedings: Incremental Deterrence

Since the 1970s, the Supreme Court has stated that the Fourth Amendment exclusionary rule is not a constitutional requirement *per se* as was suggested in *Mapp*. Instead, the Court has said that the exclusionary rule is a required remedy to deter the future misconduct of law enforcement officials. *United States v. Calandra*, 414 U.S. 338, 347 (1974).

The exclusionary rule's deterrence aim is furthered when the exclusionary rule is applied to suppress unconstitutionally-seized evidence sought to be introduced by the government in the prosecution's case-in-chief at trial. However, if police misconduct is not deterred by applying the exclusionary rule in a particular setting, the Court has stated that the rule should not be used because the social costs of the rule's application (i.e., some criminals will go free) are so great.

Forfeiture Proceedings. Many American jurisdictions have enacted statutes that permit the government to seek the forfeiture to the government of instrumentalities used in the commission of specified criminal activity (e.g., cars, boats, or airplanes used to smuggle narcotics). Such "forfeiture proceedings" are civil rather than criminal in nature. However, the Court ruled that the exclusionary rule applies with full force to suppress unconstitutionally-seized evidence sought to be introduced in such forfeiture proceedings because of the "quasi-criminal nature" of these proceedings. *One 1958 Plymouth Sedan v. Commonwealth of Pennsylvania*, 380 U.S. 693, 701 (1965).

Grand Juries. *United States v. Calandra*, 414 U.S. 338 (1974) noted the concern about permitting the exclusionary rule to prevent grand juries from hearing about illegally obtained evidence. "Any incremental deterrent effect which might be achieved by extending the [exclusionary] rule to grand jury proceedings is uncertain at best." As a result, the exclusionary rule was held inapplicable by the Court to the use of unconstitutionally-seized evidence sought to be presented to a grand jury.

Civil Proceedings. For similar reasons, the exclusionary rule does not usually apply in civil cases. *United States v. Janis*, 428 U.S. 433 (1976). In *Janis*, the Supreme Court permitted evidence seized illegally by Los Angeles police officers to be introduced in the prosecution's case-in-chief in a federal, civil tax proceeding for back taxes brought by the Internal Revenue Service. The exclusionary rule also does not apply in (civil) deportation proceedings. *Immigration & Naturalization Service v. Lopez–Mendoza*, 468 U.S. 1032 (1984).

Third-party Involvement. Because one purpose for the exclusionary rule is to discourage official misconduct, evidence illegally obtained by private persons not acting in concert with the police is admissible. For example, in *United States v. Jacobsen*, 466 U.S. 109 (1984), the Court found no Fourth Amendment violation where employees of a private freight carrier opened a damaged package, made an examination of its contents, discovered plastic bags filled with white powder, and then called a federal agent who took a trace sample of the powder and tested it. However, evidence obtained as a result of cooperative or coercive action between police officers and private citizens is subject to the exclusionary rule. See *Abel v. United States*, 362 U.S. 217 (1960).

Because the constitutional limitation on obtaining evidence is intended to deter all public officers, unlawful evidence obtained by an agent of one governmental unit does not lose its taint merely because the evidence is handed to another governmental unit on a "silver platter." For example, in *Elkins v. United States*, 364 U.S. 206 (1960), State officers, without involvement of federal officers, conducted an unreasonable search and seizure. The Court held that the evidence obtained as result of that State search is inadmissible in defendant's federal criminal trial.

Federal Habeas Corpus. The exclusionary rule does not apply to Fourth Amendment claims raised in federal habeas corpus proceedings where the petitioner had a full and fair opportunity to litigate these issues in her prior State court proceedings. *Stone v. Powell*, 428 U.S. 465 (1976).

> There is no reason to believe, however, that the overall educative effect of the exclusionary rule would be appreciably diminished if search-and-seizure claims could not be raised in federal habeas corpus review of state convictions. . . . Even if one rationally could assume that some additional incremental deterrent effect would be presented in isolated cases, the

resulting advance of the legitimate goal of furthering Fourth Amendment rights would be outweighed by the acknowledged costs to other values vital to a rational system of criminal justice. *Id.* at 493–94.

"Ker–Frisbie Doctrine". The "body" or identity of a defendant or respondent in a criminal or civil proceeding is never itself suppressible as a fruit of an unlawful or unconstitutional arrest. *Ker v. Illinois*, 119 U.S. 436 (1886); *Frisbie v. Collins*, 342 U.S. 519 (1952).

3. Impeachment

The exclusionary rule applies only to the use of unconstitutionally-seized evidence offered at a criminal trial during the prosecution's case-in-chief. It does not apply to the same evidence sought to be introduced by the prosecution at trial to "impeach" the defendant's credibility on cross-examination. *Harris v. New York*, 401 U.S. 222 (1971); *Kansas v. Ventris*, 556 U.S. 586 (2009). This "impeachment exception" was adopted because the extension of the exclusionary rule to this sort of impeachment would not create any incremental deterrence of law enforcement officers.

Courts permit the prosecution to use most illegally obtained evidence to impeach a defendant's direct testimony, *Oregon v. Hass*, 420 U.S. 714 (1975), or to impeach statements elicited on cross-examination when cross is "reasonably suggested" by the defendant's direct testimony. *United States v. Havens*, 446 U.S. 620 (1980). In *Havens*, the defendant testified at trial that he did not own an incriminating item of clothing, a T-shirt. The Supreme Court ruled that this testimony by the defendant was impeached constitutionally by the prosecution when, in response to this statement, it introduced into evidence the T-shirt to which the statements pertained, even though the T-shirt had been seized unconstitutionally by the government.

A defendant's direct or cross-examination testimony can be impeached with illegally obtained evidence bearing *directly* on the current charge (e.g., a confession admitting to the charged offense). Before a defendant can be impeached with an illegally obtained confession, the prosecution must show that the confession was given voluntarily, i.e., not in violation of Due Process. *Mincey v. Arizona*, 437 U.S. 385 (1978). The impeachment rules apply to confessions regardless of whether the police acted negligently or intentionally in eliciting the statement from the defendant.

The impeachment exception to the exclusionary rule applies only to impeachment of the defendant's testimony by the government, not to the attempted impeachment of other defense witnesses with unconstitutionally-seized evidence. *James v. Illinois*, 493 U.S. 307 (1990). Extension of the impeachment exception to all defense witnesses would compromise the deterrent effect of the exclusionary rule.

A defendant's post-arrest silence, after receiving her *Miranda* warnings, cannot be used as substantive evidence, *Wainwright v. Greenfield*, 474 U.S. 284 (1986), or for impeachment at trial, *Doyle v. Ohio*, 426 U.S. 610 (1976). When the defense successfully objects to a prosecutor's question as to why the defendant failed to reveal an exculpatory story earlier and the judge instructs the jury to ignore the question, no *Doyle* violation occurs. *Greer v. Miller*, 483 U.S. 756 (1987).

However, a reference to post-arrest silence for impeachment purposes is reversible error when it is deliberately used to impeach an explanation subsequently offered at trial or where there is a similar reason to believe that a defendant has been prejudiced by reference to the exercise of his or her constitutional right to remain silent (e.g., where the prosecutor focuses on defendant's silence in a way that is linked to defendant's testimony). This prohibition on the use of the defendant's prior silence does not apply to: (1) cross-examination that merely inquires into prior inconsistent statements, *Anderson v. Charles*, 447 U.S. 404 (1980); (2) pre-arrest silence, *Jenkins v. Anderson*, 447 U.S. 231 (1980); and (3) post-arrest silence without *Miranda* warnings, *Fletcher v. Weir*, 455 U.S. 603 (1982).

4. Good–Faith Exception

In 1984, the Supreme Court adopted a significant exception to the exclusionary rule, holding that it does not apply where a law enforcement officer has acted in reasonable "good faith" on the basis of an unconstitutional search warrant. *United States v. Leon*, 468 U.S. 897 (1984). The Court adopted this exception because police officers acting in good faith on the basis of what reasonably appears to them (even erroneously) to be a valid and lawful search warrant would not ordinarily be deterred by application of the rule.

The "good-faith exception" to the exclusionary rule is an objective test, i.e., the police officer's reliance on the otherwise invalid search warrant must be reasonable: "whether a reasonably well trained officer would have known that the search was illegal despite the magistrate's authorization." *Id.* at 922 n.23.

The good-faith exception is always inapplicable in four situations, where:

> the magistrate or judge in issuing a warrant was misled by information in an affidavit that the affiant knew was false or would have known was false except for his reckless disregard of the truth, . . . where the issuing magistrate wholly abandoned his judicial role, . . . an officer . . . rel[ied] on a warrant based on an affidavit "so lacking in indicia of probable cause as to render official belief in its existence entirely unreasonable"; . . . [and] depending on the circumstances of the particular case, a warrant [was] so facially deficient—i.e., in failing to particularize the place to be searched or the things to be seized—that the executing officers cannot reasonably presume it to be valid.

Id. at 923.

The good-faith exception to the exclusionary rule was adopted as a matter of *federal* constitutional law. A number of State courts, disagreeing with the Supreme Court's deterrence analysis, have concluded that the good-faith exception does not exist under their own State constitutions. The dichotomy thereby created is that, in some States, the unconstitutional actions of a federal law enforcement agent would be subject to application of the good-faith exception to the exclusionary rule, but the unconstitutional actions of a State or city police officer would not be.

The good-faith exception adopted in *Leon* applies only to searches pursuant to defective *search warrants*; not *warrantless* searches by law enforcement officers. The Supreme Court has extended the good-faith exception to the exclusionary rule, however, to otherwise unconstitutional actions by law enforcement officers based upon: (1) a computerized police record erroneously indicating the existence of an outstanding arrest warrant, *Arizona v. Evans*, 514 U.S. 1 (1995); (2) objectively-reasonable reliance upon a statute subsequently found to be unconstitutional. *Illinois v. Krull*, 480 U.S. 340 (1987); or (3) an officer's reliance on negligent recordkeeping by other officers leading to an illegal search. *Herring v. United States*, 555 U.S. 135 (2009). The extent to which the exclusionary rule is justified by . . . deterrence principles varies with the probability of the law enforcement conduct.

In *Groh v. Ramirez*, 540 U.S. 551 (2004), the Court distinguished *Leon* and limited the Court's application of the good faith exception in the context of a civil rights lawsuit.

5. "Knock and Announce" Violations

In *Hudson v. Michigan*, 547 U.S. 586 (2006), the Court refused to apply the exclusionary evidence rule in the context of a violation of the "knock and announce" rule. Although the police searched Hudson's house pursuant to a warrant, they waited only three to five seconds after knocking before entering. The Court held that the wait was insufficient and the question was whether the fruits of the search should be suppressed because of the premature entry. The Court answered that question in the negative, applying the cost-benefit test and noting that the exclusionary rule should not be indiscriminately applied, but rather should be reserved for situations "where its remedial objectives are thought most efficaciously served," i.e., "where its deterrence benefits outweigh its substantial social costs." Justice Scalia wrote that the knock-and-announce rule was meant to prevent violence, property damage, and impositions on privacy, *not* to prevent police from conducting a search for which they have a valid warrant.

C. STANDING

1. Constitutional Limitation

A criminal defendant must have "standing" to raise the issue of unconstitutional law enforcement conduct. Standing exists only where the defendant seeks to remedy a violation of her own personal constitutional rights, not the rights of another person. *Alderman v. United States*, 394 U.S. 165 (1969). For example, if the police arrest *A* illegally and then interrogate *A* without giving her *Miranda* warnings, any statement that *A* makes as a result of that unconstitutional conduct (arrest and custodial interrogation) could be suppressed by *A* in a criminal proceeding brought against her. But the same statement could *not* be challenged by *B*, even if the statement directly implicates him in the same (or different) criminal conduct (e.g., *A* said "*B* and I killed *C*."). *B* lacks standing because the unconstitutional conduct (illegal arrest, failure to give *Miranda* warnings) violated only *A's* constitutional rights, not *B's* constitutional rights.

Some applications of the standing rules are self-evident. For example, only the person identified can challenge her identification. Only the person who made an incriminating statement can challenge the admissibility of her statement. Only the person seized can challenge her arrest or stop, and only the person searched can challenge the search of her person.

Personal constitutional rights are violated where the constitutional harm is done to that individual personally, at a place (e.g., her home) or to some thing (e.g., her car or backpack) where and when she possessed a "reasonable expectation of privacy" (sometimes referred to as a "legitimate expectation of privacy"). *Rakas v. Illinois*, 439 U.S. 128 (1978). Therefore, a defendant does not have standing to object simply because evidence has been seized unconstitutionally from her co-defendant or co-conspirator. Standing doctrine (which is a part of substantive constitutional law) cannot be ignored on the basis of the court's inherent, non-constitutional "supervisory powers" over law enforcement. *United States v. Payner*, 447 U.S. 727 (1980).

An individual's "reasonable expectation of privacy" is the same concept used to define when police conduct is subject to Fourth Amendment requirements. However, unlike Fourth Amendment standing, which is about whether there is *a* reasonable expectation of privacy, here standing is about whether *this specific defendant* complaining about police conduct has a reasonable expectation of privacy to challenge the evidence obtained by the police conduct. "A burglar plying his trade in a summer cabin during the off season may have a thoroughly justified subjective expectation of privacy, but it is not one which the law recognizes as 'legitimate.' His presence, . . . is 'wrongful'; his expectation is not one that society is prepared to recognize as 'reasonable.' " *Rakas v. Illinois*, 439 U.S. at 143 n.12, *quoting Jones v. United States*, 362 U.S. 257 (1960), and *Katz v. United States*, 389 U.S. 347 (1967).

Rakas concerned whether a passenger in a motor vehicle has standing to challenge a search of the vehicle in which she is riding. In standing cases, it is important to isolate which police act is objectionable. If the passengers in *Rakas* had challenged the *stop* of the car in which they were riding or had challenged the *seizure* of their persons, they would probably have had standing to challenge the evidence seized as a fruit of the violation of their personal rights.

At one extreme of the standing spectrum, a hitchhiker just picked up by the driver would not have standing to challenge a later search of the car, although she would argue that her recent arrival in the vehicle negates her guilt on the substantive charge. At the other end of the standing spectrum, the owner of the vehicle would have standing to challenge a search of her vehicle, even if she was a passenger in the vehicle or absent from the vehicle at the time of the search. For any vehicle passenger, the reasonableness of her expectation of privacy would depend on such factors as the regularity of her presence in the vehicle, her ownership of the vehicle, and her relationship to the vehicle owner.

An individual does not have standing to complain about the constitutionality of the search of another person's container (containing his own drugs). *Rawlings v. Kentucky*, 448 U.S. 98 (1980). An individual also lacks standing when a police officer illegally peeps through a gap in a closed window blind when the individual's presence in that apartment was strictly as part of a commercial transaction, not as a social guest or invitee. *Minnesota v. Carter*, 525 U.S. 83 (1998). An individual does have standing to challenge the constitutionality of a search of an apartment where he was present as an "overnight guest." *Minnesota v. Olson*, 495 U.S. 91 (1990).

How does a defendant sustain the burden of proving that her Fourth Amendment rights have been violated? Factors to be considered include: (1) property ownership, (2) whether the defendant has a possessory interest in the thing seized, (3) whether the defendant has a possessory interest in the place searched, (4) whether the defendant has the right to exclude others from that place, (5) whether the defendant has exhibited a subjective expectation that the place would remain free from governmental invasion, and (6) whether the defendant took normal precautions to maintain privacy.

2. Automatic Standing

Some states have retained an automatic standing rule under their own State constitutions. Prior to *Rakas*, *Jones v. United States*, 362 U.S. 257 (1960) adopted an "automatic standing" rule for defendants charged with possessory crimes (e.g. possession of narcotics). However, the automatic standing rule was overruled by the Supreme Court as a matter of federal constitutional law, because the testimony of a defendant about her relationship to evidence sought to be suppressed in a suppression hearing cannot be used against her at trial on the issue of her substantive guilt. *Simmons v. United States*, 390 U.S. 377 (1968).

D. DERIVATIVE EVIDENCE: THE "FRUIT OF THE POISONOUS TREE" DOCTRINE

Evidence derived from law enforcement's unconstitutional activity is inadmissible in criminal proceedings not only when it is obtained as a direct result of that activity, but also when it has been derived only as an *indirect* result of such a constitutional breach. This rule is formally referred to as the "derivative evidence rule," but more commonly it is called "the fruit of the poisonous tree" doctrine [FOPT]. *Nardone v. United States*, 308 U.S. 338 (1939). For example, in *Wong Sun v. United States*, 371 U.S. 471 (1963), where police illegally entered the defendant's home, a statement made by the defendant immediately following the illegal entry and drugs discovered based on the information in the defendant's statement were inadmissible against the defendant.

FOPT is an alternative method for challenging the admissibility of evidence. Assume that the defendant was arrested and the police subsequently seized contraband from the defendant's briefcase. Typically, the defendant would move directly to suppress the admissibility of the contraband from her briefcase. FOPT doctrine enables the defendant also to challenge the admissibility of the contraband by attacking the legality of the arrest, even if the search of the briefcase was legal.

In order for a defendant to invoke the FOPT doctrine, she must demonstrate that: (1) she has standing to challenge the original violation, i.e., the tree, (2) the original police activity violated her rights, and (3) the evidence sought to be admitted against her, i.e., the fruit, was obtained as a result of the original violation (even if the fruit would be admissible in the absence of the FOPT doctrine). FOPT analysis specifically addresses the last issue. If the answer for any of the issues is in the negative, the FOPT analysis fails, and the defendant would have to rely on the direct challenge to the search yielding the contraband in order to suppress the evidence. The burden of proving that the evidence is not the FOPT is on the prosecution.

The doctrine may be especially useful for defendants who lack standing to challenge the alleged fruit of the original violation. For example, if a confession was obtained from codefendant *A* in reaction to the illegal arrest of codefendant *B*, codefendant *B* cannot directly attack the admissibility of *A*'s confession because *B* lacks standing. However, under the FOPT doctrine, *B* can prevent the admission of *A*'s confession if *B* has standing to challenge *B*'s own illegal arrest, which violated *B*'s rights, and if *B* can show a direct link between *B*'s illegal arrest and *A*'s confession.

A court will, however, admit the fruit of the poisonous tree if the prosecutor establishes that: (1) the evidence was obtained from a source independent of the primary illegality, (2) the evidence inevitably would have been discovered in the course of the investigation, or (3) the connection between the challenged evidence and the illegal conduct is so attenuated that it dissipates the taint of the illegal action.

1. Constitutional Test

The FOPT doctrine applies to both physical and testimonial evidence. *Wong Sun v. United States.* The *Wong Sun* Court made clear that the FOPT doctrine is *not* applied by using a mechanistic "but for" type of causation test (e.g., "but for" the police officer's unconstitutional activity, the government would never have discovered the hidden marijuana). Some evidence that would satisfy a "but for" test will nonetheless be deemed admissible where it was either not acquired "by exploitation" of the officers' unconstitutional activity, and/or because it was obtained "by means sufficiently distinguishable" from that unconstitutional activity to warrant such admission.

In *United States v. Patane*, 542 U.S. 630 (2004), the Court dealt with the question of whether a failure to give a suspect *Miranda* warnings necessitated suppression of physical evidence (e.g., a gun) located as a result of the suspect's unwarned but voluntary statements. A plurality of the Court refused to suppress the gun, noting that the *Miranda* rule protects against violations of the Self–Incrimination Clause, and that this clause is not implicated by the introduction at trial of physical evidence resulting from voluntary statements. Justice Kennedy, joined by Justice O'Connor, concurred, arguing that the admission of "nontestimonial physical fruits (the gun in this case) [does] not run the risk of admitting into trial an accused's coerced incriminating statements against himself." In other words, the *Patane* Court questioned the application of the FOPT analysis when the fruit is physical evidence that was located as a result of a voluntary statement.

2. Independent Source

The essence of the exclusionary rule is not merely that illegally seized evidence not be used in court, but that the prosecution should not be permitted to use such evidence at all. However, when police obtain knowledge of the same facts through an independent source, the prosecution is not barred from attempting to prove such facts. *Silverthorne Lumber Co. v. United States*, 251 U.S. 385 (1920). In other words, the fruit of the illegality was in fact located by means unrelated to the illegal source.

In *Murray v. United States*, 487 U.S. 533 (1988), the Court offered the rationale for the independent source exception to the FOPT analysis. When challenged evidence has an independent source, application of the exclusionary rule would place the police in a worse position than they would have been in the absence of any violation. If no violation had occurred, the evidence would have been admitted due to the operation of the independent legal source.

Identification evidence is a recognized context for the operation of the independent source exception. For example, if a trial judge has ruled that the police conducted an unconstitutional out-of-court identification procedure, the prosecutor still has the opportunity to show that the victim or witness can make an in-court identification that is based on what he saw at the time of the crime rather than what he saw at the improper out-of-court identification procedure. In other words, the in-court identification has a source independent of the improper out-of-court identification.

3. Inevitable Discovery

The inevitable discovery exception is a "hypothesized independent source" exception to the FOPT rule, i.e., evidence seized by unconstitutional law enforcement activity is nonetheless admissible into evidence (again, as another exception to the FOPT doctrine) where the government can prove by a preponderance of the evidence that it would have discovered this same evidence anyway or "inevitably," absent the constitutional violation. In other words, the fruit of the illegality would have been located by means unrelated to the illegality.

The Supreme Court has formally endorsed the inevitable discovery exception to the fruit of the poisonous tree doctrine. In *Nix v. Williams*, 467 U.S. 431 (1984), although the defendant's illegally obtained confession led to expedited discovery of the murder victim, because the prosecution proved that a search party was approaching the actual location of body and would have found it even if the defendant had not confessed, evidence pertaining to the discovery and condition of the victim was properly admitted. If "the prosecution can establish by a preponderance of the evidence that the information ultimately or inevitably would have been discovered by lawful means . . . then the deterrence rationale has so little basis that the evidence should be received."

4.   Attenuation

Evidence that would not have been discovered but for police misconduct may be admissible if it is sufficiently attenuated from the illegal action. In *Wong Sun v. United States*, although the defendant was initially arrested without probable cause, since he had been released for several days after the arrest and then returned voluntarily to make a statement, the statement was admissible despite the initial illegal arrest because "the connection between the arrest and the statement had become so attenuated as to dissipate the taint."

Like the inevitable discovery exception, the rationale for the attenuation exception is that an attenuated connection between the illegal activity and evidence obtained reduces the deterrent value of the exclusionary rule. Thus, the cost of excluding the evidence outweighs the benefit of deterrence. Yes, the illegality has in some manner resulted in procurement of the evidence, but the improper police activity played a *de minimis* role. The facts of each case must be examined.

The Court has noted that relevant attenuation criteria include the temporal proximity of "tree" and the "fruit," the presence of intervening circumstances, and the purpose and flagrancy of police misconduct. *Brown v. Illinois*, 422 U.S. 590 (1975). The defendant in *Brown* made a statement less than two hours after his illegal arrest. On the other hand, a statement obtained at the station house following an unlawful entry to arrest was admissible because the statement was not an exploitation of the illegal entry. *New York v. Harris*, 495 U.S. 14 (1990).

In *United States v. Ceccolini*, 435 U.S. 268 (1978), the Supreme Court held that the connection between an illegal search and live witness testimony that was the fruit of that search was sufficiently attenuated to allow admission of the testimony. The witness had freely decided to testify and a long time had elapsed between the illegal search and the witness's testimony. Excluding live witness testimony is so costly to the prosecution that only a close connection between the testimony and the illegal conduct justifies exclusion.

In another case, the Court applied the attenuation doctrine to determine the admissibility of statements made by a defendant during an illegal arrest and detention. In *Dunaway v. New York*, 442 U.S. 200 (1979), police seized, detained, and interrogated the defendant without probable cause. During the interrogation, the defendant made incriminating statements; the Court held that the connection between the unconstitutional police conduct and the incriminating statements was not sufficiently attenuated to permit use of the statements against the defendant at trial.

When the Court examined a case involving consecutive confessions, the first unwarned and the second warned, it held that a technical *Miranda* violation of failing to warn a suspect does not poison the derivative statement. *Oregon v. Elstad*, 470 U.S. 298 (1985). Despite the Court's refusal to discuss attenuation explicitly, it still found the second confession adequately attenuated from the original violation, i.e., the unwarned confession.

In *Missouri v. Seibert*, 542 U.S. 600 (2004), the Court excluded a statement when the police deliberately violated *Miranda* in hopes that they could obtain a later, "Mirandized" confession. The Court criticized the police approach of rendering the "warnings ineffective by waiting for a particularly opportune time to give them, after the suspect has already confessed." On the other hand, in *United States v. Patane*, 542 U.S. 630 (2004), the police deliberately violated *Miranda* in the hope of obtaining statements that would lead them to physical evidence. Although there was substantial evidence that the *Miranda* violation was designed to facilitate discovery of the evidence, the Court applied *Elstad* and held that the physical evidence acquired from the *Miranda* violation was admissible. The Supreme Court held that "[a]ttenuation also occurs when, even given a direct causal connection, the interest protected by the constitutional guarantee that has been violated would not be served by suppression of the evidence obtained." *Hudson v. Michigan.*

E. HARMLESS ERROR

The "Constitution entitles a criminal defendant to a fair trial, not a perfect one." *Delaware v. Van Arsdall*, 475 U.S. 673 (1986).

1. Non–Constitutional Errors

Where an appellate court finds non-constitutional trial errors, the Court has held that

> [i]f, when all is said and done, the conviction is sure that the error did not influence the jury, or had but very slight effect, the verdict and the judgment should stand. But if one cannot say, with fair assurance, after pondering all that happened without stripping the erroneous action from the whole, that the judgment was not substantially swayed by the error, it is impossible to conclude that substantial rights were not affected. The inquiry cannot be merely whether there was enough to support the result, apart from the phase affected by the error. It is rather, even so, whether the error itself had substantial influence. If so, or if one is left in grave doubt, the conviction cannot stand.

Kotteakos v. United States, 328 U.S. 750 (1946).

2. Constitutional Trial Errors

When an appellate court determines that a defendant's constitutional rights were violated at trial (or that the trial court erroneously found a constitutional violation not to have existed), the "harmless error" rule requires the defendant's conviction not be reversed automatically if the error was "harmless." Unlike non-constitutional error, the Supreme Court has held that "before a federal constitutional error can be held harmless, the court must be able to declare a belief that it was harmless beyond a reasonable doubt." *Chapman v. California*, 386 U.S. 18 (1967).

3. Constitutional Structural Defects

Some constitutional errors are so fundamental to the inherent reliability and fairness of a criminal trial that they involve "structural defects" in the criminal justice system. These errors are not subject to the ordinary *Chapman* harmless error analysis.

> The admission of an involuntary confession—a classic "trial error"—is markedly different from . . . constitutional violations . . . not . . . subject to harmless-error analysis. One of those violations [is] the total deprivation of the right to counsel at trial. [Another is trial with a trial] judge who [is] not impartial. These are structural defects in the constitution of the trial mechanism, which defy analysis by "harmless-error" standards. The entire conduct of the trial from beginning to end is obviously affected by the absence of counsel for a criminal defendant, just as it is by the presence on the bench of a judge who is not impartial. Since our decision in *Chapman,* other cases have added to the category of constitutional errors which are not subject to harmless error the following: unlawful exclusion of members of the defendant's race from a grand jury; the right to self-representation at trial; and the right to public trial. Each of these constitutional deprivations is a similar structural defect affecting the framework within which the trial proceeds, rather than simply an error in the trial process itself.

Arizona v. Fulminante, 499 U.S. 279 (1991). Since *Fulminante*, the Court has added denial of trial by an impartial fact finder and failure to disclose exculpatory evidence to the list of structural errors not subject to harmless error analysis. *United States v. Gonzalez–Lopez*, 548 U.S. 140 (2006); *Kyles v. Whitley*, 514 U.S. 419 (1995). On the other hand, in *Hedgpeth v. Pulido*, 555 U.S. 57 (2008), a conviction arising from a general verdict following jury instructions based on multiple theories of guilt (one of which is invalid) was held not to be a structural error, but instead was subject to harmless error review.

4. Federal Habeas Corpus Proceedings

The *Kotteakos* standard for assessing the existence of harmless error when non-constitutional errors are alleged also applies to claims of constitutional error in federal habeas corpus proceedings. *Brecht v. Abrahamson*, 507 U.S. 619 (1993). A federal habeas court applies the *Kotteakos* standard when reviewing a constitutional error in a state conviction, regardless of whether the state courts recognized the error or applied the more deferential "harmless beyond a reasonable doubt" standard from *Chapman*. *Fry v. Pliler*, 551 U.S. 112 (2007). The *Kotteakos* standard does not, however, apply to structural defects. *California v. Roy*, 519 U.S. 2 (1996).

EXCLUSIONARY RULE CHECKLIST

I. Suppression of Evidence as an Exclusionary Remedy

A. The exclusionary rule is a constitutional remedy that precludes the prosecution in a criminal trial from introducing evidence in its case-in-chief seized unconstitutionally by government agents.

   1. The exclusionary rule must be triggered by the defendant's successful argument of a pretrial motion to suppress.

   2. The purpose of the exclusionary rule is to deter the government from engaging in unconstitutional activity.

B. **Constitutional Origins of Exclusionary Rule**. The exclusionary rule as a federal constitutional remedy applies in both federal and State criminal cases. State courts also apply the exclusionary rule under their own State constitutions.

C. **Alternatives to the Exclusionary Rule** are not workable, including the wrath of public opinion, criminal prosecutions of offending officers, disciplinary proceedings and review boards for reviewing the actions of offending officials, and civil damage actions.

II. Limits on the Exclusionary Rule's Application

A. **Private Actors**. The exclusionary rule does not apply when physical evidence is seized by private individuals acting alone. The evidence is admissible in criminal proceedings, even if the conduct is otherwise the same as if it were undertaken by law enforcement officers.

B. **Non-criminal Proceedings: Incremental Deterrence**. Since the 1970s, courts have viewed the exclusionary rule as a required remedy to deter the future misconduct of law enforcement officials. If police misconduct is not deterred by applying the exclusionary rule, the rule sometimes is not used because of the social costs of its application (i.e., some criminals will go free).

   1. **Forfeiture Proceedings**. The exclusionary rule applies to suppress unconstitutionally-seized evidence sought to be introduced in forfeiture proceedings because of the "quasi-criminal nature" of these proceedings.

   2. **Grand Juries**. The exclusionary rule is inapplicable by the Court to the use of unconstitutionally-seized evidence sought to be presented to a grand jury.

   3. **Civil Proceedings**. The exclusionary rule does not apply ordinarily to permit the suppression of unconstitutionally-seized evidence in civil proceedings.

   4. **Different Sovereigns**. The Supreme Court has rejected the so-called "silver platter doctrine" which would permit agents of one sovereign (e.g., the State) to turn unconstitutionally-seized evidence over to agents of a different sovereign (e.g., the federal government) "on a silver platter."

   5. **Federal Habeas Corpus**. The exclusionary rule does not apply to Fourth Amendment claims raised in federal habeas corpus proceedings where the petitioner had a full and fair opportunity to litigate these issues in her prior State court proceedings. *Stone v. Powell*, 428 U.S. 465 (1976).

6. **"Ker–Frisbie Doctrine."** The identity of a defendant or respondent in a criminal or civil proceeding is never itself suppressible as a fruit of an unlawful or unconstitutional arrest.

C. Impeachment

1. The exclusionary rule does not apply to evidence introduced by the prosecution at trial to "impeach" the defendant's credibility on cross-examination, because applying the exclusionary rule to this sort of impeachment does not create any incremental deterrence of law enforcement officers.

   a. A defendant's direct or cross-examination testimony can be impeached with illegally obtained evidence bearing directly on the current charge.

   b. Before a defendant can be impeached with an illegally obtained confession, the prosecution must show that the confession was given voluntarily, i.e., not in violation of Due Process.

2. The impeachment exception applies to physical evidence.

3. The impeachment exception applies only to impeachment of the defendant's testimony, not to the testimony of any other witness.

4. A defendant's post-arrest, post-*Miranda* silence cannot be used for purposes of impeachment.

5. A defendant's pre-arrest silence or a defendant's post-arrest, pre-*Miranda* silence can be used by the prosecution to impeach the defendant.

D. Good–Faith Exception

1. There is a good-faith exception to the exclusionary rule that applies where a law enforcement officer has acted in reasonable "good faith" on the basis of an unconstitutional search warrant.

2. The "good-faith exception" to the exclusionary rule is an objective test, i.e., the police officer's reliance on the otherwise invalid search warrant must be reasonable.

3. **Exceptions to the Good–Faith Exception**. There are four exceptions to the good-faith exclusionary rule.

    a. Where the judge issuing a warrant was misled by information in an affidavit that the affiant knew was false or would have known was false except for his reckless disregard of the truth.

    b. Where the issuing magistrate wholly abandoned his judicial role.

    c. Where an officer relied on a warrant based on an affidavit "so lacking in indicia of probable cause as to render official belief in its existence entirely unreasonable."

    d. Depending on the circumstances of the particular case, where a warrant was so facially deficient, i.e., in failing to particularize the place to be searched or the things to be seized, that the executing officers cannot reasonably presume it to be valid.

    e. A number of State courts, disagreeing with the Supreme Court's deterrence analysis, have concluded that the good-faith exception does not exist under their own State constitutions.

4. The good-faith exception is not applicable to all searches and applies only to searches pursuant to defective search warrants, not warrantless searches.

E. **Knock-and-Announce Violations**. The exclusionary evidence rule is inapplicable to a violation of the "knock and announce" rule, because the deterrence benefits of excluding the evidence are outweighed by its social costs.

III. Standing

A. A criminal defendant must have "standing" to raise the issue of unconstitutional law enforcement conduct.

1. Standing exists where the defendant seeks to remedy a violation of her own personal constitutional rights, not the rights of another person.

2. Personal constitutional rights are violated where the constitutional harm is done to that individual personally, at a place (e.g., her home) or to some thing (e.g., her car or backpack) where and when she possessed a "reasonable expectation of privacy" (sometimes referred to as a "legitimate expectation of privacy").

B. Fourth Amendment standing generally relates to whether there is *a* reasonable expectation of privacy, while here standing is about whether *this specific defendant* complaining about police conduct has a reasonable expectation of privacy to challenge the evidence obtained by the police conduct.

1. A hitchhiker just picked up by a driver would not have standing to challenge a later search of the car.

2. The owner of the vehicle would have standing to challenge a search of her vehicle, even if she was a passenger at the time of the search.

3. For any vehicle passenger, her standing to challenge a vehicle search would depend on such factors as the regularity of her presence in the vehicle, her ownership of the vehicle, and her relationship to the vehicle owner.

4. An individual has standing to challenge the constitutionality of a search of a place where he was present as an "overnight guest," but not when the defendant's presence was for commercial reasons.

IV. Derivative Evidence: The "Fruit of the Poisonous Tree" Doctrine [FOPT]

A. The fruit of the poisonous tree rule: evidence derived from law enforcement's unconstitutional activity is inadmissible in criminal proceedings not only when it is obtained as a direct result of that activity, but also when it has been derived as an *indirect* result of such a constitutional breach.

B. There are three parts to the FOPT-related analysis when an allegedly illegal arrest led to a search.

1. Does the defendant have standing to challenge the source of the illegality, i.e., the arrest?

2. Was the source illegal, i.e., was the arrest illegal?

3. Is the evidence obtained during a search the fruit of the illegal arrest? FOPT analysis specifically addresses this question.

4. If the answer to any of the three questions is in the negative, the FOPT analysis fails, and the defendant would have to rely on the direct challenge to the contraband from the search to suppress the evidence.

C. Generally, the FOPT doctrine applies to both physical and testimonial evidence.

1. The following test is used to determine its application: "whether, granting establishment of the primary illegality, the evidence to which instant objection is made has been come at by exploitation of that illegality or instead by means sufficiently distinguishable to be purged of the primary taint."

2. In *United States v. Patane*, 542 U.S. 630 (2004), a plurality of the Court refused to suppress the gun located as a result of a *Miranda* violation, noting that the *Miranda* rule protects against violations of the Self–Incrimination Clause, and that this clause is not implicated by the introduction at trial of physical evidence resulting from voluntary statements.

D. **Independent Source**. The independent source exception applies to the FOPT doctrine when law enforcement officers possess an "independent source" for the information used to acquire evidence that was otherwise obtained unconstitutionally. In other words, the fruit of the illegality was in fact located by means unrelated to the illegal source.

E. **Inevitable Discovery**. The inevitable discovery exception applies to the FOPT doctrine as a "hypothesized independent source" exception to the FOPT rule.

1. The government can prove by a preponderance of the evidence that it would have discovered this same evidence anyway or "inevitably," absent the constitutional violation.

2. In other words, the fruit of the illegality would have been located by means unrelated to the illegality.

F. **Attenuation**. Because the FOPT doctrine is not a pure "but for" causation test, the relationship between unconstitutional police activity and evidence seized as an indirect result of that activity may be so "attenuated" that the FOPT doctrine does not apply. The relevant factors are the temporal proximity of the source (tree) and the fruit, the presence of intervening circumstances, and, particularly, the purpose and flagrancy of the official misconduct.

V. Harmless Error

A. **Non–Constitutional Errors**. If the error did not influence the jury, or had but very slight effect, the verdict and the judgment should stand.

B. **Constitutional Trial Errors**. When an appellate court determines that a defendant's constitutional rights were violated at trial (or that the trial court erroneously found a constitutional violation not to have existed), the "harmless error" rule is that the defendant's conviction will not be reversed automatically if the error was "harmless." The appellate court must be able to declare a belief that it was harmless beyond a reasonable doubt.

C. **Constitutional Structural Defects**. Some constitutional errors are so fundamental to the inherent reliability and fairness of a criminal trial that they are deemed to involve "structural defects" in the criminal justice system and are not subject to the ordinary harmless error analysis. Examples of structural defects include either the total deprivation of the right to counsel at trial or a trial judge who is not impartial.

D. **Federal Habeas Corpus Proceedings**. The standard for assessing the existence of harmless error when non-constitutional errors are alleged applies to claims of constitutional error in federal habeas corpus proceedings.

ILLUSTRATIVE PROBLEMS

■ PROBLEM 8.1 IMPEACHMENT ■

The defendant was tried for kidnaping. On direct examination of a police officer, defense counsel elicited that the defendant had a drug problem, that he was confused about the events when he was interrogated after his arrest, and that he was cooperative and helpful to the extent of doing everything that was requested of him. On cross-examination, the prosecutor asked whether the defendant had done everything he was asked, including giving a written statement. After a defense objection was overruled, the officer replied that the defendant, who had been given *Miranda* warnings, had declined to make a formal statement and had also stopped the questioning by asking for a lawyer. What result on appeal after conviction?

Analysis

It violates Due Process to use post-*Miranda* silence to impeach a defendant, because the defendant has been cautioned that he has a right to remain silent and that anything he says can be used against him. To then use his silence against him is considered fundamentally unfair. *Doyle v. Ohio*. Here, the defendant's silence is not being used to impeach the defendant's exculpatory story. Nor is silence being used to suggest his guilt. Rather the testimony is being used to impeach a police officer's testimony that the defendant had been cooperative and helpful when he was interrogated.

In *Wainright v. Greenfield*, the prosecutor, to impeach the defendant's claim of insanity, introduced the fact that the defendant invoked his rights three times after receiving *Miranda* warnings. The Court stated that it is fundamentally unfair to promise an arrested person that his silence will not be used against him and then to breach that promise by using his silence to impeach his testimony. *Greenfield* seems to control here.

■ PROBLEM 8.2 GOOD FAITH ■

A telephone caller, who would not give his name, told Detective Murphy that he had observed a large stash of marijuana in the basement of a home in which he had been employed as a tradesman. The caller did not mention the date of his observation, Deciding that the tip needed corroboration, Murphy conducted a surveillance at the residence in question for two hours on two successive evenings, but he observed nothing unusual. Murphy then presented the following affidavit for a search warrant to a judge:

> An anonymous telephone caller stated that he had been hired to do some work at [the home in question.] Upon entering the basement, he smelled the distinct odor of marijuana and observed what appeared to be marijuana in the basement. Questioned about his knowledge of marijuana, the caller stated that he had been a user in his younger days. He further stated that he feels the occupants are engaged in dealing as opposed to possession for their own use. Surveillance was initiated on 4–13 and 4–14, but no undue amount of traffic was observed going to the home.

After the judge issued a warrant, a search uncovered more than 300 pounds of marijuana. What result on a motion to suppress?

Analysis

In *United States v. Leon*, the Court held that suppression is not required when an officer has acted in an objectively reasonable reliance on a subsequently invalidated search warrant. The Court observed that the good faith exception to the exclusionary rule does not apply when the warrant affidavit contains knowing or reckless falsity, when the issuing magistrate fails to act in a neutral and detached fashion and wholly abandons the judicial role, when the supporting affidavit does not provide the magistrate a substantial basis for finding probable cause, so that the officer's reliance on the warrant is neither in good faith nor objectively reasonable, and when the officer has no reasonable basis for concluding that the warrant was properly issued.

Assuming the warrant was defective, the issue is whether Murphy's reliance on it was objectively reasonable. When Murphy got the tip, he realized that it needed corroboration. Yet, he conducted surveillance for only two hours on two nights, and he observed nothing unusual. Nothing, therefore, changed from the time Murphy received the tip. The judge, in issuing the warrant, relied solely on a tip from an unknown person, a tip that did not even specify the date marijuana had been seen. It may be argued that Murphy did not act on objectively reasonable grounds in relying on the warrant.

■ PROBLEM 8.3 STANDING ■

Kentucky State Police stopped a car that was weaving and that had only one headlight. The driver, Ron Jefferson, had a suspended Indiana license; the two passengers, Jefferson's brother and the car's owner, Ernest Tillis, had valid licenses. Because the brothers gave conflicting accounts of a trip to Michigan, the officers became suspicious. The officers then searched the car and found crack in the trunk. Assuming that the three men were taking turns driving home from Michigan, what result when all three move to suppress the crack?

Analysis

Tillis, as owner, clearly has standing, even though he was not driving at the time of the search. A present owner can always show a reasonable expectation of privacy in the vehicle. Jefferson, the driver, is just like the passenger in *Rakas*. The fact he was driving at the time of the police intrusion is irrelevant. He has to make some showing of an expectation of privacy in the place searched. (It would make no sense to have standing depend upon the fortuity of who was driving at the time of the search.) Jefferson's brother was clearly a passenger in the *Rakas* sense of the word at the time of the search; accordingly, he falls squarely within the holding of *Rakas*.

The defendants would not get standing by claiming that they owned the drugs. *Rawlings*. To challenge a search, a person needs a reasonable expectation of privacy in the place searched. Had Jefferson and his brother stashed the drugs without Tillis's consent, they wouldn't have had any reasonable privacy expectations.

■ PROBLEM 8.4 FRUIT OF THE POISONOUS TREE ■

An informant and an undercover narcotics agent arranged to purchase narcotics from William Drosten. When they arrived at Drosten's apartment, they were greeted by Dobby Barrett, whom the informant had previously met, and whose identity and address the informant had given the police. Barrett informed them that Drosten was out, but that they should call his beeper. The informant, who had previously given Drosten's beeper number to the police, went to a phone booth, contacted Drosten by using the beeper number, and arranged to meet him back at the apartment.

As they were returning to the apartment, the agent became suspicious that Drosten "was on to them." He then ordered the surveillance officers to move in and to search the apartment. The officers made a warrantless entry, arrested Drosten, found and questioned Barrett and Howard Gray, and seized a beeper. The officers were unaware of Gray or his presence before entering the apartment.

Alleging that the warrantless entry was illegal, Drosten moved to suppress the beeper and Barrett's and Gray's testimony. He also moved to suppress the testimony of Rubin Stone. Stone, who leased the beeper, allowed Drosten to use it as long as Drosten made the monthly lease payments. The police learned Rubin's identity by tracing the beeper's serial number; they also could have learned his identity by using the beeper number. What result?

Analysis

In *United States v. Ceccolini*, the Court indicated it will be very hard to suppress a witness's statements, in part because witnesses often come forward with evidence on their own volition. The police had an independent source for Barrett. The informant had previously given Barrett's identity and address to the police. The police also knew that Barrett was at Drosten's apartment on the night in question. The illegal search (if it was illegal) in no way brought Barrett to the attention of the police. Moreover, there is no evidence that the police exploited their illegality in getting Barrett to testify. Barrett's testimony should be allowed under *Ceccolini*.

The police were unaware of Gray or his presence before the illegal search. Their surveillance team would have eventually uncovered Gray's identity. (But how long would Gray have been there, and how long would the surveillance team have been there?) Prior to the night in question, the informant had given Drosten's beeper number to the police. This number could have led them to Rubin Stone, who leased the beeper. Instead, they found Stone by tracing the serial number that they learned in the illegal search. The government was investigating the beeper, and it seems they would have learned Stone's identity without the serial number.

POINTS TO REMEMBER

- The exclusionary rule precludes the prosecution from introducing evidence seized as a result of unconstitutional activity in its case-in-chief.

- The exclusionary rule does not apply to the actions of private actors.

- The exclusionary rule is justified primarily because of its deterrent effect on future law enforcement unconstitutional activity.

- Where no incremental deterrence of unconstitutional law enforcement activity is obtained, the exclusionary rule does not apply.

- The exclusionary rule does not apply where police officers act in objectively-reasonable "good faith" in executing an otherwise defective search warrant.

- In order to raise an issue relating to unconstitutional police activity in a motion to suppress, the moving party needs to possess "standing," i.e., her own personal constitutional rights must have been violated.

- The exclusionary rule applies both to evidence seized as a direct result of unconstitutional police activity, as well as to additional evidence derived indirectly from that activity.

- The FOPT doctrine does not apply when the government proves by a preponderance of the evidence that it would have discovered unconstitutionally-seized evidence anyway if there had been no constitutional violation.

- The relationship between unconstitutional police activity and evidence seized as a result of that activity may be so "attenuated" that the FOPT doctrine does not apply.

CHAPTER 9

Entrapment

The entrapment defense regulates participation by government agents in criminal acts during undercover investigations. The defense is raised when a defendant claims that the only reason he committed the crime was because government agents entrapped him into engaging in that conduct. The defense developed before modern Due Process law limited police conduct during interrogations, searches, and seizures. Defendants who cannot satisfy the requirements of the entrapment defense try to use Due Process as an alternative protection from "outrageous government conduct." Due Process may ban certain types of police entrapment activities, but the Supreme Court has yet to uphold a Due Process claim of this type.

A. THE ENTRAPMENT DEFENSE

The Court recognized the entrapment defense in federal criminal law in *Sorrells v. United States*, 287 U.S. 435 (1932), endorsing the "subjective" test for entrapment. Most State courts follow the Supreme Court standard, but about one third of State courts use an "objective" test.

Under the "subjective" test, a defendant must prove a sufficient governmental "inducement" for her to engage in criminal activity. The prosecution can rebut this proof with evidence of the defendant's "predisposition" to commit the crime beyond a reasonable doubt. The purpose of those inquiries is to distinguish situations where government agents "merely afford opportunities" for crime from entrapment situations where crime occurs as "the product of the creative activity" of those agents. The "objective" test does not consider the defendant's "predisposition," and focuses solely on governmental inducement.

The Supreme Court applied the "subjective" test for entrapment in *Sherman v. United States*, 356 U.S. 369 (1958), holding that the defendant was entrapped as a matter of law. The *Sherman* defendant's proof of inducement was clear, and the government's proof of predisposition was found to be inadequate. The defendant met the government informant while seeking treatment for addiction. The informant feigned an addiction and repeatedly pleaded with the defendant to help him obtain drugs for his addiction. The defendant initially refused to help the informant, but ultimately agreed. The defendant became addicted again after sharing drugs with the informant. The government's evidence of predisposition was two prior drug convictions, but there was no evidence of the defendant's "readiness" to traffic in drugs.

A plurality in *Sherman* criticized the majority's "subjective" test for entrapment and advocated an "objective" test that would treat predisposition as an irrelevant consideration. The objective test requires a case-by-case analysis, using factors like the setting of the inducement, the type of crime involved, and the method by which the actual crime usually occurs.

Several decades after *Sherman*, the Court signaled a new readiness to scrutinize predisposition evidence. In *Jacobson v. United States*, 503 U.S. 540 (1992), the Court found that as part of its burden of proof of predisposition, the government must show that the defendant was predisposed to commit the crime "before being approached by government agents." Two types of predisposition evidence satisfy this showing: 1) evidence developed prior to the first government contact, or 2) evidence developed during the course of the investigation before the commission of the crime.

Proof of the *Jacobson* defendant's predisposition was insufficient because he became predisposed only after two and a half years of repeated mailings from fictitious government entities in a child pornography sting operation. Based on the evidence of his inducement, his entrapment defense was upheld as a matter of law.

The new element in the "subjective" test required the government to prove that predisposition is "independent and not the product of the attention that the Government [directs] at" a target defendant during an undercover investigation. The Court in *Jacobson* concluded that the new proof requirement for predisposition was necessary to protect people like the defendant, "an otherwise law-abiding citizen who, if left to his own devices, likely would never run afoul of the law."

What *Jacobson* requires, which *Sherman* did not, is judicial scrutiny of the conduct of government agents from the moment of first contact with a defendant until the moment the defendant commits the crime. *Jacobson* was concerned about a pattern of repeated government contacts, as denying the government the power to prosecute defendants whose predisposition was "created" by the government.

B. DUE PROCESS AND "OUTRAGEOUS GOVERNMENT CONDUCT"

The Court has observed that "due process principles" may prohibit some "outrageous" entrapment-style conduct of government officials. *United States v. Russell*, 411 U.S. 423 (1973). But the Court has not described specific Due Process limits on such conduct. In cases when predisposition evidence may have precluded entrapment under the "subjective" test, defense counsel wanted to expand entrapment to include governmental conduct that showed "an intolerable degree of governmental participation in the criminal enterprise," thereby violating Due Process.

The defendant in *Russell* argued that the "criminal conduct would not have been possible" if the undercover agent had not "supplied an indispensable means to the commission of the crime that could not have been obtained otherwise through legal or illegal channels." Specifically, the agent supplied bottles of a chemical used in manufacturing methamphetamine, in return for the right to purchase part of the finished product.

Russell rejected the defendant's argument on three grounds: 1) the ingredient was possible to obtain, and the defendant obtained it from other sources; 2) the ingredient was a harmless and legal substance; and 3) during the process of "infiltration" of drug "rings" by government agents, "the supply of some item of value that the drug ring requires" must be permissible in order for an agent to be "taken into the confidence of the illegal entrepreneurs." The law enforcement tactic was not fundamentally unfair or "shocking to the universal sense of justice" under Due Process precedents.

In *Hampton v. United States*, 425 U.S. 484 (1976), the Court observed that Due Process limitations "come into play only when the Government activity in question violates some protected right of the [d]efendant." A plurality of the Court conceded that the agents "played a more significant role" in *Hampton* than in *Russell*. One agent supplied defendant with illegal drugs; another agent acted as the buyer. The *Hampton* plurality held that these differences were insufficient for a Due Process violation, because the defendant was predisposed to act with the agents.

The *Hampton* dissenters disagreed, concluding that there was a Due Process violation because the government was "buying contraband from itself and jailing the intermediary." The crime was "the product of the creative activity of its own officials." Lower courts have applied the *Hampton* dissent to develop a case-by-case approach for the evaluation of Due Process claims. The focus is on such factors as

> [w]hether the police conduct instigated a crime or merely infiltrated ongoing criminal activity, whether the defendant's reluctance to commit a crime was overcome by pleas of sympathy, promises of excessive profits, or persistent solicitation, whether the government controls the criminal activity or simply allows for the criminal activity to occur, whether the police motive was to prevent crime or protect the public; and

whether the government conduct itself amounted to criminal activity or conduct "repugnant to a sense of justice."

State v. Lively, 921 P.2d 1035 (Wash. 1996).

ENTRAPMENT CHECKLIST

I. **The Entrapment Defense**. The defense regulates participation by government agents in criminal acts during undercover investigations.

A. The Court recognized the entrapment defense in federal criminal law in ***Sorrells v. United States***, 287 U.S. 435 (1932), endorsing the "subjective" test for entrapment.

    1. Under the "subjective" test for entrapment, a defendant first must show a sufficient governmental "inducement" for her to engage in criminal activity.

    2. The prosecution must prove that the defendant was predisposed to commit the crime "before being approached by government agents."

    3. The showing may be made by evidence developed either prior to the first government contact or during the course of the investigation before the commission of the crime.

B. The "objective" test for entrapment does not consider the defendant's "predisposition," and focuses solely on governmental inducement.

    1. The objective test requires a case-by-case analysis.

    2. The relevant factors are "the setting in which the inducement took place," the "nature of the crime involved," and "the manner in which the actual criminal business is usually carried on."

II. Due Process and "Outrageous Government Conduct"

A. The Due Process test differs from the subjective test of entrapment. Due process principles may prohibit some "outrageous" entrapment-style conduct of government officials, even though predisposition evidence may preclude entrapment under the "subjective" test.

B. The Court has never upheld a Due Process claim.

   1. Governmental conduct may be so outrageous that dismissal of a criminal charge is appropriate, even though the defendant was predisposed to commit the crime.

   2. Lower courts have developed a case-by-case approach for evaluating Due Process claims, when the crime was the result of creative governmental activity.

ILLUSTRATIVE PROBLEMS

■ PROBLEM 9.1 ENTRAPMENT ■

It is illegal to sell or purchase "sport caught" fish, fish that have not been caught commercially. After hearing that this law was being violated, the State police randomly called dozens of caterers and restaurants, using assumed names, and offered to sell fresh fish at a price well below that of commercially available fish. The police left a message to this effect on the answering machine at Sharp's restaurant. Before making these calls, the police had no information that any of the people they contacted had made illegal purchases of fish. When Sharp returned the call on his machine, he and an undercover officer negotiated a sale. During the conversation, the officer asked for and received assurances that the police would not be present when the fish were delivered. Sharp indicated that the fish should be carried into his restaurant in a black bag. Before his arrest, Sharp made four separate purchases of fish from the officer. What result under the majority view of entrapment?

Analysis

When the government has induced a defendant to commit a crime, it must prove beyond a reasonable doubt the defendant's predisposition prior to the government's first approaching the defendant. In the typical sting operation, the government merely offers the defendant the opportunity to commit a crime, and the defendant's ready commission of the crime amply demonstrates his predisposition. In such a case, it would be unlikely that entrapment would warrant a jury instruction. Here, the government agent left a phone message with the proposed illegal sale of fish, and the defendant responded without hesitation. This is a mere offer to the defendant of an opportunity to commit a crime and the defendant's ready commission of it. The entrapment defense does not apply.

■ PROBLEM 9.2 DUE PROCESS OUTRAGEOUS CONDUCT ■

The sheriff, with the prosecutor's knowledge, entered into an agreement with informant Berger, who agreed to sell several hundred pounds of marijuana that the county had seized in prior cases. The sheriff also agreed to let Berger keep 10% of all forfeitures arising from successful criminal prosecutions relating to his sales. To collect the 10%, Berger agreed to testify in the criminal prosecutions. Pursuant to the agreement, Berger sold over 100 pounds of marijuana to the defendants. Shortly thereafter, the sheriff's deputies arrested the defendants and seized more than $80,000 in cash, subject to forfeiture. What result on the defendants' motions to dismiss the criminal charges and to have the money returned? Do the defendants have any plausible Due Process defense?

Analysis

Is this one of the rare cases in which the government conduct is so outrageous as to violate Due Process? It is difficult to see the outrageousness in the government's conduct. Clearly, the informant's fee was contingent on successful prosecutions and forfeitures, and this created an interest in the outcome that could affect the informant's credibility. But to say that this perhaps unwise policy was so outrageous so as to violate Due Process may be a stretch.

POINTS TO REMEMBER

- Under the "subjective" test for entrapment, the defendant must prove sufficient "inducement," and then the prosecution must prove the defendant's "predisposition" beyond a reasonable doubt.

- Under the "objective" test for entrapment, the defendant's predisposition is irrelevant. The defendant should prove that the police created an inducement that produced a substantial risk that such an offense would be committed by persons other than those who were ready to commit it.

- When proving predisposition in a "subjective" test jurisdiction, the prosecution must show that the defendant was predisposed to commit the crime "before being approached by government agents."

- It is not a violation of Due Process for one government agent to supply the illegal drug to a defendant and arrange for another government agent to buy the same drug from the defendant.

Conclusion: General Examination Tips

Now that you have the full set of checklists for each of the topics that you will be covering on your examination, there are some bits of advice to help you ace your criminal procedure examination:

Before the Examination

- Prepare early for examinations by reviewing information learned as you go along rather than waiting until the end of the semester.

- Review the material by working on hypothetical problems. It is important to gain experience answering and writing out answers to problems before the examination.

- Meet with your professor regularly to gain useful insight into what he or she feels is important about particular topics and to develop a deeper understanding of the material. This time can also be used to obtain information regarding what type of analysis the professor expects on an examination.

- Synthesize the material by recognizing the connections between different topics covered within the course to develop a more comprehensive view of the material.

- Do not neglect information regarding the policy under-pinnings or implications of various legal principles learned in the course. These policy issues become important in giving you the ability to resolve tough questions and to provide rationales for particular legal outcomes.

- Do not rely on a mere mastery of the substantive material to prepare for the exam. What is equally important is a deep understanding of the material which will enable you to engage in high level analysis of the problems that you will face on the exam.

During the Examination

- Before writing an essay to a question, be sure you understand precisely what the professor is asking you to do, e.g., giving the arguments on both sides of an issue or on behalf of only one party, assuming the role of the judge writing an opinion in the case. Outline the answer to facilitate your ability to provide a clear, organized response and to structure your thinking about the question to ensure that your answer covers all of the issues that need to be addressed.

- On the exam, professors are not simply looking for students to apply the law they have been taught to a given set of facts to achieve a result. In addition, superior exam takers demonstrate a depth of understanding beyond the black-letter law. The recognition of difficult questions and reference to underlying policies is the mark of a good answer.

- Always identify your assumptions. If you are assuming certain facts as the basis for your answer, make those assumptions explicit.

- Unless the question asks for a very brief answer, never give a simple conclusion regarding the proper result as your answer on an exam. Provide a full explanation showing your analysis. How you reach your conclusion is much more important than the conclusion.

- Rather than simply reaching a particular result because a certain case calls for that result, reason toward a conclusion by identifying key facts in the question, similar facts in other relevant cases, and any policy issues that support the outcome you intend to reach.

- Regardless of how difficult the question may seem, an answer to an examination question must reach a result. Do not equivocate, unless a factual ambiguity invites you to explore alternative analytical paths. Use legal judgment, reasoning, and analysis to identify a superior position and provide arguments for your choice.

- Generally, consider the arguments on both sides of an issue and state them. Then take the opportunity to apply your understanding of the principles and policies involved as well as any relevant precedent to side with a particular result.

- When deciding between two competing approaches to resolving an issue, clearly state which approach you intend to apply and articulate the arguments for why that is the better approach.

- Distinguish yourself by engaging in an analysis that demonstrates depth of knowledge and true understanding rather than rote memorization or dexterity with available source material (for open-book exams).

- In addition to the quality of one's answer, make sure to provide an answer that identifies all of the issues raised in the question. Working on practice questions is a good way to develop the ability to spot issues, making it critical that you work with practice questions prior to the exam.

After the Examination

Don't waste time talking with other classmates about the exam. You'll just create more anxiety for yourself. Focus on the next exam; or, if criminal procedure is your last exam, celebrate being done!

Appendix:

Mini–Checklists

In this Appendix, students will find brief versions of the checklists for each topic, for quick reference and use when it is necessary to find something quickly under a time crunch during an exam. These reduced versions cover the key points that need to be checked in your analysis. Proper use and understanding of these "mini-checklists" requires a complete understanding of the full checklists presented in the main text of this book.

INCORPORATION AND RETROACTIVITY

I. Incorporation

    A. **Application of the Bill of Rights to the States**. The rights included in the first ten amendments to the United States Constitution do not all apply to the States.

    B. **Fundamental Rights Approach** applies when a right is "implicit in the concept of ordered liberty."

    C. **Total Incorporation** involves an application of *all* parts of the Bill of Rights to the States through the Fourteenth Amendment Due Process Clause. The Court has rejected total incorporation.

    D. **Selective Incorporation**. Fourteenth Amendment Due Process includes only those rights in the Bill of Rights which are essential to "ordered liberty."

        1. Look at the entirety of the right, not just as it applies to a particular set of facts, and whether the provision is fundamental to Anglo–American jurisprudence.

        2. Most of the rights in the Bill of Rights apply to the States using selective incorporation.

II. Retroactivity

    A. **Retroactivity** is about the application of a new constitutional rule to others whose cases involve the same issue when the case announcing the new rule was decided.

    B. **Cases Pending and Not Yet Final**

        1. A new rule is to be applied retroactively to all cases, State or federal, pending on direct review or not yet final.

        2. Generally, new constitutional rules of criminal procedure are not applicable to cases which have become final before the new rules are announced.

RIGHT TO COUNSEL

A. **Appointed Counsel for Indigents**. Criminal defendants who cannot afford an attorney have a constitutional right to appointed defense counsel under the Sixth Amendment.

   1. Indigent defendants do not have the right to choose which defense attorney will be appointed to represent her.

   2. **"Day in Jail" Rule**. An indigent defendant who has a right to counsel cannot be imprisoned unless she had the opportunity to have appointed counsel.

B. **Retained Counsel**

   1. A criminal defendant with sufficient financial resources generally has the right to be represented at trial by any attorney she chooses to employ.

   2. The right to retained counsel must yield to overriding governmental interests, such as counsel having a conflict of interest or not being admitted to practice law.

C. **Waiver of the Right to Counsel**. The right to counsel may be waived knowingly and intelligently.

D. **Representing Oneself**. A defendant has the right to proceed *pro se*, but standby counsel may be appointed.

E. **Ineffective Assistance of Counsel** applies not only to trial, but also to guilty pleas, sentencing, and a first appeal of right. If there is no right to counsel, no right to effective assistance exists.

   1. A defendant may claim that her defense counsel was guilty of *per se* or "extrinsic ineffectiveness."

   2. **Actual Ineffectiveness**. A defendant must show *both* that her defense counsel performed deficiently *and* that the deficient performance actually prejudiced her defense.

3. Strategic choices are not regarded as constituting deficient performance

4. The right to effective assistance may be violated when a defendant loses out on a good plea offer because of her counsel's wrong advice or failure to communicate the offer.

F. **Conflicts of Interest**. A lone attorney's representation of codefendants is not *per se* unconstitutional.

1. When counsel timely alerts the trial court about the risk of a conflict of interest, the trial judge must decide whether to appoint separate counsel.

2. A defendant who did not object at trial must show that an actual conflict of interest adversely affected his lawyer's performance.

G. **The *Griffin–Douglas* Doctrine**. Indigent prisoners appealing a conviction as a matter of right in State court are constitutionally entitled to a free trial transcript and to counsel on a first appeal, but indigents undertaking *discretionary* appeals do not.

SEARCH AND ARREST WARRANTS

A. **Warrants Preferred**. Courts prefer search warrants, i.e., searches without warrants are *per se* unreasonable under the Fourth Amendment, subject to a few specific exceptions.

B. **Probable Cause** for a search warrant requires a showing by the government of "a fair probability" that the specified items sought are evidence of criminal activity and that those items are presently located at the specified place described in the search warrant application. Probable cause for an arrest warrant exists when there is a fair probability that a crime has been committed and that the person to be arrested committed the crime.

   1. **Informant Information**. A "totality-of-the-circumstances" test applies for probable cause, looking at factors like the basis for the information, why an informant is credible, and corroboration of some of the informant's factual details.

   2. **Staleness**. Probable cause information that is stale cannot support the issuance of a search warrant.

   3. **Anticipatory Warrants**. A search warrant may issue based only upon a showing of prospective probable cause.

C. **Obtaining Warrants**

   1. **Affidavits** contain information supporting issuance of a warrant that must be disclosed to the issuing judge at the time of the application for a warrant.

   2. **Challenging Affidavits**. Affidavits can be challenged "on their face" or because some or all of the statements in that affidavit were false.

   3. **Issuing Judges** must be neutral, detached, and capable of determining whether probable cause exists for a requested arrest or search.

D. **The Particularity Requirement**. The warrant must describe the place to be searched and the persons to be arrested or things to be seized.

E. **Execution of Search Warrants** may be either by the specific law enforcement officers directed in the warrant itself or by any other law enforcement officers authorized by applicable statutes in that jurisdiction.

  1. **Time Limits**. Search warrants must be executed both within the jurisdiction's maximum time limit for execution and prior to the time the probable cause information supporting the warrant grows stale.

  2. **Knock-and-Announce Doctrine**. Police generally must announce their presence and purpose before going into a building to serve a warrant, unless to do so would be dangerous or futile.

  3. **Post–Execution Requirements**. Executing officers must leave a copy of the search warrant and a receipt for items seized at the search premises.

F. **Seizures Pursuant to Warrant** are items specified in a search warrant as evidence of crime as well as non-described items that they see in "plain view."

  1. **Where Seizures Can Be Made**. Executing officers may search anywhere on the search premises that the items particularly described in the search warrant may be hidden.

  2. **Duration of Search**. Once all of the objects particularly described and sought under a warrant have been found, no further searches are permissible under that warrant.

  3. **Persons and Their Property on or Near Search Premises**. Anyone on the search premises may be detained.

G. **Burden of Proof**. The prosecution has the burden of proving the validity of the warrant, and the defendant then has the burden of demonstrating its invalidity.

FOURTH AMENDMENT ACTIVITY

A. **Reasonable Expectation of Privacy** requires compliance with the Fourth Amendment, (e.g., probable cause).

B. No reasonable expectation of privacy exists when a person conveys information to third parties who then provide that information to the police.

C. **"Curtilage"** is the land "immediately surrounding and associated with the home" and it generally is a protected area.

D. **"Open fields"** are considered to be the area beyond the curtilage and can be entered and searched without a warrant or probable cause.

E. **Human Surveillance and Enhanced Surveillance**.

    1. No reasonable expectation of privacy exists in garbage placed in opaque trash bags on the curb and searched by police.

    2. Canine sniffs by narcotics detection dogs of luggage in a public place do not violate a reasonable expectation of privacy.

    3. Tracking beepers are acceptable as a substitute for visual surveillance when the beeper is not used to reveal information about what was going on inside the defendant's home.

    4. Aerial surveillance cases indicate no reasonable expectation of privacy from some police "fly overs" of property.

    5. A homeowner has a reasonable expectation of privacy from the use of a thermal imaging device.

    6. Police installation of a GPS tracking device on a vehicle and warrantless use of the device to monitor the vehicle's movements constitute a "search" and violate a defendant's Fourth Amendment rights.

WARRANTLESS SEARCHES AND SEIZURES

A. **Warrantless Searches and Seizures** are disfavored and are *per se* unreasonable, subject to specific exceptions.

B. **Plain View Exception** requires that police are in a place where they have the right to be and the items seized are incriminating on their face, (e.g., seizure of a car is invalid when the incriminating character of the car or its contents are not immediately apparent).

C. **Search Incident to Legal Arrest**. When police make a legal arrest, they have the right to search the arrestee and the area within her immediate control, contemporaneous with the arrest.

D. **Booking Searches**. Jail officials can remove both contraband and valuables to prevent personal items from being stolen, to protect police against false claims of theft, and to prevent the arrestee from introducing contraband, etc. into the jail.

E. **Automobile Exception**. When there is probable cause to search an automobile, police may search every part of the vehicle and its contents that may conceal the object of the search.

F. **Inventory Exception**. When a vehicle has been legally impounded, police may search the passenger compartment, the trunk, and closed containers.

G. **Consent**. Consent searches are permissible when the prosecution proves that consent was freely and voluntarily given.

    1. To determine the validity of consent, a "totality-of-the-circumstances" test is applied, using a variety of factors peculiar to the suspect and factors that suggest coercion.

    2. When a third party consents to a search, a court must decide both that consent was voluntarily given and that the third party could consent to the search.

    3. Police are entitled to believe that the consenting party had "apparent authority" to consent based on the facts before them.

H. **Administrative Inspections**. "Administrative" probable cause enables inspection of all places in a particular area, and no warrant is necessary in emergency situations.

I. **Stop and Frisk**. A police officer may stop a person when the officer has reasonable suspicion to believe that criminal activity may be afoot.

　　1. A frisk is a "protective search for weapons" of the suspect's outer clothing.

　　2. If the police officer feels something beneath the clothing that feels like a weapon, she can reach beneath the clothing to retrieve the weapon.

　　3. To conduct a frisk, the officer must have reasonable suspicion that the suspect is "armed and dangerous."

J. **Other Issues Relating to Investigative Searches and Seizures**.

　　1. An investigative seizure may occur when police grasp or apply physical force with lawful authority.

　　2. The validity of an investigative seizure is based on whether a reasonable person would have believed that she was not free to leave and is evaluated under the totality of the circumstances.

　　3. **Scope and Length of Investigative Seizures**. Limits on the length of an investigative seizure are based on the length and intrusiveness of the seizure and the time reasonably needed to effectuate the purpose of the seizure.

K. **Exigent Circumstances** include the existence of probable cause, plus a need to enter either to assist persons who are seriously injured or threatened with such injury, or to apprehend a suspect.

　　1. Hot pursuit.

　　2. Gathering evidence from suspect's body.

3. Special needs cases.

4. Special rules for school-age children.

L. **Burden of Proof.** Warrantless arrests, searches, and seizures are presumed to be illegal, with the burden on the prosecution to prove that the intrusion is justified under some exception to the warrant requirement.

POLICE INTERROGATION AND CONFESSIONS

A. **The *McNabb–Mallory* Rule** prohibits confessions obtained during the period of unnecessary delay when arrestees are not taken promptly to a judicial officer after arrest.

B. **The Fifth Amendment and *Miranda* require warnings for an interrogated person in custody.**

   1. After the warnings, a suspect may knowingly and intelligently waive these rights and agree to answer questions or to make a statement.

   2. Statements taken in violation of *Miranda* may nevertheless be used to impeach the defendant.

   3. **Custody** under *Miranda* is determined by how a reasonable person in the suspect's shoes would have understood the situation.

   4. **Interrogation under *Miranda*** occurs when the police use any words or actions that they should know will reasonably elicit an incriminating response from the suspect. Exceptions are for questioning:

      a. for "routine booking,"

      b. by undercover agents, and

      c. for public safety.

   5. **Adequate Warnings** are evaluated by whether the "totality" of the warnings adequately conveyed the meaning of the *Miranda* rights.

   6. **Waiver of *Miranda* Rights** must be "voluntary, knowing and intelligent," looking at the totality of the circumstances.

   7. **Invocation of Silence** does not permanently end the interrogation, if the police "scrupulously honor" the suspect's invocation at a later interrogation session.

8. **Invocation of Counsel** requires that the interrogator immediately stop the interrogation until the suspect re-initiates further conversation. If a suspect is released from custody after invoking his right to counsel, the prohibition on police questioning lasts for fourteen days.

9. *Miranda*-**defective evidence** may nevertheless be used to impeach a defendant if the confession is otherwise voluntary.

C. **Sixth Amendment Right to Counsel** prevents police from deliberately eliciting incriminating statements from a defendant at or after the start of adversary judicial proceedings against her.

1. Unlike the Fifth Amendment, the Sixth Amendment right to counsel is "offense-specific."

2. The Court has not identified significant differences between *Miranda* "interrogation" and "deliberate elicitation" under the Sixth Amendment when defendants are questioned by police.

3. Deliberate elicitation exists in the undercover informant-cellmate context when the informant is an active participant (rather than a passive listener) in conversations with the defendant.

4. The standard for waiver of Sixth Amendment rights is the same as for Fifth Amendment waiver.

D. **Due Process** applies a case-by-case approach in which there must be coercive police activity that overcomes the suspect's free will, using a totality of circumstances analysis.

E. **Burden of Proof.** The prosecution has the burden of proving the voluntariness of custodial statements by a preponderance of the evidence.

IDENTIFICATION PROCEDURES

A. **Sixth Amendment Right to Counsel** applies to any corporeal identification at or adversary judicial criminal proceedings have begun against the defendant.

    1. Counsel is not constitutionally required to be present when an eyewitness is shown a photographic display which includes a photo of the defendant.

    2. When the right to counsel is denied at a pretrial confrontation, the witness cannot testify at trial about the out-of-court identification but may nevertheless make an in-court identification.

B. **Due Process** has two parts in relation to any identification procedure.

    1. The first part of the test is whether the pretrial identification procedure was impermissibly suggestive. Judicial inquiry into the reliability of an eyewitness identification is required only when the identification was procured under unnecessarily suggestive circumstances arranged by law enforcement.

    2. If so, the court must assess based upon the totality of the circumstances, the possibility that the witness would make an irreparable misidentification at trial.

C. **Burden of Proof**. The prosecution has the burden of proving the circumstances under which a pretrial identification was made.

EXCLUSIONARY RULE

A. **The Exclusionary Rule** precludes the prosecution in a criminal trial from introducing evidence in its case-in-chief that was seized unconstitutionally by government agents.

B. **Limits on the Exclusionary Rule's Application**

    1. **Private Actors**. The exclusionary rule does not apply when physical evidence is seized by private individuals acting alone.

    2. **Non-criminal Proceedings: Incremental Deterrence**. Courts view the exclusionary rule as a required remedy primarily to deter the future misconduct of law enforcement officials.

    3. **Impeachment** of a defendant's credibility with illegally obtained evidence may occur when exclusion of the evidence does not create any incremental deterrence of law enforcement officers.

    4. **Good–Faith Exception** applies when a law enforcement officer has acted in reasonable "good faith" on the basis of an unconstitutional search warrant.

    5. **Knock-and-Announce Violations**. The Court refuses to apply the exclusionary evidence rule in the context of a violation of the "knock and announce" rule, because the deterrence benefits of excluding the evidence were outweighed by its substantial social costs.

C. **Standing** is required for a defendant to raise the issue of unconstitutional law enforcement conduct.

    1. It exists only where the defendant seeks to remedy a violation of her own personal constitutional rights, not the rights of another person.

    2. Personal constitutional rights are violated where the constitutional harm is done to that individual personally, at a place or to some thing where and when she possessed a "reasonable expectation of privacy."

D. **Derivative Evidence: The "Fruit of the Poisonous Tree" Doctrine [FOPT].** Evidence derived from law enforcement's unconstitutional activity is inadmissible in criminal proceedings not only when it is obtained as a direct result of that activity, but also when it has been derived as an *indirect* result of such a constitutional breach. There are three parts to the FOPT-related analysis when an arrest led to a search:

1. The defendant has standing to challenge the original violation, i.e., the tree.

2. The original police activity violated her rights.

3. The evidence sought to be admitted against her, i.e., the fruit, was obtained as a result of the original violation. FOPT analysis specifically addresses this last issue.

4. Exceptions to application of the FOPT Doctrine:

   a. Independent Source,

   b. Inevitable Discovery, and

   c. Attenuation.

E. **Harmless Error** applies to affirm a conviction when, despite a violation of the defendant's constitutional rights, the violation was harmless beyond a reasonable doubt because of the overwhelming amount of admissible evidence against the defendant. Some constitutional errors, however, are so fundamental to a fair trial that they constitute "structural defects" in the criminal justice system and are not subject to ordinary harmless error analysis.

ENTRAPMENT

A. **The Entrapment Defense** may be shown by a subjective approach or an objective approach.

  1. The"subjective" test for entrapment focuses on whether the defendant was predisposed to commit the crime.

  2. The "objective" test for entrapment does not consider the defendant's "predisposition," but focuses solely on governmental inducement.

B. **Due Process and "Outrageous Government Conduct"** prohibit some "outrageous" entrapment-style conduct of government officials, even though predisposition evidence may preclude entrapment under the "subjective" test.

†